THE AMERICAN SECRETARY

THE AMERICAN SECRETARY

The Colonial Policy of Lord George Germain, 1775–1778

BY GERALD SAXON BROWN

ANN ARBOR / THE UNIVERSITY OF MICHIGAN PRESS

To Dorothy and Cathy

PREFACE

Lord George Germain was secretary of state for the American Department from 1775 to 1782. In this capacity he exercised a decisive influence upon the formation and the execution of British policies during the War for American Independence. Few periods of history have been more intensively investigated than the American revolutionary period, and during the last fifty odd years a substantial measure of agreement has been reached among American and British scholars with respect to the major developments and personalities of those fateful years. In a most emphatic way this general agreement has included the policies, activities, and personality of Germain. He has appeared, with few exceptions, in our studies of the Revolution as a stubborn reactionary, inflexible and vindictive of temper, heir to most of the vices and few of the virtues of eighteenth-century political life. Above and beyond these defects of temper and intellect, he has been judged singularly inefficient and maladroit in the administration of his high office.

These judgments may be found scattered throughout both the general histories of the period and the more detailed monographs. After my study was completed Alan Valentine's *Lord George Germain* (Oxford University Press, 1962) appeared. Mr. Valentine states in his preface: "This is not the first preface in which an author has tried to anticipate his critics and to disarm them in advance. I confess my emotional handicap as a biographer of Lord George. To write about a man one cannot bring oneself to like is to court disaster, yet I could not resist his compulsive fascination. In the effort to avoid doing him injustice, I have searched for every episode and interpretation that could be turned in his favor, but though I have found enough to temper my distaste I have not found enough to remove it. If my portrait of Lord George seems harsh, I believe it is his features and not my prejudices that have made it so." I have felt no "emotional handicap" in writing upon Germain. My purpose has been to record an account of Germain's part as a policymaker and as an administrator during the revolutionary struggle. The attempt has been made to construct this study as nearly as may be from the documents of the time, and, most importantly, from Germain's own papers, and to raise queries at points where the results of this examination differ materially from the generally accepted view. There has been no purpose to rehabilitate Germain, but my study comes to very different conclusions from those Mr. Valentine draws, and for purposes of evaluation the two works should be read side by side.

This study does not go beyond 1778. Its whole emphasis is on the colonial policy of Germain; as bearing significantly upon that policy, his court-martial after the battle of Minden (1759) and his early contacts with the American question in the 1760's have been treated in the first two chapters. The period 1775–78 has a unity of its own. During those years Germain was directing a war which had the character of a civil war within the Empire. He was sometimes known as a colonial minister, and down to 1778 it is appropriate to consider his colonial policy. After that critical year the war broadened out to include France, Spain, and the Netherlands, and the theaters of operation expanded from the mainland and coasts of North America to include the West Indies, Central America, the Atlantic, the Mediterranean, the English Channel, and, in a contingent way, the sea lanes to the East Indies. The war had changed essentially in its nature: the colonial phase was over, and issues emanating in the state system of Europe had come to share, and to a large degree to dominate, as determinants in the War for American Independence.

There are many of my colleagues and friends to whom I owe a debt for insights and shared interests, but I should like especially to mention three scholars to whom I owe most in this study for their encouragement and criticism. They are A. L. Burt, emeritus professor at the University of Minnesota, Verner W. Crane, emeritus professor at the University of Michigan, and Professor William B. Willcox of the University of Michigan. Any errors of fact or judgment are wholly my own. Howard H. Peckham, director of the William L. Clements Library, and his staff have been unfailingly efficient and courteous and have greatly aided me in my researches. I wish also to acknowledge and to express my appreciation for the financial aid in the preparation of this study extended to me by the Horace H. Rackham School of Graduate Studies at the University of Michigan and the Institute of Early American History and Culture at Williamsburg, Virginia.

CONTENTS

CHAPTER 1

MINDEN AND THE COURT-MARTIAL, 1759–66

Lord George Germain, the third son of the first Duke of Dorset— and known until 1770, when he was fifty-four, as Lord George Sackville—became secretary of state for the American Department on 10 November 1775.[1] He remained in office for more than six years, resigning under crushing opposition after the fall of Yorktown. During the whole of the revolutionary struggle, he was virtually War minister in the British cabinet. Upon him, more than upon any other man, fell the weight and responsibility of mobilizing the imperial forces for that great struggle in America, the failure of which signalized the end of the First British Empire.

The whole of his public life was embittered and conditioned by the national memory of his court-martial and conviction in 1760 on the charge of disobedience of orders at the Battle of Minden (1 August 1759).[2] Contemporaries regarded his appointment to the high office of secretary of state with surprise and some indignation, and historians since that time have generally agreed that it was a characteristic act of impolicy on the part of George III. Any reference to Germain in the enormous historical literature of the American Revolution is almost invariably prefaced by a brief or extended account of the Minden affair. The great notoriety attaching to Sackville as a result of his court-martial, together with the failure of his policy toward the American colonies, has come near to making him, as a recent writer has noted, "the whipping boy for all the British errors in the Revolution." [3] Since the "Ghost of Minden" was used as a continuous reproach to Sackville during his period of office as American secretary, it deserves a full examination in any appraisal of his public policy toward the American Revolution.

No adequate study has ever been made of all the factors involved in Sackville's conduct at Minden, and even today the documentation for such a study is in part defective.[4] Materials, however, are available now which make possible an analysis that takes into consideration the broad implications of Minden in British politics rather than focusing upon the rather narrow possibilities, much disputed, of a military problem.[5]

The key to the understanding of his conduct at Minden lies, on the political side, in the inveterate hostility between George II and his grandson George, Prince of Wales.[6] The stakes men played for in choosing one side or the other in this quarrel were high. Favor with the Prince and the "Young Court" at Leicester House meant the chance for preferment in the next reign; favor with the king and the "Old Court" meant possible advancement at the moment, but it jeopardized the future. Around this constant of politics, men's fortunes rose and fell, and the general effect of the orientation one way or the other, is clearly seen in the case of Sackville.

As early as 1757 he had become involved in this intricate play of politics. In June of that year, Henry Fox, the father of Charles James Fox, attempted and failed to form an administration designed to save the King from advisers who were subservient to the Prince. Sackville was asked to take part in this projected administration, but he refused, and thus identified himself with the interests of the "Young Court." [7] Pitt remained in office.

The German war provided a real issue between Leicester House and the King. The Prince and Lord Bute were bitterly anti-Prussian, and, as such, opposed the sending of an expeditionary force to fight on the Continent. They advocated a policy of raids against the French coast—a policy of diversions and sideshows in preference to the commitment of a major British force in the continental warfare.[8] Pitt followed Leicester House in this policy in 1757 in the expedition against Rochefort,[9] and again in 1758 in two further raids against the French coast.[10] In the first of these raids of 1758, Sackville participated under the command of the Duke of Marlborough.

The raids obtained no significant results. They reflected no credit either on those who planned them or upon those who carried them out. Pitt had begun, in the early summer of 1758, to re-evaluate the situation. He came by stages to favor the participation of a British force in the German war. In June, 9,000 troops were sent to the Continent and reinforcements followed.[11] Pitt had reversed his old policy of attacks upon the periphery of French power and committed himself to send British troops in strength to the Continent in an effort to strike at the enemy's main armies in the field.[12] This meant in the long run that Pitt had deserted the policy of the Prince and Bute and had gone over to the King. Pitt's reversal was not immediately apparent, however, as the policy was decided upon piecemeal and implemented in the same way.

Sackville sought and obtained the post of second in command of the British troops sent to the Continent under the Duke of Marlborough. The rift between Pitt and Leicester House was not clear and decisive in the summer of 1758, and Pitt was willing to conciliate the Young Court by the appointment of Sackville.[13] He went to Germany thinking that he had the support of Pitt. It also seems reasonably clear that he understood his position with the army on the Continent as one which would represent the interests of the Prince and Bute. He was to observe and to report whether the British army was being used to serve purposes other than those which were vital to the British nation. His function was that of critic and regulator.[14]

From this time on the Prince and Bute were glad to hear of bickerings between the officers of the allied armies under Prince Ferdinand, and Sackville satisfied them in this particular.[15] On the other hand, Pitt and the King were now behind a vigorous and united effort in Germany. The lines had been clearly drawn, and the Prince had given up hope that he could count on Pitt to support his policy: "I am certain he has given himself either up to the K. or the D. of N., or else he could not act the infamous and ungrateful part he now does." [16] The war in Germany had become the King's war, Pitt's war, or Prince Ferdinand's war; it was not the war of Leicester House.

On 28 October 1758 the Duke of Marlborough died and Sackville became the commander of the British forces serving in Germany. The new instructions sent out to him were similar to those which had been issued to Marlborough, except that the authority, so important to the prestige of a military commander, of posting officers to vacancies was denied to him.[17] Flattering explanations of this came from Ligonier, the commander in chief, who asserted that all the ministers, and he himself, had exerted every influence to secure for Sackville the same authority as that entrusted to Marlborough. The King had been adamant. It was not, Ligonier asserted, a reflection upon Lord George Sackville; the same would have happened to any officer who took the command.[18]

Sackville was sensitive to what he considered an effort to reduce the importance of his command, and, in consequence, to elevate the importance of Prince Ferdinand. He wrote immediately to Pitt to express his dissatisfaction and told him frankly that if difficulties arose because of the belief on the part of the army that their commander lacked support at home, he would count on Pitt's friendship to make it possible for him to retire honorably.[19] The accounts which Sackville received from Bute made him still more suspicious that his position in the allied army was being made small in order to make the position of his German commander great. Bute wrote, "I rejoice extremely at your having the command, it was your due every way. At the same time, I observe with indignation that it is given by halves, but you'll guess where the hitch was, as Lord Ligonier assures me every method was taken by your friends to make it compleat." [20] The Prince and his family had a cordial dislike of the ducal family of Brunswick, and, aside from the politics of the war, Prince Ferdinand, as belonging to that family, was an object of suspicion and ill will.[21] It is entirely possible that the "hitch" referred to in Bute's letter was the opposition offered by Prince Ferdinand to Sackville.[22] He had, therefore, upon taking over the command of the British forces, some grounds to suppose that Prince Ferdinand had intrigued to make his post a subordinate one. He had also every reason to expect the support of the Prince and Bute in his resentment of this situation.

There were further elements of friction in the situation perhaps even more fatal to unity than the difficulties arising out of Sackville's command. Both Prince Ferdinand and he were men of high temper and dominating personality. They were bound to clash. Lord Granby, who was now second in command to Sackville, was a very popular soldier with the army, having an open purse and an easy manner of living. He was more pliable in the hands of Prince Ferdinand than was Sackville, and, though inferior to the latter in talents, he might well excite his jealousy. In addition, there were real issues beside temper and personality between Sackville and Ferdinand. Sackville felt that the British were made to pay exorbitant prices by the impositions of German agents. He was bold enough to bring this to Ferdinand's attention, perhaps in too sharp a manner.[23] Again, there was a strong suspicion that the commander in chief was subordinating British to Prussian interests and that it was the duty of Sackville to watch him closely.[24] These divisions were known in England, and, as early as December 1758, Prince George in his letters to Bute spoke of Sackville as one of those who might rule in the next reign.[25]

The lines of political and party spirit had thus been projected from London to the allied army in Germany. Many men of the time had their eye on the next reign, and a man of the strong ambition and aggressive character of Lord George Sackville was certainly keenly aware of every shade of political opinion which might lead to preferment. Lord Shelburne gave it as his opinion that, if Sackville had not met with checks to his military career, there was nothing which would have stopped him from becoming prime minister.[26]

The summer of 1759 saw a further deterioration of relations between Prince George and the King. During the invasion scare of that summer,[27] the Prince had written a very dutiful, and indeed humble, letter to the King requesting that he might take an active part in the defense of the kingdom.[28] The King thanked him shortly and formally, and put him off to "a proper occasion." [29] This seeming unconcern for the Prince gave rise to real resentment. He wrote hotly to Bute: "You will see by H. M. letter how shuffling it is and unworthy of a British monarch: the conduct of this old K. makes me ashamed of being his grandson; . . ." and then added characteristically, "I am going to carry a copy of this unworthy letter to my mother." [30] Pitt also was suspected of being a party to the slight upon Leicester House, and "this insolence of Pitt's" was carefully observed.[31]

Meanwhile, Sackville was in correspondence with Bute and reflected in his letters a critical attitude toward both Prince Ferdinand's strategy and his intentions. His advice had been set aside and, in consequence, the French had profited:

I confess, in my poor opinion, Marshal Contades has fairly outwitted us. It would be a presumption in me to think we could have done better, but,

I own, when we were at the camp of Dissen, the enemy did seem to have given us an opening which I then wish'd and expected would have been taken . . .

Prince Ferdinand acted as he did, in Sackville's opinion, above all in order to keep open his communications with Prussia; as a result the British army had been cut off from its shortest communication with England and Holland. In addition, the army had given up great quantities of supplies and lost winter quarters in a country which was capable of supplying forage with no expense to the public. Having thus sacrificed real advantages for communications with Prussia, Sackville was pessimistic of any aid from that power. He wrote: "I only wish we may ever see assistance come from that quarter. We certainly must not expect it without some great previous success on that side." [32] In an official letter to Holdernesse of the same day Sackville did not give expression to any of these critical sentiments.[33] The two parties in England were receiving substantially different accounts of the operations of the allied armies in Germany.

The general action of Minden was fought on 1 August 1759.[34] It was a significant allied victory, though the failure of the British cavalry to advance promptly at a critical moment is generally judged to have made the defeat of the enemy less complete than it ought to have been. The British Horse was under the command of Sackville, and repeated orders from Prince Ferdinand failed to put it in motion. At his subsequent court-martial, Sackville defended himself essentially on the following grounds: (1) that there was a contradiction in the orders from Prince Ferdinand: one set of orders directed him to bring up all the cavalry, the other set to bring up only the British cavalry and on the left; (2) that a wood impeded his march; (3) that he was on the alert and was in fact the first on horseback upon hearing the French artillery; (4) that Prince Ferdinand, through the neglect of the Prince of Anhalt, had not had adequate information of the approach of the French, and (5) that only a short space of time, at the most eight minutes, had been lost.[35]

On the day after the battle Prince Ferdinand issued an order of thanks to the army, and, in the order, he went so far as to observe that if the British cavalry had been under the command of Lord Granby the victory would have been even more decisive. Sackville wrote Ferdinand on that very day protesting this pointed rebuke.[36]

His commander, however, was not disposed to alter his position, but instead declared:

Je vous ai fourni la plus belle occasion pour profiter et pour faire decider le sort de cette journée, si mes ordres avoient été rempli au pied de la lettre. Le temoignage que j'ai rendu à my lord Granby je le lui dois par ce qu'il le mérite à tous égards et qu'il me l'a marqué dans tant d'occasions. Ce n'est pas une règle que puisque je loue l'un que je blame l'autre. Mais il ne me peut pas être indifférent si mes ordres ne s'executent point . . .[37]

Prince Ferdinand also sent a full report to England.[38]

Sackville, up to this time, had been reasonably confident that he had the support of both Leicester House and Pitt, who, he believed, would follow the lead given by the Prince and Bute. He was not aware of the break which had occurred over the question of the Prince's application for active service.[39] Apparently, Pitt still hoped to keep on good terms with the heir apparent, and yet to run the war himself. But it also seems clear that if he had to make a choice, he was determined that the direction of the war should not be allowed to slip from his hands. On 6 August he wrote to Bute that he had done his best to secure an honorable post for the Prince, but that "repugnancies hard to be eradicated in age" [i.e., the King] had made him almost despair of success.[40] Bute replied coldly that the Prince "complains bitterly of the extreme neglect he ever meets with . . ." and that he, Bute, would not make himself answerable for the consequences.[41] With this Pitt took his stand for the prosecution of the war in Germany under his direction and complete support of the brightest instrument of that policy after Minden—Prince Ferdinand.

On 11 August Bute received a letter from Sackville explaining his side of the Minden affair and enclosing a letter to Holdernesse asking permission to return to England.[42] He left it to Bute's discretion either to send the letter on to Holdernesse or to hold it. Bute approved the letter and it was forwarded.[43] The Prince immediately took the part of Sackville and condemned the conduct of Ferdinand. On the day that Bute received Sackville's letter, the Prince wrote: ". . . unless P. Ferdinand is very certain of what he alledges, he acts most impiously in this attack and let the thing be as it will, I think it is pretty pert for a little German Prince to make publick any fault he finds with the English Commander without first waiting for instructions from the King on so delicate a matter." He was deeply aggrieved over the matter, more particularly as he had thought Lord George might be a very useful man.[44]

Sackville was given permission to return to England.[45] On the next day Pitt took the opportunity to inform Bute of the fact and to emphasize that the government was acting in a humane manner. But he was careful to point out that the humanity extended only so far as the public good would allow.[46] Pitt clearly meant to indicate that he had no intention of shielding Sackville from the censure of Prince Ferdinand.

Lord George arrived in London at the beginning of September to find public opinion completely aroused against him, the King disposed to take violent measures, and himself wholly lacking in ministerial support.[47] He had a hard decision to make. He might have sought safety in obscurity had he felt that his conduct at Minden would not bear examination. The subsequent unwillingness of the government to grant a court-martial showed clearly enough that it would have been content to let the matter rest. The result of an unfavorable verdict of a military court, as the late case of Admiral Byng showed only too clearly, might be the capital sentence. Public opinion and almost all the influential elements of English society were against him. Yet, despite this dark prospect, Sackville, supported by the advice of Bute,[48] determined upon the bold action of requesting a court-martial. His letter to Holdernesse containing this request is spirited and dignified:

... I therefore most humbly request that I may at last have a public opportunity given me of attempting to justify myself to His Majesty and to my country, by a court martial being appointed, that if I am guilty, I may suffer such punishment as I may have deserved, and if innocent that I may stand acquitted in the opinion of the world, but it is really too severe to have been censured unheard, to have been condemned before I was try'd, and to be informed neither of my crime nor of my accusers.[49]

On the next day he was informed that the King would consider his request.[50]

He determined, now that he had resolved upon his course of action, to discover unequivocally where Pitt stood. He wrote him a letter enclosing his own requesting a court-martial. If he had entertained any hope that Pitt might support him, that hope was effectively dashed by Pitt's reply:

You are pleased to make very undeserved acknowledgements for such good offices only of common candour and humanity, as I judged it consistent with my duty to the King and zeal for the service to employ; but those offices went no further than using my endeavors that your Lordship might return from your command by his Majesty's *permission*, not by *order*.

He went on to observe that, though his own ignorance of military matters might make him incompetent to pass upon Sackville's conduct, still that conduct was such as to make it difficult for him to approve and support.[51] Sackville knew now beyond all doubt that he could expect no help from the minister. He wrote Bute that, if anything could have made him doubt his own innocence, this strong declaration of Pitt's would have done so. He was, nevertheless, confident that truth would prevail and that Bute would find him worthy of his friendship and backing.[52]

There was, however, to be no speedy resolution of the case. On 10 September Holdernesse informed Sackville that he could not be granted a court-martial at that time because officers who would act as witnesses were on duty in Germany. Nevertheless, if Sackville still wished it, the King would grant his request when the necessary officers had returned to England.[53] On the same day he was officially informed that his services as lieutenant general and colonel of Dragoon Guards were no longer required.[54]

He was thus forced to let the matter lie for a time until a court could be constituted and the requisite officers to act as witnesses could be brought from Germany. It is entirely likely that no further steps would have been taken by the government had Sackville not brought the whole question up again on 1 December by writing to Holdernesse to inquire, in view of the fact that the army had gone into winter quarters, whether the King would not now grant him his request and summon a court-martial.[55] Holdernesse replied that a doubt had arisen as to whether Sackville was legally amenable now to a court-martial. This question was under consideration, and, if he were judged subject to military law, the King would comply with his request.[56]

On 15 January 1760 Holdernesse wrote a quite extraordinary letter to Sackville. He enclosed a copy of the report of the attorney and solicitor general giving it as their opinion that Sackville might properly be tried by court-martial. He then went on, "as there is no specific charge exhibited against his Lordship, and he has requested the court martial to justify his conduct, he is desired to state in what manner he proposes to take the benefit of the same." [57] Sackville was, in fact, asked to charge himself before the court. Surely this was meant strongly to suggest to him that the government had no desire to press any charges—no specific charge had been made— and that the whole affair might now be allowed to rest by mutual, if tacit, agreement.

Sackville had taken the initiative in September by requesting a court-martial; it was put off then by the government. He raised the question again in December at which time seemingly the original governmental objection to the trial no longer existed and still no move was being made by the Crown. He was now asked to exhibit charges against himself. Even in this situation he continued to insist on a court-martial, though indeed he professed surprise that the King should have stripped him of all his military offices and shown him the strongest marks of disfavor, and had yet omitted to lay any charge against him. But he pressed his request "that his Majesty will be pleased to direct him to be prosecuted for whatever crime he is supposed to be guilty of. As he is conscious of no crime, he must wait to hear the accusation before he can offer his defense." [58]

The motivation is difficult to follow here and the puzzle remains. By forcing the trial in the face of his great unpopularity, the hostility of the court and the army, and the lack of any support from ministers, he seemed to defy his fortune. Horace Walpole, who remembered those days, declared: "For my own part, I would sooner pronounce Lord George a hero for provoking his trial, than a coward for shrinking from the French. He would have been in less danger by leading up the cavalry at Minden than in every hour he went down to the Horse-guards as a criminal." [59] The King sent Sackville a message telling him that he would put into execution the sentence of the court whatever it might be "without delay or mitigation." [60]

On 22 January he was informed that the King had given orders for the appointment of a court-martial,[61] and on 27 January the judge-advocate wrote him that the charge against him was disobedience to the orders of Prince Ferdinand. He was asked to furnish the names of any witnesses he wished to summon.[62] He replied with a list of eighteen witnesses, noting that he might have asked for witnesses of greater rank (the highest rank was that of colonel) but that he feared that their absence from the army might inconvenience the King's service. If, however, any general officers should be in England at the time of the trial, he hoped he might call on them.[63]

Since Sackville was a member of the House of Commons, the whole matter came up in that body as a matter of privilege. Lord Barrington, on 28 February, informed the House that Lord George had been placed under arrest for disobedience of the orders of his superior while serving with the army in Germany. The Speaker and, indeed, many members of the House were strongly against allowing one of their members to be brought before a military court when he was no longer in the army. However, Sackville had instructed his brother-in-law, Lord Milton, to assure the House that the trial was what he most earnestly desired, and though it is fairly clear that an issue could have been made, Sackville's own wish in the matter was respected by the House. After objection on the part of only a few members, a motion was agreed to thanking the King for his respect for the privileges of the House. Lord George had been active again in bringing on the trial, and in clearing away any obstacles which the government might have met with in regard to its legality.[64]

The court-martial began on 7 March and continued, through several adjournments, until 5 April. From the beginning to the end of the trial, Lord George conducted himself in a spirited and aggressive, even an arrogant, manner. He treated the judges, the attorneys, the witnesses, in a very high style, giving the impression that he felt they were all inferior to him in parts and in understanding. There was nothing timid, nothing hesitant, in his attitude. Walpole says: "An instant of such resolution at Minden had established his character forever." [65] He appeared confident that the trial could have but one result—his complete acquittal.[66]

However, the court found him guilty of disobedience of orders and declared him "unfit to serve His Majesty in any military capacity whatever." [67] The King confirmed this verdict and went beyond it.

He struck his name from the Council Book, forbade him the Court, and directed that the sentence of the court-martial be given out in all army orders, with the comment that it was "worse than death." [68] The King's actions went beyond the court, and violated the old maxim that "no man ought to be punished beyond his sentence." [69]

The political implications of the whole affair came out clearly with the reactions of the "Young Court." After the trial it was currently reported that the Prince intended to receive Sackville at Leicester House.[70] On 23 April the Lord Chamberlain informed Bute that Lord George had been forbidden the Court,[71] and the vice-chamberlain was sent also to acquaint him of the prohibition.[72] The Prince and Princess Dowager were also notified that Sackville was not to be received. The Prince was very angry that he should be treated in this manner. He declared that the whole "harsh affair" would bring credit to Sackville and show the public that somebody is "both judge and party." [73] He felt that the proceedings against Lord George were the most unusual and the most unconstitutional he had ever known. The reason the ministers acted as they did toward Sackville was, however, clear to him. It was because Lord George was a "drawn sword" in Bute's hand—a sword to keep the ministers in order. A man of Sackville's force with a clear reputation would have been of great value to the Prince and Bute. The whole affair made him resolve to take a bolder course: to take a course which would attract men to his side. He spoke boldly of men following "my banner." [74] Nevertheless, Leicester House did not receive Sackville despite the Prince's protestations.[75]

The net result of the trial and conviction were, for Sackville, something very nearly approaching personal disaster. He never escaped from its implications during the rest of his life. For fifteen years it effectively barred him from responsible office, and, during his period as secretary of state (1775–82), the ignominy of the sentence was constantly cast in his teeth by a provoked and vindictive opposition. It pursued him into retirement and it was sought to bar him from his seat in the House of Lords on the grounds that his presence was an affront to the dignity and honor of that body.[76] He spoke of Minden to his friend, Cumberland, during the last days of his life. This is the account which Cumberland gave:

It was in that same day, after dinner, as I well remember, the evening being most serene and lovely, we seated ourselves in the chairs that were placed out upon the garden grass-plat, which looks towards Crowberry and the forest. Our conversation led us to the affair of Minden; my friend most evidently courted the discussion; I told him I had diligently attended the whole process of the trial, and that I had detailed it to Mr. Doddington; I had consequently a pretty correct remembrance of the leading circumstances as they came out upon the evidence. But I observed to him that it was not upon the questions and proceeding agitated at that court, that I could perfect my opinion of the case; there must be probably a chain of leading causes, which, though they could not make a part of his defence in public court, might, if developed, throw such lights on the respective conduct of the parties, as would have led to conclusions different from those which stood upon the record.

To this he answered that my remark was just; there were certain circumstances antecedent to the action, that should be taken into consideration, and there were certain forbearances, posterior to the trial, that should be accounted for. The time was come when he could have no temptation to disguise and violate the truth, and a much more awful trial was now close at hand, where he must suffer for it if he did. He would talk plainly, temperately, and briefly to me, as his manner was, provided I would promise him to deal sincerely, and not spare to press him on such points as stuck with me for want of explanation. This being promised, he entered upon a detail, which, unless I could give as taken down from his lips, without the variation of a word, so sacred do I hold the reputation of the dead intrusted to me, and the feelings of the living, whom any error of mine might wound, that I shall forbear to speak of it except in general terms. He appeared to me, throughout his whole discourse, like a man who had perfectly dismissed his passions; his color never changed, his features never indicated embarrassment, his voice was never elevated, and being relieved at times by my questions and remarks, he appeared to speak without pain, and in the event his mind seemed lightened by the discharge. When I compare what he said to me in his last moments (not two hours before he expired), with what he stated at this conference, if I did not from my heart and upon the most entire conviction of my reason and understanding, solemnly acquit that injured man, now gone to his account, of the opprobrious and false imputations, deposed against him at his trial, I must be either brutally ignorant, or wilfully obstinate against the truth.

At the battle of Fontenoy, at the head of his brave regiment, in the very front of danger and the heat of action, he received a bullet in his breast, and being taken off the field by his grenadiers, was carried into a tent belonging to the equipage of the French King, and there laid upon a table, whilst the surgeon dressed his wound; so far had that glorious column penetrated in their advance towards victory, unfortunately snatched from them. Let us contemplate the same man, commanding the British cavalry in the battle of Minden, no longer in the front of danger and the heat of action, no longer in the pursuit of victory, for that was gained, and can we think with his unjust defamer, that such a man would tremble at a flying foe? It is a supposition against nature, a charge that cannot stand, an imputation that confutes itself.[77]

It is impossible now to solve the enigma of that day. It is clear that an interpretation in terms of personal cowardice is quite as inadequate as one in terms of personal rancor against Ferdinand—"he sacrificed himself to sacrifice Prince Ferdinand." [78] The whole affair must be seen against the background of the extraordinarily bitter political controversies of that day—controversies occurring at the end of a reign for the very basis of power in the British state. It must also be judged in terms of what eighteenth-century wars meant. Minden, and similar battles of the Seven Year's War on the fields of Germany, may have been the instrument for the up-building of the British Empire. They were not conceived in the terms of the great patriotic wars of our times; the animosities aroused between belligerents were less bitter, and the conduct of the generals was more formal, more conventional. The animosities between men on the same side, however, were as bitter then as now, and ambition was as compelling a motive. In such a situation, the extension of issues of domestic politics to the soldiers in the field and to the sailors at sea, bound up as they were with these issues, was perhaps inevitably part of the system. As inevitably, service trials came to partake of party controversy—Byng in 1757,[79] Sackville in 1760, and Palliser and Keppel in 1779.[80]

Clearly, Lord George continued to regard himself as an innocent man. Years later, speaking in the House on an intended inquiry into the conduct of Lord Mansfield, he said: "I could never oppose the minutest scrutiny into my behavior. However much condemned by the envy and malevolence of enemies, I would at least show that I stood acquitted in my own mind—'Qui fugit judicium, ipso teste, reus est!' " [81] So prominent a soldier as General James Murray,[82] and so prominent a sailor as Admiral George Rodney,[83] both gave their opinions for Sackville.

On 25 October 1760 George II died. Immediately on receiving

news of this event, Sackville wrote to Bute to inquire whether it would be proper for him now to pay his respects at Court.[84] He came to the first Court after the accession on the invitation of Bute.[85] His appearance, however, gave great offense to the ministers of George II, and Bute and the King came to the decision that it was too soon to attempt his rehabilitation. However, Bute secured from the King an undertaking to do something for Lord George as soon as the war was over. In the meantime, Sackville went into retirement though he attended the House and spoke upon occasion.[86]

Bute carried on negotiations with France during the summer of 1762, and in November the preliminaries of peace were signed. Sackville took this opportunity to remind the King and Bute of his situation and expectations. The King took the view that he could not be restored to his military commands and that a civil appointment would suit him best. Even that would be impossible until the end of the session: "... how much should not we hear again of the unlucky day of Minden if he were in the profession again," the King added, as though it were an afterthought.[87]

In April 1763 Sackville, through his friend Sir Henry Erskine, brought himself and his position again before Bute, and this time Erskine, whether authorized or not, hinted that Lord George might join himself with others if he did not receive some mark of the King's favor.[88] This implied threat aroused Bute, and he replied that if Sackville was that kind of man, he was not worthy of the good opinion which the King held of him—a good opinion which Bute had taken every opportunity to instill. He reported that he had had a long conversation with the King, who was very sensible of the ill-treatment Sackville had suffered and who had hoped, long before this, to be able to do something for him. However, to move in this direction would cause such resentment now as to threaten the government. If Lord George came to Court "he would soon be convinced of this, and that at a proper opportunity, offices might be open to him that would lead to higher ones, and then what appeared dangerous now would become easy and indeed palatable." [89] Sackville was by no means satisfied, and he confided to Erskine that the time had come, set by Bute himself, when he ought to have been "released from that situation to which I was reduced by the violence and iniquity of the last reign." [90]

In any case he took the hint and came to Court. He was received on 20 April, and the King showed him particular attention. He also came the next day and the King was not so pleased.[91] His rehabilitation had begun.

The Bute administration was replaced in May 1763, by one formed under George Grenville. Although Sackville was later to count himself as a follower of Grenville, the connection between the two was not established until Grenville was out of office. He held no government post during the period of slightly more than two years that Grenville was in power and embarked upon an American policy which culminated in the Stamp Act (22 March 1765).

During July 1765 negotiations were on foot to form an administration under Rockingham.[92] Charles Townshend took part in the political maneuvers antecedent to the formation of this administration, but he declined to take office upon its eventual formation. It was he, however, who brought Sackville forward and who pointed out most flatteringly that the time had come when "necessity had removed the prejudices which reason ought to have conquered with respect to you." [93] The upshot was that in December 1765 Sackville was given the post of joint vice-treasurer for Ireland, a relatively unimportant post, but a highly lucrative one. More gratifying to Sackville, however, than this minor Irish post was the fact that on the day of taking office he was again sworn of the Privy Council. Five years had passed since his name had been struck from the Council book by George II with all the humiliating consequences of public disgrace. Officially, his re-establishment was going forward, perhaps slowly, but nevertheless progress was being made. He met the Hereditary Prince of Brunswick, the kinsman of Prince Ferdinand, at the levée and the Prince put himself out to speak in the most courteous manner.[94] However, the public had not forgotten, and a part of the press greeted Lord George's return to office with abuse. One of the grounds taken in the press was that the Hereditary Prince, being in London at the time, would regard it as an insult to him.[95] Minden was in the past, if not forgotten, and the American Question loomed as the problem for the future.

CHAPTER 2

THE AMERICAN QUESTION, 1766–75

Sackville's interest in problems relating to America dated from his period of office under Rockingham. When Parliament assembled after the Christmas recess (14 January 1766) Pitt brought forward a demand for the repeal of the Stamp Act and precipitated the great debate upon this measure and the Declaratory Act—a debate which absorbed the interest of both Houses until March. It was during these debates that Sackville formed his first decided opinions on legislative supremacy, opinions which, with slight modification, he held to the end of the American War.

He listened with interest and attention to Pitt's views; but he rejected them completely. The distinction between the representative capacity of the British Parliament—in virtue of which it may levy taxes—and its legislative capacity—in virtue of which it may control trade and commerce—were distinctions wholly incomprehensible to him. To assert, as Pitt did, that the Parliament of Great Britain might in its legislative capacity, through external taxes, properly regulate the trade and commerce of the American Colonies, whereas in its representative capacity, being defective in colonial representation, it might not levy internal taxes seemed to Sackville both dangerous and absurd.[1]

Grenville's rebuttal of these views had his full approval, and he felt that Grenville showed as deep a knowledge of the Constitution as Pitt did, and that, in addition, he had a better informed judgment.[2] The Rockingham ministry, however, committed itself to the repeal of the Stamp Act, and many members of the administration looked to Pitt for a lead. Conway, secretary of state for the Southern Department, went so far as to announce in the House that he would be happy to serve under Pitt. Grenville on the other hand came more and more to represent opposition to Pitt's views and to stand forward as the champion of legislative supremacy. This doctrine was congenial to Sackville, and, as the debates progressed,

17

he found himself drawn toward Grenville. This was not because Grenville had made any overtures toward him. In fact, the opposite had been the case, and Sackville had commented upon his indifference.[3]

The Declaratory Bill, asserting the full power of the British Parliament to legislate for the colonies, was bound up as a companion measure with the repeal of the Stamp Act.[4] Sackville favored this measure and found himself again in opposition to Pitt and on the side of Grenville. In debate Pitt contended that if the Parliament proceeded to tax the colonies without representation, then the contract between the Sovereign Power and the Americans would be broken, and the latter would be justified in using force to resist such unconstitutional action. Sir Fletcher Norton, who was later to join Sackville as a follower of Grenville, declared that such opinions were criminal and Lord George fully agreed with him.[5] He was further concerned and agitated to hear Pitt go on to assert boldly that, if he were an American, he would not thank the British Parliament for the repeal of the Stamp Act, unless on the principle that that body had no constitutional right to levy an internal tax. This simply scandalized Sackville to whom it meant that the colonial assemblies would appropriate for themselves the exclusive legislative right of taxation. It seemed to Lord George that when ideas so subversive of the authority of the Parliament found a spokesman of such eminence in the Commons itself, legislative supremacy ought to be given strong expression in the Declaratory Act, so that these unorthodox and disquieting constitutional doctrines might be put to rest.[6]

During the debates on repeal Grenville began to make those friendly overtures to Sackville which resulted in their acting together until Grenville's death in November 1770.[7] Through a friend Grenville let Sackville know that he approved of his taking office and he gave a flattering explanation of the reasons why Sackville had not been approached before.[8] Throughout the debates of the rest of the session, Sackville reported Grenville's speeches fully to his friend Irwin and always spoke of his views with respect and approval.[9] He followed Grenville so far as to vote against repeal (11 March 1766) and to part company with the government.[10] He had thus at the very beginning of his active interest in the American question taken the side of strong measures against colonial discontent.

He had accepted the position from which he did not deviate during the long controversy preceding the war nor during the bitter war years.

With the repeal of the Stamp Act and the passing of the Declaratory Act in March, Parliament took up other business and the American question was not debated further during that session. Parliament was prorogued on 6 June and did not meet again until 11 November.[11] During July a protracted negotiation was undertaken, the end result of which was the formation in August of a new administration under Pitt, now made Earl of Chatham.[12] As a result Sackville was dismissed from his Irish office on 30 July.[13] In any case his allegiance to the Rockingham ministry had been little more than formal, and, on the important American issues, he had broken abruptly with his party. It was, in fact, on the question of America that Sackville found his real leader in George Grenville, and, though the relations of the two men appear to have been purely political and formal, they acted together effectively and without friction. During the maneuvers which preceded the formation of the new administration, when the situation was still confused, Sackville gave it as his opinion that only Grenville could form a government which would have those elements of strength necessary to make it other than an "Administration of Parade." This opinion was dutifully passed on to Grenville and served to emphasize the unity of purpose and ideas between the two.[14]

Parliament reassembled on 11 November 1766, and, from the beginning of that session, Sackville worked closely with the Grenville party. The most effective members of this group were Sir Fletcher Norton, Wedderburn, Sackville, and Grenville himself.[15] They were ever on the lookout for an issue which might make it possible for them to urge measures in line with their "strong" American policy. The brilliant but unstable Townshend, as chancellor of the Exchequer, soon gave them the opportunity they sought. Late in January, during the debates on the military establishment in America, Grenville proposed that the colonies should bear the whole cost of that establishment. This proposal was made with little expectation that it would receive any attention from the ministers. Townshend, however, to the great surprise of everybody, and not least his own party, declared that a revenue could be raised in America which would largely defray the expenses of the troops stationed there. This undertaking was seized upon by the Grenville group, and they determined to press it upon the minister. Sackville noted it as an announcement which would serve them well, and one which, in future debates, would not be forgotten.[16] It was the genesis of the Townshend duties passed in June.

Meanwhile, Sackville and his friends acting together with the Rockingham party, and with the support of the landed gentry, scored a spectacular victory over Townshend. Advocating a reduction of the land tax from four shillings in the pound to three, they were successful, early in March, in defeating a money bill of the ministry.[17] This had not happened since the Revolution, and it seemed clear that the government would be forced out of office. The defeat, however, had been accomplished by a combination of unstable elements in opposition and the ministry remained in power. The unlucky Townshend went on to devise his expedients for raising a revenue in America. Adopting Grenville's ideas of colonial financial support of the military, he proposed duties on glass, paper, paints, and tea imported into the colonies. The revenue from these duties was to be used first to help meet the expenses of the civil government and the administration of justice, and the remainder was to be paid into the British exchequer, to be disposed of, on the authority of Parliament, for the support of the military establishment in America. This measure was passed without opposition on 2 June 1767.[18] As Sackville had remarked in February, Townshend's unguarded declarations on the necessity for raising a revenue in America had, indeed, for the Grenville party, been "of use in future debates." [19]

During the summer of 1767 an attempt was made to form an administration based on the union of the Rockingham and Grenville parties. By Grenville's direction, Sackville was kept minutely informed of the progress of this negotiation.[20] On two questions, principally, agreement was found impossible: the American question, and the appointment of Conway to office. On the first point some accommodation might have been found, as it appeared Rockingham was prepared to retreat from the position he had occupied at the time of the repeal of the Stamp Act. However, no real agreement on this problem was attempted, as the Grenville party would not consent to giving high office to Conway, and indeed, in the apportionment of offices, the Rockingham party stipulated for so large a share that, as Sackville said, there were only "the scraps for those who belonged to Mr. Grenville and Lord Temple." [21] The whole affair seemed to turn more upon the question of employment than upon any large issues of policy either with respect to America or with respect to any other political question. Nevertheless, insofar as principle was concerned, Grenville stood for the assertion and establishment of the sovereignty of Great Britain over her colonies; the Rockingham party, not wishing to go so far, had stood out for the maintenance and support of that sovereignty.[22] Sackville interpreted this to mean that Grenville had made the issue of "public measures" the paramount matter for consideration, and that, on this issue, he had the firm support of all his friends.[23]

The Townshend duties came into operation 20 November 1767 and resulted in discontent and disturbance in America. Two regiments were ordered from Ireland to Boston, and Sackville, in the summer of 1768, declared himself in favor of strong measures. Nothing, he felt, was so apt to lead to trouble and confusion as "vigour unably exerted." [24] In December of that year, during the debate on a petition from Pennsylvania complaining of taxation without representation, Sackville spoke strongly against the petition, and Grenville spoke still more strongly. The latter declared that if the Parliament had no right to tax, it had no right to "bind" in other things. "If you mean to give way, give way universally, give way at once. Put an end to this question one way or other." [25]

From the beginning of 1769 down until the spring of 1774, insofar as the record is complete, Sackville was inactive on questions relating to America.[26] This, in large measure, is accounted for by the death of his leader, George Grenville, in November 1770. In writing to Irwin in October 1770, when the news of Grenville's health was giving genuine concern to his friends, Sackville had remarked: "If any accident should happen to him, it will require very serious consideration what part we are then to take. It would be the greatest mortification for me to act upon different ground than Wedderburn. If that was to happen, I should think as little as I could of public business, and I cannot say that my inclination at present leads me much to enter into the bustle and trouble of it." [27] Following Grenville's death, Wedderburn took office in the North administration (formed in 1770) as solicitor-general; hitherto he had been one of the most bitter enemies of the ministry. Thurlow and Suffolk, also Grenvillites, went over to the government.[28] Sackville remained, during the next few years, loyal to his old chief and did not join the relatively large defection from the Grenville group.[29] However, he took less and less part in politics, seeing little prospect arising from opposition, but he confided to Irwin, almost a year after Grenville's death, that, when the time came, he would show that he was not likely to change his views easily on "men or measures."[30]

In February 1770, Sackville assumed the name of Germain by act of Parliament.[31] He did this in compliance with the terms of the will of Lady Betty Germain who died in December 1769, leaving to him the extensive country estate of Drayton and £20,000 on the condition of his changing his name to Germain.[32] Cumberland has left us this pretty, idiosyncratic sketch of his country life:

As sure as the hand of the clock pointed to the half-hour after nine, neither a minute before nor a minute after, so sure did the good lord of the castle step into his breakfast room, accoutred at all points according to his own invariable costume, with a complacent countenance, that prefaced his good-morning to each person there assembled; and now, whilst I recall these scenes to my remembrance, I feel gratified by the reflection, that I never passed a night beneath his roof, but that his morning salutation met me at my post. He allowed an hour and a half for breakfast, and regularly at eleven took his morning's circuit on horseback at a foot's pace, for his infirmity would not admit of any strong gestation; he had an old groom, who had grown gray in his service, that was his constant pilot upon these excursions, and his general custom was to make the tour of his cottages to reconnoitre the condition they were in, whether their roofs were in repair, their windows whole, and the gardens well cropped and neatly kept; all this it was their interest to be attentive to, for he bought the produce of their fruit-trees, and I have heard him say with great satisfaction that he has paid thirty shillings in a season for strawberries only to a poor cottager, who paid him one shilling annual rent for his tenement and garden; this was the constant rate at which he let them to his laborers, and he made them pay it to his steward at his yearly audit, that they might feel themselves in the class of regular tenants, and sit down at table to the good cheer provided for them on the audit day. He never rode out without preparing himself with a store of six-pences in his waistcoat pocket for the children of the poor, who opened gates and drew out sliding bars for him in his passing through the inclosures; these barriers were well watched, and there was rarely any employment for a servant; but these six-pences were not indiscriminately bestowed, for as he kept a charity school upon his own endowments, he knew to whom he gave them, and generally held a short parley with the gate-opener as he paid his toll for passing. Upon the very first report of illness or accident relief was instantly sent, and they were put upon the sick list, regularly visited, and constantly supplied with the best medicines administered upon the best advice; if the poor man lost his cow, or his pig, or his poultry, the loss was never made up in money, but in stock. It was his custom to buy the cast-off liveries of his own servants as constantly as the day of clothing came about, and these he distributed to the old and worn-out laborers, who turned out daily on the lawn and paddock in the Sackville livery to pick up boughs and sweep up leaves, and in short do just as much work as served to keep them wholesome and alive.

To his religious duties this good man was not only regularly but respectfully attentive: on the Sunday morning he appeared in gala, as if he was dressed for a drawing-room; he marched out his whole family in grand cavalcade to his parish church, leaving only a sentinel to watch the fires at home, and mount guard upon the spits. His deportment in the house of prayer was exemplary, and more in character of times past than of time present: he had a way of standing up in sermon time for the purpose of reviewing the congregation, and awing the idlers into decorum, that never failed to remind me of Sir Roger de Coverly, at church: sometimes, when he has been struck with passages in the discourse, which he wished to point out to the audience as rules for moral practice worthy to be noticed, he would mark his approbation of them with such cheering nods and signals of assent to the preacher, as were often more than my muscles could withstand; but when to the total overthrow of all gravity, in his zeal to encourage the efforts of a very young declaimer in the pulpit, I heard him cry out to the Reverend Mr. Henry Eatoff in the middle of his sermon—'Well done, Harry!' it was irresistible; suppression was out of my power: what made it more intolerably comic was, the unmoved sincerity of his manner, and his surprise to find that anything had passed that could provoke a laugh so out of time and place. He had nursed up with no small care and cost in each of his parish churches a corps of rustic psalm-singers, to whose performances he paid the greatest attention, rising up, and with his eyes directed to the singing gallery, marking time, which was not always rigidly adhered to, and once, when his ear, which was very correct, had been tortured by a tone most glaringly discordant he set his mark upon the culprit by calling out to him by name, and loudly saying, 'Out of tune, Tom Baker!' [33]

From this point on, it will be appropriate to use the name Germain in place of Sackville.

The period 1770–73 was characterized by no outstanding dispute between Great Britain and her colonies. It was a time of calm, and many on both sides of the Atlantic felt that, the stormy days of the 1760's having passed, the relations between the mother country and the colonies might adjust themselves through usage and custom without some great constitutional or legislative solution. It was also a time of prosperity and this acted to assuage grievances.

But the quiet was not to continue, however, for on the night of 16 December 1773 occurred the Boston Tea Party. The news of the violent actions of the people of Boston brought the whole American question before Parliament again. Germain took a leading part in the debates on the Coercive Acts and developed his opinions more thoroughly than he had ever done before. They were not different from those he had held when he followed Grenville. They were, however, more pungent, more forceful; they more nearly approached a system of opinion.

Being of a logical and clear mind, Germain began by assigning a cause for the late troubles in America. They arose from the fact that the Stamp Act had been repealed. If this had not been done there would have been no Boston Tea Party, the people would have "returned to their obedience," and the colonial question would have received its solution.[34]

However, since it was now necessary for Parliament to deal with a situation and not to lament a lost opportunity, Germain had specific views on the measures which ought to be enacted. He developed these views in a speech in Parliament on 28 March 1774.[35] First he declared that there was a "degree of absurdity" in the election of the council in the colony of Massachusetts Bay. He would remedy this by placing the council there on the same footing it was in other colonies; he would make it appointive. He would go on from that and abolish the town meetings: "I would not have men of a mercantile cast every day collecting themselves together, and debating about political matters; I would have them follow their occupations as merchants and not consider themselves as ministers of that country."[36] The next step would be to give all the corporate authority to certain people in each town; this was the case in Great Britain. In this manner, it would be possible to secure subordination, authority, and order. The grand and petty jury system led to great abuses, since these juries were open to public pressure; they were totally different from those in the mother country and ought to be strictly regulated. Chancery suits should be heard before chancery courts and not, as in the colonies, before the assembly. The assembly itself in Germain's view was "a downright clog upon all the proceedings of the governor." [37] In fine, there was no government; it was "the proceedings of a tumultous and riotous rabble, who ought, if they had the least prudence, to follow their mercantile employment, and not trouble themselves with politics and government which they do not understand." [38] Some objected to the charters being broken. Germain advocated not the breaking of the charters but rather their correction and regulation. He was for free government, but not a government which asserted its rights by words, and then denied its own authority and prevented the execution of the laws. Rather "by a manly and steady perseverence, things may be restored from a state of anarchy and confusion, to peace, quietude, and a due obedience to the laws of this country." [39]

This speech made a considerable impression upon Lord North, who spoke after Germain, and referred with approval, and in a most complimentary manner, to the cogency of argument and fruitfulness of suggestion which had characterized the preceding speech.[40] Germain was, in fact, being considered by North for office. His ability in debate was striking, and, particularly on American questions, North urgently needed such support in the House. His strong advocacy of the government's coercive legislation, at a time when it was being hotly assailed by the opposition, was a real acquisition. This was so noticeable that Shelburne wrote to Chatham that the rumor was that Germain was to be offered a post in the government. "He has certainly put himself forward of late, and met with great encouragement from the ministry. . . ." [41]

In May, he again came to the support of the government. He declared that America at that time was nothing but "anarchy and confusion"; that both the governor and the council were at the mercy of a "lawless rabble." [42] He adjured the House to support its own supremacy and to understand that legislation was a part of that supremacy. He ended by a clear assertion of his support of the measures put forward by government:

It is incumbent on every man to give his opinion from his own breast upon this great occasion; but, Sir, I cannot help once more condemning that mob of people, which, under the profession of liberty carries dark designs in its execution; but my utmost wish is, that these measures, in their consequences, may turn out well and contrary to what has been apprehended.[43]

Parliament was prorogued on 22 June 1774.[44] The government's coercive legislation had been passed, and a strong policy, strongly supported by Germain, had been written into the public law of Great Britain. It remained to be seen what success this legislation might have. In the meantime, the members dispersed for the summer recess.

The next session, the first of the fourteenth Parliament, assembled on 29 November, but Germain took no part in the debates until after the Christmas holiday. On 29 January 1775, he spoke in support of the series of coercive laws passed during the last session.[45] He based his argument upon the Declaratory Act and professed to address himself only to those who agreed with its principle. The assertion of the right to legislate implied the propriety and, indeed, the necessity of exercising that right. If the Americans complained of the late legislation as a grievance, they ought to petition for its repeal. He would be the first to welcome and examine such a petition. If, however, repeal were demanded as a right, and the authority of the mother country was thus drawn in question, he declared that he favored the enforcement of the Acts "with a Roman severity." [46] The government's majority was large and well disciplined, and efforts to modify or to repeal the Intolerable Acts were unavailing.[47]

Late in May 1775, the news of Lexington and Concord reached England. It caused an immediate stir and engaged Germain's full attention.[48] Early accounts did not reveal the serious loss which the British troops had sustained. When the gravity of these losses became generally known, it was widely rumored that the ministry would fall. Germain did not subscribe to this view. He felt, to be sure, that Dartmouth, secretary of state for the American Department, might fail to give "the necessary orders for decisive and vigorous measures." [49] This, however, would not mean the defeat of the government. He, himself, saw clearly what ought to be done. A local force should be armed and a body of Canadians marched to the frontiers of New England. Strong measures undertaken immediately might prevent the fatal consequences which would be the sure result of delay. But his conclusion was gloomy: "... I still think we shall not dare to take bold and decisive measures till we are drawn into them by degrees, and when, perhaps, it may be too late...." [50]

By midsummer 1775, Germain's position on the American question had been fully developed both in Parliament and in private letters to his friends. He was a "man of principle" and his consistent and uncompromising adherence to "a plan of coercion" [51] marked him off strongly from those who preferred to equivocate and to temporize.

Suffolk, secretary of state for the Southern Department, and his undersecretary, the influential Eden, were both in correspondence with Germain during that summer. In the middle of June, Suffolk had written to Germain with respect to Lexington and Concord and the effect of events in America upon the political situation in England. [52] He asked Germain to give him plainly his ideas on the position of affairs. In a long letter of reply, Germain entered into a detailed analysis of the American situation, and put forth clear-cut suggestions as to the course of action that ought to be followed. [53] He noted the parallel between the action at Concord and the defeat of Braddock during the Seven Years' War. At that time, measures had been taken to introduce a new discipline appropriate to the irregular character of warfare in America, and these had proved effective. The same course should now be followed. Further, to strengthen the military position, Gage ought to be replaced. He is "in a situation of too great importance for his talents." [54] Howe knew the principles of warfare which would be effective in America and would soon teach them to the army. [55] Germain reverted also to one of his favorite ideas —the use of Canadian troops: "... I believe the Canadians would be very ready to chastise their neighbors under the sanction of government." [56] The prime object, however, ought to be the retaking of New York. This city was the most strategic post in America and was absolutely essential to successful military operations. The whole tone of this letter is unmistakable: it is written with the freedom and precision of detail of one who is confident of the advice he gives and of one who knows that the ground has been prepared for the reception of that advice. Germain was not, however, convinced that the ministry would have the resolution to act, for "... as they love delay, they may wait for the resolves of Congress." [57]

News reaching England in July seemed to indicate that whatever colonial unity had resulted from open conflict with the British authorities was fast dissolving. Suffolk reported to Germain that the southern colonies were hard hit by the stopping of their trade and could not hold out much longer. The delegates from Massachusetts, so Germain heard, were disgusted, and Dr. Franklin was losing his influence because of his moderation. Germain was convinced that one decisive action by land and then the inexorable pressure of blockade would end the business.[58] In September he declared: "As there is not common sense in protracting a war of this sort, I should be for exerting the utmost force of this Kingdom to finish this rebellion in one campaign." [59]

Eden continued to keep Germain informed of developments in America and, during September, their correspondence became much fuller.[60] Eden's letters appear to be quasi-official reports of government policy. On 3 October 1775, he wrote to Germain at the special request of Lord North.[61] After detailing the preparations which the government was undertaking to secure the submission of America—preparations which would be pressed forward vigorously—Eden told Germain of the other part of the government's plan. The organization of a large military and naval force was to act as a threat; the setting up of a commission was to constitute the olive branch. The government wished to indicate that it was equal to the emergency and was prepared to use force unflinchingly and with annihilating effect. On the other hand, an accommodation was to be offered by a single commissioner endowed "with ample powers to settle everything in dispute with any colony which either fear, interest, fickleness, or duty might bring to submission." [62] In order that Germain might be fully informed of the character of the commission proposed and its relationship to the whole policy of the ministry, Eden enclosed, in strictest confidence, a tentative outline of the King's speech which was to be delivered at the beginning of the next session. This speech did not attempt in detail to define the powers which would be granted to the commissioner, but Germain was asked to consider what powers would be proper and necessary. Eden then came to the real reason for his letter:

There never perhaps was a commission of such importance for any individual in the annals of mankind, and I shall proceed to tell your lordship without form or flattery that Lord North (and I believe, every person equally well informed and equally honest in wishes and declarations) thinks you the fittest man in the Kingdom. He also *knows* that nothing would make your friend Howe so happy as to see you in such a situation.[63]

This is a unique and largely neglected aspect of the history of the many ill-fated commissions projected and realized in the revolutionary period. It raises many questions, not least among them being the question of the sincerity of the British government in setting up such commissions, or, alternatively, the question of the government's judgment of the whole American situation. It would be idle to examine whether or not the government were sincere, since there is no tangible evidence to adduce. However, to select Germain, who was so clearly associated with the advocacy of "strong measures" toward America, as the sole commissioner to conciliate and to adjust the large and the increasingly bitter controversies existing between the mother country and the colonies *after* Lexington and Concord seems almost incredible. Surely, this proposition to Germain augurs that North and his colleagues had utterly no judgment of the realities of the situation.

Germain congratulated Eden upon the draft of the King's speech. He hoped that Britain would exert her full force against America and bring on a decision either one way or the other. However, with a better conception of the real position of affairs in America than either Eden or North had displayed, he declined the commission on grounds of health.[64] The whole transaction, however, emphasized the closeness of Germain to administration, and the great confidence reposed in him by those in authority. Shortly after receiving Germain's refusal, Eden wrote: "...we have no longer any idea of any one person fit to fill so large a Vice-Royalty, and, unless your Lordship will help us, must divide the burthen and reduce it too." [65]

Parliament came into session on 26 October 1775, and the speech from the throne contained the outlines of the proposed commission. As the result of Germain's refusal to accept the position of sole commissioner, it had been determined to appoint several persons. The commissioners were to be empowered, at discretion, to grant general or individual pardons, to receive the submission of any colony, and to restore to such colony its trade and commerce.[66] Germain spoke during the debate on the Address of Thanks, and supported the policy of government as laid down in the King's speech.[67] Of course, he had already seen the rough draft of the speech and approved it before it had been delivered. Colonel Barré followed Germain in the debate and criticized North severely. He asserted that North had no views of his own and adopted all of Germain's; he ought to resign his post to him as the abler man. The Address was adopted at four in the morning by a vote of 279 to 108.[68]

The North administration had now come to the decision to use real force against the colonies. Germain had been the steady advocate of a resolute policy toward America from the first. This fact, together with his abilities in debate and his reputation as an able administrator, determined North to seek his support and to offer him the high office of secretary of state for the American Department.[69] The appointment of Germain, as successor to the indecisive Dartmouth in the American Department, served notice upon the colonies and the world that the British government intended to adopt force, in the measure necessary, to secure a proper acknowledgment of the supremacy of the mother country. Germain accepted the appointment early in November [70] and the King's warrant was issued to him 10 November 1775.[71] His own comment was, "Pity me, encourage me, and I will do my best." [72]

CHAPTER 3

THE STATUS OF THE AMERICAN
DEPARTMENT UNDER GERMAIN

I

Germain's coming into office was preceded by one of those complicated arrangements among leaders of fractional groups in the House of Commons, which made the tenure of power of any ministry most uneasy. It is not surprising that researchers in this period, looking through the voluminous correspondence, should "come away bewildered by the cross threads of home politics, by the names remembered or forgotten of statesmen, by the fall and reconstruction of ministries, by the crises of Whigs and Tories." [1] Beneath all this, however, there is the reality of politics; these changes and these jarrings of interest represented by individuals, often themselves selfish in motive, are the outward signs of tendencies which have a long-range importance in the political and administrative history of Great Britain. Such was the case in a rather remarkable degree in the circumstances surrounding the appointment of Germain and its sequel. [2]

The original intention of the King and North was to bring Germain into the cabinet to replace Dartmouth as secretary of state for the American Department. Dartmouth, unhappy in his office, was prepared to accept this arrangement on the condition that he should be made Lord Privy Seal. [3] However, Lord Weymouth, who was Groom of the Stole, also laid claim to the Privy Seal and, through his connection with Lord Gower and the Bedfords, threatened to wreck the administration. Lord North, in a characteristic gesture, offered to resign. [4] The King refused this offer, called North his "sheet anchor," and held out to him the hope that by continuance in office he would secure solid advantages to his family. The King, nevertheless, was well aware of the awkwardness of breaking off with Germain in a negotiation which had gone so far. He hoped that Dartmouth, being cooler than either Weymouth or Germain, would come around to his view and accept the Groom of the Stole in the place of the Privy Seal, the former office being, in the King's view, the equal of the latter.[5] However, Dartmouth was unwilling to make an accommodation along these lines. At this point it appeared that a way out of the dilemma had been found in the willingness of Lord Rockford, "who continues very low," to vacate his office as secretary of state for the Northern Department, it being understood that he would receive certain specified and very solid equivalents elsewhere within the gift of the King.[6] The thought now was to give Dartmouth the Northern Department, make Weymouth Privy Seal, and Germain American secretary.[7] Even these rather notable and far-reaching changes failed to give satisfaction to the Earl of Dartmouth, whom North represented to the King as being desirous either of being made Privy Seal or remaining where he was, namely in the American Department.[8] The King now began to see what was behind the obstinacy of Dartmouth "who abstracted from his conduct on this occasion I really respect, and trust that in this affair, he is guided by others and not his own sentiments." Dartmouth had come in fact, the King considered, to believe that he was being ousted from his office through the influence of Lord Suffolk, secretary of state for the Southern Department. This had hurt his pride.[9] It was, indeed, commonly believed at the time that Suffolk wished to see Germain in the cabinet as a preliminary move in the formation there of a bloc of power upon which he could base his claim to be the King's first minister.[10] Suffolk thought of Germain, it would appear, as a supporter of his in the cabinet, not as an equal. This view is borne out by the rather elaborate correspondence stretching over the previous six months between Suffolk, his undersecretary Eden, and Germain.[11]

The tangle of cross purposes was cleared up by Weymouth. He told North that he would "without the least regret" take the seals of secretary of state for either the Northern or the Southern Department,[12] and the final arrangement saw Weymouth given the Northern Department, Dartmouth made Lord Privy Seal, and Germain American secretary.[13]

This whole affair, perhaps tedious in detail, is worth recording because of its relationship to the developing theory of the secretariat. The American Department had been created in 1768 with the Earl of Hillsborough as its first secretary.[14] He was succeeded in August 1772 by the Earl of Dartmouth. The commissions of both these

noblemen contained a limiting clause in the preamble which set
forth the reason for establishing the third secretaryship. The relevant
part of the preamble was couched in the following terms: "Whereas
the public business of our colonies and plantations increasing, it
seemeth expedient to us to appoint one other principal secretary
of State beside our two ancient secretaries." [15] This limiting clause
seemed to indicate that the secretary of state for the American Department was a new office. In that case, because of the Place Acts
of Queen Anne, no member of the House of Commons could hold
the post.[16] Since both Hillsborough and Dartmouth were peers, no
problem arose with respect to them. However, Germain was a commoner, and if the American Department was indeed a new office he
would be debarred from his seat in the House of Commons.

It was further urged that the preamble in the commissions of
Hillsborough and Dartmouth limited the function and authority of
the new office. Since the Board of Trade had continued to function
after the creation of the American Department, and since both
Hillsborough and Dartmouth had presided at the Board, they were
held not to be the equals of the two "ancient secretaries," but only
first Lords of Trade with the Seals and the cabinet, lacking the full
measure of authority to transact any of the King's business. It was a
restrictive secretaryship, an *ad hoc* creation for expediting the affairs
of America. Weymouth had refused the post at the time Dartmouth
took it (1772) because he did not believe the office to rank as a full
secretaryship.[17]

In addition to these two problems there was still a further difficulty
raised by the opponents of the third secretaryship. It was contended
that the secretariat was in fact in commission, since it had been
divided in the days of Henry VIII. If this were the case then the
17th section of the 6th of Queen Anne applied. This stated that "no
greater number of commissioners shall be made or constituted for
the execution of any office than have been employed in the execution
of such respective office at some time before the first day of this
parliament," viz., 23 October 1707.[18] As the argument was then
made, this would have made it impossible for there to be more than
two secretaries of state: [19]

The office of the King's Principal Secretary is an ancient office, having
legal as well as political functions. It is but one office since the reign of

Henry the 8th. It may be exercised by two Secretaries, but more cannot be joined in it.[20]

There thus appear three separate problems in administrative and constitutional history raised by the office of the American Department and in particular by Germain's appointment to that Department. *First:* Could a commoner hold that office—was it a new office? *Second:* Did the preamble in the commissions of the first two secretaries limit their authority to matters pertaining to America, and thus bar them from the plenary authority within the scope of the necessity of the King's business which the two "ancient secretaries" enjoyed? *Third:* Did the law and custom of the constitution limit the exercise of the functions of the secretariat to two officials?

It was an easy matter to meet the difficulties presented by the first two problems. The telltale preamble in the commissions of Hillsborough and Dartmouth might be simply omitted in the case of Germain. It was expected that Suffolk and Weymouth might object to this as tending, by the raising of the status of the American Department, to derogate from the status of their own office. Suffolk, at the outset, was in an awkward position. He was a prime mover in bringing Germain into the cabinet; it would seem an ungracious and undiplomatic act on his part to raise objections to a line of action which would make it possible for Germain to take the American secretaryship and retain his seat in the House. He and Eden thought they saw a way, through an arrangement noted below, by which they could acquiesce in the omission of the preamble and still maintain the primacy of the two "ancient secretaryships." The King took the lead in circumventing any opposition which Weymouth might offer. When the Privy Council met to swear in the new officers, the Lord President, Gower, moved the King that Weymouth be sworn as secretary of state. The King replied that there were two secretaries of state to be sworn and that they should be sworn together. This, in fact, was done, and after the ceremony, Weymouth, sensing now the King's intent, took Germain aside to tell him that he had understood that some difficulty was being made about his right to sit in the Commons on the ground that his office was a new one. Weymouth assured Germain that there should be no difficulty if his commission was in the same terms as the other secretaries. Weymouth, having abandoned his opposition, Germain's commission was prepared in Suffolk's office in identical terms with those of the "ancient secretaries." [21] This stroke made it possible for Germain to take his seat in the Commons as it made it clear that his office was not a new one, and it seemed equally to indicate that in the discharge of his duties he was not limited to American affairs.

Suffolk and Eden, however, were not prepared to accept this as the final solution. They determined to seek a delimitation of the authority of the American Department through a royal directive, which Wedderburn described as a "barrier treaty" between Cleveland Row and Whitehall.[22] This remarkable document is in the hand of Eden and though undated was clearly under consideration at the middle of December 1775—about a month after Germain had taken office.[23] In this document the King was to be made to declare that the American secretaryship

is always to be considered as separate from the other two, and that the Ministers filling the Northern and Southern Departments shall in all events be considered as the two Principal Secretaries of State at whatever period they may be appointed. And further, it is my pleasure that my secretaries for the Northern and Southern Departments shall exclusively as heretofore transact all matters respecting the interior of Great Britain or any other parts of my dominions and all other matters which have been executed within said Departments subsequent to Lord Hillsborough and Lord Dartmouth being made Secretaries of State. And it is equally my pleasure that my Secretary for the colonies shall transact exclusively all matters in his own Department in the same manner as has been hitherto done by his predecessors therein.

It was hoped that the King would sign this document and deliver it to each of the three secretaries as the definitive statement of the function of each. As it clearly was a derogation of Germain's position, and as his opposition could be presumed, Eden attempted to persuade Germain's friends to urge him to accept this arrangement. He began by approaching Wedderburn, an old friend of Germain, who, together with him, had been a Grenvillite in the late sixties, and who had preceded Germain by some years in coming over from the Opposition to the Government. Eden wrote Wedderburn that it was the intention of Germain and his friends to raise the American Department above the other departments of government, and that, in the end, it would be the only department. This was being done too, he asserted, in direct opposition to the interests of those who had contributed most to the bringing of Germain into office. Now that he was in office, he had a different set of friends from those whom he had cultivated before, and among these latter, Eden counted himself. He explained that the purpose of the "barrier treaty" was to calm troubled waters.[24]

Wedderburn took an uncompromising stand against the treaty and replied to Eden in most explicit terms:

I should advise him to resign his Seals rather than submit to an explanation not called for, not attempted on two former occasions, and one that can only be proposed (as you know it only is) to make him submit in the first place to an indignity and afterwards hold the exercise of his office at the discretion of the other officers and at his own risk; for to give as a fixed line the usage of seven or eight years is only establishing a rule the extent of which is to be disputed on every case and which the powers of the two to one will be decided for his office when troublesome and against it when pleasant.[25]

Faced with all-around opposition, from the King, Germain, and the latter's friends, the project of the "barrier treaty" was dropped and not heard of again.[26]

Had this effort to limit the divisibility of the secretariat been successful in 1775, it might well have barred for good one of the main lines along which the modern cabinet has developed. For it has been precisely along this line of the infinite divisibility of the office of the secretariat, with the retention of full responsibility and authority for all the King's business, that the modern cabinet system has evolved. In the last quarter of the eighteenth century, it was by no means clear that this would occur. These were formative years in the growth of that uniquely flexible and British system of fused powers, king-in-cabinet government. When Germain declared that

he was Secretary of State at large, and not connected with the Board of Trade, though he sometimes attended as first lord,[27]

and that the office he held

was neither that of third Secretary of State, nor secretary for the colonies: but one of His Majesty's principal Secretaries of State,[28]

when he took this position, he was the spokesman for the future. It is, perhaps, an irony that a man who has always been judged the exponent of prerogative notions of government should thus have taken so important a part in the development of the institution which more than any other ensured the control of the executive by Parliament.

II

Germain took office at a critical time in the history of the first British Empire. At Boston one British army was under close siege and before the year was out another British force, having retired to the bastion of Quebec, would have to fight for its very life in the face of the converging columns of Montgomery and Arnold. Upon Germain rested the primary responsibility for mobilizing the forces of the empire against the serious and mounting threat of the revolution in America. For seven years he carried that burden and that responsibility, and the ill success of his policy has led even a distant relative and friendly historian of the Sackvilles to dismiss her kinsman with the tart comment that he was first a soldier and then a statesman, both disastrously.[29]

At his first session in the House of Commons as one of His Majesty's principal secretaries of state, Germain sat on the Treasury Bench between Lord North and Wedderburn. He confessed some feeling of awkwardness during this first sitting (16 November), but he continued in the House for the fourteen hours of the debate [30] and spoke on Burke's motion for composing the troubles in America.[31] He met with no abuse and felt satisfied with his reception by the House.[32] Indeed, he was in the way of being the man of the hour, and Horace Walpole reported that he "engrosses all tongues." He reminded Walpole of some lines which Lord Lansdowne had written while confined in the Tower: "Some fall so hard, they bound and rise again." [33]

Germain was now in his sixtieth year. At this period he enjoyed good health and was capable of withstanding the fatigue, mental and physical, attendant upon the long hours of sitting in the House of Commons, which, combined with the running of a great department of state, made exacting demands upon his strength and energy. He had keen eyesight, which Lord North notably lacked, and upon taking his place in the House, it was the habit of Germain to examine carefully the Opposition benches, noting who was present and who was absent, and in this way forming a pretty accurate judgment as to how the business of the day would proceed. He often said that for a man with good eyesight, everything was to be *seen* in the House, whereas little except declamation was to be *heard*.[34]

In height he was almost six feet and, though his features were pronounced and saturnine, he would be counted a handsome man. Shelburne, who was no friend of his, described him as

a tall man, with a long face, rather strong features, clear blue eyes, a large make, though rather womanly, not too corpulent, and a mixture of quickness and a sort of melancholy in his look, which runs through all the Sackville family, such as is seen in the antique statues often to accompany great beauty.[35]

In bearing and manner Germain was proud, reserved, and maintained an air of aristocratic hauteur.[36] His high birth, grave manner, and air of command did not invite intimacy, though Wraxall, who knew him well and often dined at his house, related that

no man in private society unbent himself more. In the midst of his family—for he rarely dined from home, except for Cabinet dinners—and in the company of a few select friends, he soon forgot the toils annexed to public life, the asperities of debate, and the vexations of office. Even after the latest nights in the House of Commons, he always sat down to a delicately served table, drank a pint of claret, unbent his mind and passed in review the incidents of the preceding evening.[37]

Cumberland, secretary at the Board of Trade, also vouched for his coolness of manner upon first meeting, but declared that upon acquaintance he was a warm, cordial, and sympathetic friend.[38]

He was educated at Westminster School and Trinity College, Dublin, but he was never a reading man. He had a fine library at his country home, Drayton, but he rarely took a volume from the shelves.[39] He was, however, intimately acquainted with the history of England from the Stuart period down to his own day. During this time, one or another of his ancestors had occupied prominent places in the councils of the sovereign, and his mind was stored with out-of-the-way information and anecdotal history. His mother had been a maid of honor for Queen Anne and his father remembered King William. But he was a stranger to the classical education which formed the minds of educated men of his time and he lacked interest either in the reading or writing of creative literature. "I have not," he wrote, "genius sufficient for works of mere imagination." [40]

In his own correspondence, however, both official and private, there is freshness and vigor. He used idiomatic language with a dash, and there is a directness and force in his writing which has real attraction. If his mind was not stored with the classic images and ideas so common in his day, neither was his style corrupted by them. It is perhaps a negligent and impetuous style, not studied or refined, but it was a fit instrument for unambiguous exposition. Cumberland wrote of his manner of conducting affairs:

A very short time sufficed to confirm the idea I had entertained of Lord George's character for decision and dispatch in business; there was at once an end to all circumlocutory reports and inefficient forms, that had only impeded business, and substituted ambiguity for precision; there was (as William Gerard Hamilton speaking of Lord George, truly observed to me) no trash in his mind; he studied no choice phrases, no superfluous words, nor ever suffered the clearness of his conceptions to be clouded by the obscurity of his expressions, for these were the simplest and most unequivocal that could be made use of for explaining or dictating his instructions.[41]

A large part of the routine correspondence of the office of the American Department was carried on under the general direction of Germain, but the letters were very often prepared by the under-secretaries.[42] In these matters he rarely made changes, although at times some characteristic opinion of his emerged in his suggestions: "I have made a little alteration in your letter to Mr. Howe, for I could not say I approved of a cartel with rebels, tho' I am glad the prisoners are to be exchanged...," [43] or perhaps, less often, a personal animus was evident:

I like the letter to Sir G. Carleton very well in general. I had rather not have said that the information which Haldimand was to receive could not fail of being of the greatest use in his administration. As I do not believe a word of that sentence, you must absolve me from the crime of signing what I do not think is true.[44]

In general, however, Germain confined himself to "capital leading cases," [45] and it is in the great state documents of the time, embodying significant policies at the cabinet level, that we find Germain's own language strong, forceful, sometimes careless, but almost always effective.

In the House of Commons, Germain was a real support for the ministry. The general opinion of the day was that he was an able administrator but an even more able debater.[46] He was assiduous in his attendance, and Lord North relied upon him when problems touching America came before the House. With his convictions, he was more vehement and dogmatic on these questions than his predecessor, Lord Dartmouth, had been. In addition, he was thoroughly and minutely acquainted with the extremely complex political situation in the House of that day. This resulted, in part, from his early introduction into the highest levels of society in public life and the army; in part, from his own quick perceptions and judgment; and in part, though less assuredly, from the fact that he belonged to a coterie of men who had been contemporaries at Westminster School, and who came in an astonishing degree to influence and to dominate some of the great figures of the age. Among this group was the austere figure of Lord Mansfield.[47] There is a curiously macabre scene drawn by Richard Cumberland of an interview between Lord Mansfield and Germain which occurred during the last days of Germain's illness when he was suffering a great deal:

He wished to take his last leave of the Earl of Mansfield, then at Tunbridge Wells; I signified this to the earl, and accompanied him in his chaise to Stoneland; I was present at their interview. Lord Sackville, just dismounted from his horse, came into the room, where we had waited a very few minutes, and staggered as he advanced to reach his hand to his respectable visitor; he drew his breath with palpitating quickness, and, if I remember rightly, never rode again: there was a death-like character in his countenance, that visibly affected and disturbed Lord Mansfield, in a manner that I did not quite expect, for it had more of horror in it than a firm man ought to have shown, and less perhaps of other feelings than a friend, invited to a meeting of that nature, must have discovered, had he not been frightened from his propriety.

As soon as Lord Sackville had recovered his breath, his visitor remaining silent, he began by apologizing for the trouble he had given him, and for the unpleasant spectacle he was conscious of exhibiting to him in the condition he was now reduced to; 'but my good lord,' he said, 'though I ought not to have imposed upon you the painful ceremony of paying a last visit to a dying man, yet so great was my anxiety to return you my unfeigned thanks for all your goodness to me, all the kind protection you have shown me through the course of my unprosperous life, that I could not know you was so near me, and not wish to assure you of the invariable respect I have entertained for your character, and now in the most serious manner to solicit your forgiveness, if ever in the fluctuations of politics or the heats of party, I have appeared in your eyes at any moment of my life unjust to your great merits, or forgetful of your many favors.'

When I record this speech, I give it to the reader as correct; I do not trust to memory at this distance; I transcribe it: I scorn the paltry trick of writing speeches for any man, whose name is in these Memoirs, or for myself, in whose name these Memoirs shall go forth, respectable at least for their veracity; for I certainly cannot wish to present myself to the world in two such opposite and incoherent characters as the writer of my own history, and the hero of a fiction.

Lord Mansfield made a reply perfectly becoming and highly satisfactory: he was far on in years, and not in sanguine health or a strong state of nerves; there was no immediate reason to continue the discourse; Lord Sackville did not press for it; his visitor departed, and I stayed with him. He made no other observation upon what had passed than that it was extremely obliging in Lord Mansfield, and then turned to other subjects.[48]

Germain's speeches, even in the incomplete form in which they appear in the pages of Hansard, read well. There is little declamation and they contain practically no quotation from authors ancient or modern. They are addressed directly to the subject in hand, and their appeal is almost wholly to the commonsense view of the matter. With respect to America, as with respect to most problems, he contented himself with forming a plain judgment. There is no subtlety, no intricacy in his thought. His mind had taken hold of the idea of legislative supremacy, and it became the basis for almost the whole of his political thinking and of his exegesis. There is perhaps some justice in Shelburne's remark that he

was used to content himself with taking up the corner of an argument upon which he used to declaim with great decision and a great deal of seeming force, and for the most part judged his time and place admirably well.[49]

If we amend this, perhaps out of context, to imply that he took a bare and oversimplified view of problems which, in history and life, were overlaid with complexity and variants beyond his understanding and knowledge, we may discover more of the truth of his position than Shelburne meant to indicate. There can be no doubt that he judged his time and place well for, though he was an unpopular man in his day, he knew the House of Commons and the proper management of debate in that assembly. This may be no very high praise to give, and the old unreformed House was far from being a democratic institution, but it was, to a degree, representative, virtual or otherwise, of the British people, and in this medium Germain worked effectively.

In one respect Germain was not a very good parliamentarian. He could be goaded into indiscreet statements in the House when the more imperturbable North would have remained silent before the most provoking attacks of the Opposition. Fox, during the debates over the capture of St. Eustatius, alluded to

the unwary frankness of the Secretary of State (Lord George) as a quality for which he was sometimes praised in the House of Commons and blamed *out* of it.[50]

On one occasion when the government was under severe attack for not having properly supplied Gibraltar with gunpowder, and it was reported that Lord Darby had had to strip the ships of his relieving squadron of that essential item in order to leave two thousand barrels at the fortress, Germain reacted characteristically. Members of the Board of Ordnance had attempted to deny the story or to plead want of information. Lord George, however, rose in his place and declared that, though he had no official information, he believed the report was true. If it were true, in his opinion, Lord Darby had acted very properly and was the more to be praised. North remained silent in the face of this avowal and took no part in the debate.[51]

Aside entirely from his tendency toward a dangerous frankness in the House on public questions, Germain could be, and often was, baited on account of his court-martial for disobedience of orders at Minden. On 14 December 1770, Germain had declared in the House, while supporting a motion which he regarded as important, that it was "for the honour of the nation in which he did declare he greatly interested himself." Governor Johnstone later in the debate, while Germain was outside the chamber, declared in bitterly provocative language "that he wondered that noble Lord should interest himself so deeply in the honour of his country, when he had hitherto been so regardless of his own." When this language was reported to Germain he determined to force its retraction or to have his satisfaction.

He, therefore, sent his second, Mr. Thomas Townshend, to Johnstone, who, refusing to retract, offered to satisfy Germain in the point of his honor by agreeing to a duel. Accordingly, the duel was arranged to take place in the ring in Hyde Park, and, as Germain declared, since "in affairs of this kind, all times were alike, the present was, in his opinion, as good a one as any." Everything proceeded with the most perfect politeness and decorum. Each man fired two shots; the last shot by Johnstone shattered Germain's pistol. Governor Johnstone "afterwards declared to his friends, that in all the affairs of the kind which he ever knew, or was ever concerned in, he never found a man behave with more courage and coolness than Lord George did on this occasion." [52]

In 1778, a violent scene took place in the House between Germain and Mr. Temple Luttrell, in which again the provocation arose from a vindictive reference to Minden and the court-martial. Germain declared that old as he was he would have his revenge. The affair was quieted by the insistence of the House.[53] When Germain was elevated to the peerage in 1782, the Marquis of Carmarthen moved that his presence in the Lords, suffering as he still did from the verdict of 1760, was derogatory to the dignity of the House of Lords. The motion was lost.[54] Germain in this case, according to Cumberland, also intended to send a challenge to protect his honor, but was dissuaded from doing so by his friends, notably Lord Amherst, who made themselves responsible for his honor.[55]

CHAPTER 4

GERMAIN IN OFFICE:
THE PLAN OF COERCION, 1775–76

I

This is the man who on 16 November 1775 made his first statement of policy as a minister.[1] He stood up in his place to say that
he had been straight and consistent in his policy and conduct toward
America from the beginning. He entered office with his principles
unchanged and he hoped he would always be "decisive, direct, and
firm." On the question of legislative supremacy he took the view
that it was founded on the constitution, but as to one aspect of it—
taxation—though he would never concede that the Parliament lacked
the right to tax, he would by no means object to restraining the
exercise of that right provided that "other modes could be adopted."
However, "if we are to have no peace unless we give up the right, the
contest is brought to a fair issue, we are equal to the contest; our
internal resources are great; and we can never despair of that assistance which we may want." It was probably unfortunate that Germain, in his first speech as a minister, should have raised this whole
question of taxation and have used such strong language on a matter
which was bound to be provocative. He was indeed "direct and firm"
but it tended to show him forth as Walpole described him, breathing
fire and sword against the Bostonians, "like that second Duke of
Alva, the inflexible Lord George Germain."[2] Conway charged Germain with reviving the whole question: "He thought the fire had been
smothered, but since that noble lord came into office, he had uncov-
ered the ashes and blown the flame afresh."[3] Germain gave color to
this opinion by declaring that he hoped to draw a revenue from
America either by taxation or in any other way that the Americans
might suggest which would ease their "fears and jealousies." He was
rather patronizing on this point: "Let them be happy. Nobody can
wish them more so than I do." This happiness, however, was to be
enjoyed within the rigid bounds of the legislative supremacy of

Great Britain. He had never changed his view on that essential and "what I always held, I now stand in office to maintain."

Having stated in clear and unequivocal terms his principles upon entering office, Germain went on to consider what forces might be necessary to maintain the supremacy of Great Britain over her colonies. He had been brought into office as a war minister, and it was the hope of the government that he might be an "architect of victory" as the elder Pitt had been.[4] He was staunch in his proposals: let the officers on the spot measure the magnitude of the task; let them send to him their requisitions for force. What they should require, insofar as his advice could be effective, should be sent—"not to be insulted." He made the pledge that the forces necessary to re-establish and maintain "the power of this country in America will not be wanting." His speech had been short as it had been completely certain. He stood forth from his first day in office to his last, as a "man of principle."[5]

Two days after making his first speech as American secretary, Germain wrote his first dispatch to Sir William Howe.[6] Howe's dispatches of early October had been brought to England by Gage, who arrived in London on 14 November. These dispatches contained Howe's ideas on the forthcoming campaign, and Germain was glad to have them so soon after his coming into office. He had told the House that the forces which would be sent to America would be determined by the opinions and estimates of the officers on the spot. He had now something concrete to deal with. He must fit his thinking into the plans already formulated, though with no exactitude, by his predecessor, Dartmouth, the recalled General Gage, and the acting General Howe.

Germain himself had been in close touch with the developing situation in America since early summer. On 16 June he had set down in a letter to Lord Suffolk his conception of the position of affairs there and what ought to be undertaken by the administration.[7] After mentioning the need for light infantry, made clear by Braddock's defeat in the late war, he pointed out that General Howe had then been in command of the light troops. He confessed that he had great misgivings about the ability of Gage. Howe would soon teach the army to be as formidable in loose open fighting as it had formerly been. He expected that the most immediate assistance ought to come from Canada, and he advocated a diversion from that province by a force of regulars and Canadians who "would be very ready to chastise their neighbors under the sanction of government." His great point, however, related to New York. He lamented that Gage had withdrawn all his forces to Boston:

> ... as long as you maintained New York the continent was divided, at present there is a free communication between all the disaffected.... Now that post is lost the importance of it will be known, and had I the honour of advising administration, I should say that till that post was regained I could see no prospect of ending the war with success and I had rather act upon the defensive in New England and make my first and most vigorous efforts in establishing the troops in that center from whence I could occasionally act offensively against any of the rebellious provinces.

Germain had seized thus early upon the major objective for the campaign of 1776 and had also named the man—Howe—who would command in that campaign.[8]

At the end of July important decisions were made relating to the command in America. Gage was to be recalled, Howe was to take his place, and Carleton was to be informed of the bearing of these changes upon his position.[9] On 2 August, Dartmouth gave these decisions official form in dispatches to Gage, Howe, and Carleton.[10] Gage was told that since he himself had indicated that nothing further could be accomplished in that campaign in America, he was to return home for consultation with the government.[11] Both the King and Dartmouth felt that it was necessary to enter into full explanations with Carleton. Howe was junior to Carleton and the possibility that the two armies might join had to be taken into account. If this did happen in the course of the campaign, Carleton was assured that because of his seniority the over-all command would be his. The King was not satisfied with his commanders either by sea or by land. He wrote sourly to North: "I do think the Admiral's [Graves] removal as necessary, if what is reported is founded, as the mild general's." [12]

In a separate letter to Gage of 2 August,[13] Dartmouth made a survey of the situation in America and raised four queries. *First:* Whether in the next campaign, the whole British force should be used in New England. *Second:* Whether New York should not be taken and the Hudson Valley made the seat of the next campaign. *Third:* If this should not be expedient, whether a part of Gage's forces should not be put on transports and various raids made along the coast which would at least yield a supply of livestock and provisions.[14] *Fourth:* Whether, if Boston was not tenable, it ought not to be evacuated and the whole army posted at Halifax and Quebec until the events of the winter should make clear what course of action ought to be pursued. Dartmouth left no doubt that he, as well as "many judicious and well informed persons," felt that the taking of New York would be by far the most telling blow which the British might hope to strike in the next campaign. It is worth noting that Germain in June had advocated the recall of Gage, the appointment of Howe to that command, and the setting of New York as the major objective for the next campaign. In less than two months the administration had virtually adopted the whole of his program.

Dartmouth's letter to Gage was received at Boston on 26 September. He had directed Gage to leave it with Howe when he embarked for home. Gage answered it on 1 October,[15] and Howe on 9 October,[16] and both letters arrived in England on 14 November, four days after Germain had taken office.

Gage answered all four queries directly: *First:* That no offensive operations could be profitably carried on from Boston. *Second:* That it had always seemed to him that New York and the Hudson Valley offered the best opportunity for carrying on the war. Taking possession of the Hudson River would divide the eastern from the western colonies, as well as providing a fine water carriage. In addition the government might also find many friends in that area who would be useful in arms as well as in supplying the army. By a campaign in this area, communication might be opened with Canada and during the winter season the troops might be employed to the southward. *Third:* That raiding expeditions along the coast might have some utility. *Fourth:* "I am of opinion that Boston would be tenable in the winter without hazard."

Howe was not so direct or simple in his reflections upon Dartmouth's letter of 2 August. On the first point he was clear enough; Boston was no place from which to start a campaign. This was true for a variety of reasons, the chief of which were: the natural strength of the country, the entrenched position of the rebels, the great number of the latter, their ability to get plentiful supplies, and the difficulty of maintaining communications between the army and the town of Boston. On the point of the second query with respect to New York as the prime objective, there is an interesting ambiguity in Howe's letter to Dartmouth of 9 October. He wrote, "Your Lordship's second query regards the division of the army for the possession of New York and this town. I am humbly of opinion that our strength at present is not adequate to the undertaking. The Generals Gage, Clinton, and Burgoyne, having declared the same, I am to await his Majesty's further pleasure on this head, . . ." Howe said neither yea nor nay to the proposition.

Some light is thrown on this by the correspondence of Lord Howe with Germain in England the previous summer.[17] Lord Howe acted as an intermediary between his brother, General Howe, at Boston, and Germain in England.[18] On 29 July, Lord Howe wrote to Germain enclosing a letter from the general describing the situation at Boston.[19] His own comment was:

> Most of the particulars (in Gen. Howe's letter enclosed) I have reason to suppose have been communicated to government from a similar relation by another channel. But I fear without the effect to have been hoped for, as from discourse I had with the Secretary of War, I suspect that instead of the active measures your Lordship may think the crisis demands, a languid idea of withdrawing the troops from Boston may prevail.

Less than ten days later, however, the situation appeared to Lord Howe to have improved greatly, and this in large part due to Germain.[20] He had learned from Germain's letter written some days before that Gage was to be recalled and his brother made commander in chief in America, with the exception of Canada. Since the King had not come to this determination until 28 July, and since Lord Howe had, because of his absence from home, not received Germain's letter informing him of this change "until yesterday," it appears that Germain must have had almost instant knowledge of the King's decision. He may well have been instrumental in helping to make that decision. Lord Howe at least thought so, assuring Germain of the satisfaction which General Howe would derive from Germain's views and "if the spirit in carrying the late arrangements into execution partakes of the vigor that gave birth to the measure, he [General

Howe] will have reason to applaud his good fortune in the essential support."

The close liaison thus established between Howe and Germain makes it reasonable to conclude that Howe was kept in touch with Germain's ideas and opinions on America. Since June 1775, Germain had been a strong advocate of taking New York and pushing the campaign from that quarter. By late August, General Howe had come to this opinion as well. His brother reported to Germain that the general had now concluded that it was absolutely essential to change the theater of the "now inevitable war" to New York. In order to carry out this strategic concept the general judged the following forces necessary: 15,000 for New York; 4,000 regulars, together with Canadians and Indians to act on the side of Canada and keep open the communications between Quebec, Montreal, and Crown Point; 5,000 to occupy Boston and the posts necessary to its security. This would make a total force of 24,000, exclusive of Canadians and Indians. The general, in all modesty, professed that he thought this was a plan of larger scope than he was competent to deal with and suggested that a viceroy with unlimited powers should be sent out from England to carry through so large a design, and, "in his consideration for the public service, if his dominion were absolute in the case, your Lordship, I find would be called away from your country retirement." [21] How closely this corresponds with Germain's ideas: a diversion from Canada, with the aid of Canadians, and the main army to take New York and push the war forward from there!

General Howe had, therefore, before he took over the command at Boston, and before he wrote his letter of 9 October to Dartmouth, made known his views on the next campaign. These views had been forwarded to his brother and had been in Germain's possession since late September. Howe's official and responsible summing up of the situation on 9 October was directed to Dartmouth, but was delivered to Germain by Gage on 14 November. Germain was, therefore, familiar with the concepts Howe had formed, and, as it appears, may have had considerable influence upon their actual formation.

But Howe's plans had changed somewhat in emphasis between 20 August and 9 October.[22] On the eve of taking over the command from Gage, he outlined the forces necessary for a successful cam-

paign as follows: *First:* If Boston was to be held, it would be necessary to post 5,000 troops there; such a force could hold it in the
face of 10,000 rebels. However, he advised that this force of 5,000
troops would be more profitably employed by taking Rhode Island.
Either at Boston or Rhode Island, that army would divert approximately the same proportion of the rebel army, but at Rhode Island
it would act as such a threat to Connecticut that the army supplied
from there would be kept at home. Howe had thus brought forward
the idea of establishing a post at Rhode Island. The accomplish-
ment of this task over the subsequent years was to cost the British
dearly in blood and treasure. *Second:* The major objective was to remain the same: the taking of New York and the establishment of
communications with Canada. For this effort a force of 12,000 would
be necessary. *Third:* A force of 3,000 regulars together with 3,000 to
4,000 Canadians and a few hundred Indians would be left for the
service from the Canadian side. Howe did not presume to say
whether this would be a sufficient force for operations from Canada,
since his command did not extend to that province. After the two
armies (Howe's and Carleton's) had opened communications between Canada and the Atlantic seaboard and established proper
posts to protect this route, they might take separate routes into New
England. Of course, the basic concept of the campaign of 1777 is
clearly foreshadowed here and the same ambiguity existed. Did
"opening the communications" mean the actual junction of armies?
Did a diversion fulfill the meaning of "conjunct operations"?

The plan of operations set forth in early October by Howe required a force of only 20,000 troops as compared with the 24,000
anticipated in his earlier letter to his brother.[23] It also anticipated a
move—the evacuation of Boston—which had been determined upon
in England a month earlier and put in the form of an official dispatch by Dartmouth.[24] The troops thus evacuated were to be transported to New York or "some other place to the southward." This
letter was not received at Boston until 9 November and at that
time Howe refused to obey his orders because of the lateness of the
season, the deficiency of transport (11,602 tons), and the apparent
safety of the army in Boston.[25]

Dartmouth undertook one further commitment about two weeks
before quitting his office. On 22 October he wrote Howe that, because

of representations made by Governor Martin and Lord Dunmore, it appeared to the government that a small force sent to the Carolinas would in a short time, with the help of the local people, re-establish constitutional government. In consequence, a force was being sent out from England for this purpose and would embark from Cork about the middle of December. Howe was directed to send one of the generals under his command in a ship of war to the vicinity of the Cape Fear River and there await the force being sent from home. When that force arrived off the coast of North America the general selected by Howe would take command, by which time "he will probably have been able to collect such information and materials as may enable him the better to judge of the plan of operations to be pursued." This force of regular troops, it was hoped, would successfully complete its task by the time that the navigation on the North Atlantic coast had become practicable and would then join Howe's army for the campaigns of that year. The whole success of the operation, limited in force as it was, must depend upon the disposition of the local inhabitants, and the commander detached by Howe must use his judgment to determine in which of the provinces to the southward force of this kind might be most profitably employed.[26]

Dartmouth's letter reached Howe on 30 December. The general immediately made clear his opposition: "I am free to own my opinion to your Lordship, which has been, to leave the southern provinces in the fullest persuasion of their security until the rebels have been defeated on the side of New York." [27] Nevertheless, he gave orders to Clinton to proceed southward and that general sailed from Boston on 20 January.[28] This was the beginning of that ill-fated expedition against Charleston under Clinton and Sir Peter Parker. It was determined upon, as far as the evidence extends, entirely apart from Germain. However, he inherited this commitment upon coming into office and in his first official dispatch to Howe (18 November) [29] he wrote: "All the advices which have been received of the state of the southern provinces, since the first idea of that expedition was taken up, tend to show the propriety of it, and to confirm us in our hopes, that it will be attended with advantage and success." [30]

What then was the situation of Germain upon taking over the office of American secretary on 10 November 1775? He had a general he wanted in command at Boston and he was familiar in bold outline with the plans for 1776. He had in fact taken a part in shaping these plans. He had on his hands the expedition to the southward, which he did not plan, but of which he approved. In Canada, General Carleton was under close siege at Quebec and plans had to be laid for his deliverance. But those animosities, so bitter and destructive of cooperative effort, which later developed between himself and Carleton were not yet evident. In the House of Commons he had a disciplined majority. He had successfully asserted the rights of the American secretaryship against the "ancient secretaries." He was a "man of principle" and stood forward, "decisive, direct and firm." If indeed the "Ghost of Minden" was brought forth occasionally neck and shoulders [31] to frighten him, he had yet a strong position.

II

It was during Germain's early days in office (20 November) that Lord North introduced the Prohibitory Bill in the House of Commons.[32] This bill was designed to prohibit all trade and intercourse with the thirteen colonies so long as the rebellion continued. The bill was debated from time to time in the Commons until 21 December when it was passed. In the last stages of the debate Germain spoke in favor of the measure.[33] He took a characteristic line asserting that the colonists had brought their troubles upon themselves. The gentlemen in opposition had asked why the government in Massachusetts had not discovered the first rioters and punished them. The answer was simple: the council had refused to cooperate with Governor Hutchinson who had done all in his power to persuade it to adopt the proper measures. The Prohibitory Bill, then before the House, was the best means to use to bring the colonists back to their senses. By the terms of this legislation, as soon as a colony "submits" its ports would be opened and its trade restored. He allowed himself, somewhat complacently, to look forward to the restoration of peace. He declared that, no matter how small his part might be in the achievement of this great end, the consciousness that he had played a part would give him "the greatest pleasure and happiness." In conclusion he grew defensive and asked the members to note "that I never sought the office I have now the honor to fill, nor wished for it further than I flattered myself I might be serviceable to my country."

This speech, notable for its lack of understanding of the issues involved, was one of Germain's least distinguished performances. It is dull and dreary to read and puerile in argument. It has none of his customary vigor. During the debates, Fox, Burke, and the opposition made an excellent case against the legislation. Fox pointed out that in a rebellion the proper course to pursue was to punish individuals and spare the country; in a war against the enemy you spare the individual and lay waste the country. The government in its policy toward America was adopting the latter course instead of the former. This had been clear since the time of the Coercive Acts.[34] Despite the poor showing made in debate, the administration had no trouble in carrying the measure on 21 December. It was a fateful measure and, as Channing has pointed out, brought "many an American conscience to consent to secession." [35] It is not surprising that Germain joined himself with those who advocated this legislation. It is surprising that he did so with so little force and ability.

Parliament was in recess from 21 December until 15 February. During this period Germain was deeply engaged in the consideration and formulation of plans to supply the army in America with those reinforcements necessary to strike a heavy, and perhaps a decisive, blow at the Revolution. On 27 December 1775 Germain received from Burgoyne's hands Howe's letter of 26 November.[36] This letter was largely devoted to an explanation of Howe's reasons for not evacuating Boston in response to the orders of Dartmouth of 5 September.[37] He did, however, go on to elaborate his ideas on the next year's campaign. Howe's letters of 20 August, 9 October, and 26 November contain the essentials of his proposals for 1776 and were only modified in detail by subsequent developments. The new element in the situation was the accepted determination to evacuate Boston. Howe had advised this on 9 October and had advocated taking post at Rhode Island. The decision, having now been definitely taken, Howe submitted a specific distribution of troops for the theaters under his command:

	Battalions
Halifax and Newfoundland	1
Near Nantucket Road	1
Rhode Island	10
New York	16
Virginia, Halifax and St. Augustine	1
East and West Florida	1
West Indies	1
Total	31

Each battalion was estimated at 500 men fit for duty in the field; a total of 15,500. He then went on to say: "But this army, though complete in the spring must have between six and seven thousand recruits, and of the worst kind, if chiefly composed of Irish Roman Catholics, certain to desert if put to hard work, and from their ignorance of arms, not entitled to the smallest confidence as soldiers." This would make an army of between 21,500 and 22,500. Even an army of this size, in Howe's opinion, would not be strong enough to act offensively in a campaign against Rhode Island and New York. There should be added 4,000 further troops—Howe suggested Russians—1,500 to be added to the force acting at Rhode Island and 2,500 to the force at New York. This would bring the over-all force to between 25,500 and 26,500. But it is to be noted that Howe strongly discounted the effectiveness of the Irish Roman Catholics.

Germain replied to this letter on 5 January 1776 in his first comprehensive dispatch to Howe.[38] After having approved of Howe's failure to evacuate Boston, he plunged immediately into a discussion of the vital topic of reinforcements. He was familiar with Howe's three previous estimates of the numbers necessary for a successful campaign in 1776—estimates of 20 August (24,000), 9 October (20,000), and 26 November (25,500–26,500). Germain now set forth the expectations of the administration: it would supply a reinforcement of 4,400 British troops and a separate corps of not less than 10,000 foreign troops. Howe had in Boston a force of about 7,500.[39] Germain thus put himself on record as being prepared to undertake the campaign of 1776 with approximately 22,000 in the army under Howe. This was between 3,000 and 4,000 short of the gross number Howe had requested in his last letter, but it was very close to his two former estimates. In addition, since Howe had put little faith in the

Irish troops he had suggested, and since these were to be replaced by German troops, it might seem that the combat efficiency of his army would be as high as, if not higher than, he himself had contemplated.[40]

Germain was under the strict necessity of keeping in view the needs of both Howe and Carleton. He pointed out to Howe that the situation at Quebec was critical. The government had to prepare to face two possibilities in that command: either the relief of Quebec, if it was still in British hands, or its recapture if it had fallen before the forces of Montgomery and Arnold. To provide for both of these possibilities, every effort would be made to send to Quebec, independent of the large reinforcements preparing for Howe, a force of 10,000 men.[41] It was hoped that this force would embark during the first or second week of March. Howe had originally proposed a force of 6,000 for that service.[42]

The American secretary had to consider the over-all design. He was proposing to provide for the American war total reinforcements to the number of 24,500. Howe's original official estimate covering both the Canadian and Atlantic seaboard theaters had been for 20,000. He had pointed out at that time (9 October) that, since he did not command in Canada, he could not say whether the force he suggested (3,000 regulars) would be sufficient. The total picture revealed a heavier reinforcement than Howe had then asked. However, the emphasis had changed. The Canadian situation, judged to be so grave, was to have a much larger share of the available forces than Howe had counted upon. Germain was, in essence, undertaking to supply an army for service under Howe, which in fighting efficiency, if not in numbers, was the equal of that demanded by the commander. He was, on the other hand, substantially increasing the forces for the northern army. Since both forces had as their prime objective the crushing of rebellious resistance, it was a question of judging the most effective distribution. From London the operation was a single whole; Germain had to view it in this light. He saw the incursion of rebel forces beyond their own frontiers into a province only recently conquered, and, moreover, a province alien in language, religion, laws, and historical tradition, as an alarming threat to the whole British position in America. He chose to support strongly the army charged with the duty of turning back that threat and carrying the war into the enemy's own territory. This, too, was effective support for Howe.[43]

Evidence of the serious construction put upon the situation in Canada and the preoccupation of government in the position of affairs there, is supplied by Germain's next dispatch to Howe of 1 February.[44] The most significant part of this letter related to the threat posed by the rebel incursion into Canada and the preparations being taken to meet this threat both with respect to reinforcements and command. The position of that province was put prominently to the fore by Germain: "The unfortunate events which have happened in Canada make it necessary that we should not only exert every endeavor for the relief of Quebec, as early as possible, but also for having a force there ready to commence its operations as soon as the season will admit." It was expected that the reinforcements for Howe would sail before the end of March, and those for Canada much sooner. The fact of two substantial armies operating in America naturally raised the problem of command. Four individuals were involved: Carleton and Howe, with Carleton the senior; Clinton and Burgoyne, with Clinton the senior. Out of this conflict of seniority and overlapping command there developed among British general officers some of the most dangerous and fatal tensions of the whole war. These tensions extended to Germain as the responsible minister of the Crown, upon whom the duty devolved of conveying the King's pleasure with respect to the allocation of duties and responsibilities. It is not an exaggeration to state that the resulting conflicts of personality and ambition poisoned the relationships between the generals in the field and between them and the American secretary in London. This conflict resulted in the most extreme bitterness and contributed heavily to the defeat of British arms in the American war. In his dispatch of 1 February, Germain took up this problem for the first time without fully sensing its implications.

He informed Howe that it had been the King's intention to appoint Clinton as second in command to Carleton. It was, however, now expected that Clinton had already sailed to take command of the southern expedition.[45] The King had appointed Burgoyne to act as second in command to Carleton in the large army being sent to Canada. He would sail from Ireland on or about 20 March. Burgoyne was thus being placed over the head of Clinton in a command which promised to be active and one which was receiving the very large support of government. Clinton was posted to a command which, even in its inception, was regarded as a distinctly secondary one. This was the beginning of bitter friction. Burgoyne, both in 1776 and in 1777, partly because of the fact that he was the man on the spot, superseded as the active general officer, men his senior in rank: Clinton in 1776 and Carleton in 1777.

Germain also informed Howe that in case Quebec had fallen before relief should have reached it, and Carleton had, unhappily, not survived the loss of that city, Howe was to be commander in chief of all British armies in America. This was a natural looking forward to possible eventualities, and indicated only the normal effort, when means of communication were so slow, to provide beforehand a solution for all contingencies.[46] If Howe should succeed Carleton in this manner, it would remain within his discretion to keep Burgoyne in command of the army in Canada or place Clinton in that post. These were the first tentative efforts to deal with this difficult problem and they appear quite unexceptionable. If Clinton had been passed over, he was already committed to an operation, and provision was made for a reconsideration of his claims.

In the meantime every effort was being put forward to equip and to embark the reinforcements for Howe and Carleton. The severity of the weather, "almost beyond what has ever been known in this country," held up preparations, and in addition the Opposition had attempted to block the passage of the treaties with the German states, treaties which provided for an essential part of the forces destined for the campaign of 1776. Germain had early believed that, if the rebellion continued, recourse would have to be had to foreign troops.[47] During the debates on the treaties, Germain defended government policy and showed, by bringing forth historical data, that in every war or rebellion England had had to employ foreigners "to fight our battles and to support our government."[48] Lord Barrington, secretary at war, who followed Germain in this debate took a very practical view which Germain no doubt would have endorsed: that recruits were simply not to be had, and that the agreements under discussion, though certainly not advantageous, were the best which could be had. "They had prescribed the terms and we were compelled by necessity to accept them."[49] After heated debate on 29 February, the House approved of the treaties by a vote of 242 to 88, and the Lords did likewise on 5 March by a vote of 100 to 32.[50] The treaties provided for the following troops: Brunswick—4,636, Hesse-Cassel—12,000, Hanau—668, making in all a total of 17,304 for use by His Majesty either in Europe or America.[51] Germain regarded this problem, as most others, in a completely practical way. He would have preferred to recruit British troops for these essential military operations, but this could not be done, and, in consequence, troops had to be sought and obtained where they were available.

Before the passage of the treaties, Germain had written to Carleton (17 February) that, in addition to British troops, he would be supplied with a reinforcement of 5,000 foreign troops.[52] He also told Carleton that Burgoyne had been fully instructed as to the operations which ought to be undertaken from the side of Canada. Six weeks later (28 March), when the situation had become further clarified, Germain wrote more in detail to Howe.[53] He enclosed copies of the treaties with the German states and indicated the distribution of forces between Howe and Carleton. Howe was to have 12,200 of the foreign troops, a detachment of Guards (1,098), and the Highland Corps of two regiments (3,466 men), making a total reinforcement of 16,764.[54] Transports for the first division of foreign troops (8,200) were already fully prepared at Spithead, and the Guards detachment had begun its march to Portsmouth. It was hoped that these two forces would be ready to sail at the same time and might proceed together to America. The Highland Corps would be ready to sail by 20 April.

Carleton was to have the balance of the foreign troops (5,000), nine British battalions and McLean's corps, a total reinforcement of about 10,000 men.[55] These were considerable operations, and they were proceeding on an impressively exact time table. Germain was infusing new vigor into the office of American secretary, and his execution compared favorably with his January commitments.

The news of the defeat and repulse of the American forces before Quebec on New Year's Eve 1775 had reached England, and it gave Germain grounds to hope that the northern army might be able, not only to clear Canada of the enemy, but pursue him beyond the frontiers of that province into his own territory. He was now forming expectations, not unjustified by the scale of preparations undertaken, that the campaign in 1776, through operations from New York and Canada, might bring the contest to a decision. This view may now appear oversanguine and events were to deny it utterly. But these events came on independently of Germain, and the conduct and temper of the army commanders, particularly to the north, were perhaps the key to the frustration of his expectations.

Determined to neglect no opportunity to bring force against the rebellion, Germain drew Howe's attention to the use of Indians: [56]

As far as I can judge of what is likely to be the general plan of operations in North America, and indeed in all events the securing of the affection and assistance of our old friends and allies, the Indians of the Six Nations, is a consideration of no small importance; and I hope Colonel Guy Johnson, who is now here, and is preparing to return by the first ship, will be found useful.

Colonel Johnson was to be given the same authority as had been given to Sir William Johnson in 1756. He was to be completely under the control of Howe.

This raises an extremely controversial problem and one which has given rise to much bitterness. Germain had dealt with the problem in a minor way before he wrote to Howe in March 1776. Shortly after coming into office (23 December) he had written to Governor Tonyn to congratulate him upon preventing a defection of the Creek Indians.[57] In that letter he had been at pains to warn Tonyn against the indiscriminate use of Indians against the rebels. They were to be used only in the event that they were first employed by the rebels themselves.[58]

On 28 March Germain wrote Burgoyne as well as Howe on the problem of Indians.[59] This amounted to canvassing the situation in Canada as well as in the revolted provinces, as Burgoyne was then on the point of embarkation. He pointed out to Burgoyne that, regardless of the fate of Quebec, the disposition and temper of the Canadians and the Indians were a matter of first-rate importance. The good will of the Indians appeared to be assured "if they are managed with attention and proper persons are employed to negotiate with them."

Indians were used by the British and with Germain's sanction during the Revolution, notably by Lieutenant Governor Henry Hamilton who commanded the British post at Detroit.[60] It has been contended, in an effort to rehabilitate the reputation of Henry Hamilton with respect to the use of Indians in 1777, that there is no proof that he recommended the use of Indians to the home government. "He has been charged with recommending to the home government the employment of Indians even though his immediate superior, Governor Guy Carleton was opposed. Lord George Germain wrote to this effect and Carleton believed him, but no letter of Hamilton's seems to exist which would prove the point." [61] The background of this situation is somewhat complex. On 2 September 1776 Hamilton wrote from Detroit to Dartmouth.[62] He described to him a four-day council which had been held by the Indians at Detroit. They were considering their relations with the Virginians who had solicited their support through the ceremony of sending belts. The Indians concluded that the Virginians were not well disposed toward them, and Hamilton who was pleased with this conclusion of the matter, in a kind of symbolical provocation tore up the letters, messages and speeches of the Virginians and cut their belts before the eyes of some 200 Indians. However, though the inclination of the Indians was for war, Hamilton restrained them, for he had received a letter from Carleton, written on 19 July 1776, in which Carleton had described sending the Ottawas back home, with directions to be ready the next spring to cooperate with the British forces.[63] In line with this Hamilton directed the Indians at Detroit to watch the Virginians carefully and, if attacked, to act as a unit against the Virginians. Despite this, he fully expected that the Indians, in small parties, would fall upon scattered settlers along the Ohio and its tributaries. With an air of pious disapproval but resignation Hamilton wrote: "A deplorable sort of war—But which the disloyalty and impudence of the Virginians has justly drawn upon them." Further on, he ventured the hope, which he obviously did not believe would be realized, that "the colonists will open their eyes before the clouds burst that hang heavy over their heads."

It is this letter of Hamilton's which Germain referred to in his controversial letter to Carleton of 26 March 1777.[64] It will be recalled that at the time Germain wrote it was the very spring toward which Carleton had looked in the previous summer when he had asked the Ottawas to be prepared to cooperate with the British forces. Germain accurately summarized the substance of Hamilton's letter to Dartmouth of the previous September, and added one deduction which he had drawn from that letter: that Hamilton had proposed diversions by the Indians, under proper leaders, upon the frontiers of Pennsylvania and Virginia. In precise terms Hamilton had not made that proposition, but it is clear that he believed that the "disloyalty" and "impudence" of the Virginians had justly drawn upon them the scourge of Indian war. But in any case Germain needed no persuasion as he now directed Carleton to instruct Hamilton to utilize the Indians in the frontier war, for "it is His Majesty's resolution that the most vigorous efforts should be made, and every means employed that Providence has put in His Majesty's hands for crushing the rebellion and restoring the constitution." [65]

Germain's public defense of his Indian policy was made in the House of Commons on 6 February 1778 in speaking on Burke's motion relative to the employment of Indians in the war in America. He declared that:

the matter lay within a very narrow compass; the Indians would not have remained idle spectators; the very arguements used by the hon. mover were so many proofs that they would not; besides the rebels by their emissaries, had made frequent applications to the Indians to side with them; the Virginians particularly; and some Indians were employed at Boston in the rebel army. Now taking the disposition of the Indians with the applications which had been made to them by the colonies, it amounted to a clear undisputed proposition, that either they would have served against us, or that we must have employed them. This being the alternative, he contended for the necessity of employing them, and was ready to submit his conduct on that ground to the judgement of the House.[66]

Again, as with the employment of foreign troops, he rested his case on wholly practical grounds. He did not enter upon the possible moral implications of his Indian policy. Burke, in introducing his measure, had given a three-hour speech, highly rhetorical and condemnatory in its character. He had considered the moral problem and declared that the result of such an Indian policy was

that our national honour had been deeply wounded, and our character as a people debased in the estimation of foreigners, by those shameful, savage, and servile alliances and their barbarous consequences.[67]

Germain's reply consisted in pointing out that the necessities of the situation justified the policy adopted.

CHAPTER 5

GERMAIN IN OFFICE:
THE PLAN OF CONCILIATION, 1776

I

Late in March 1776, Germain informed General Howe of the appointment of his brother Lord Howe to the naval command in America.[1] Lord Howe was at this time engaged in England in a protracted negotiation with the ministry relating to the form and substance of the proposed commission to conciliate the differences between the colonies and Great Britain. Both Howes regarded this commission as an integral part of their "mission" to America in 1776; their function, as they saw it, was not only to bring force to bear upon the Revolution, but also to be the bearers of an "olive branch." The campaign of 1776 has both a coercive and a conciliatory character, with the Howes emphasizing conciliation and Germain coercion.[2]

The idea of a commission was not new. Germain had been thought of as a sole commissioner in September 1775, but when he refused that post, it was determined to divide the commission and reduce its scope.[3] This policy took official form in the King's speech at the opening of Parliament on 26 October 1775. After outlining the large preparations on foot to coerce the rebellion, the King declared that it was his intention to

give authority to certain persons upon the spot to grant general or particular pardons and indemnities in such manner and to such persons as they shall think fit; and to receive the submission of any province or colony which shall be disposed to return to its allegiance. It may be also proper to authorize the persons so commissioned to restore such province or colony so returning to its allegiance, to the free exercise of its trade and commerce, and to the same protection and security, as if such province or colony had never revolted.[4]

Germain had seen the draft of the King's speech before it was delivered and had approved it.[5] The policy laid down required a good deal of submission before pardon, and held out no offer at all of negotiation with the revolutionary movement itself. This was Germain's policy, and he was one of the first ministers of the Crown to defend the proposed commission. On 16 November 1775, six days after taking office, he presented his views in the House. He saw the commissioners as empowered not only to grant pardons but to inquire into grievances. If the Americans wished to come to terms—"not with arms in their hands"—the commissioners might, upon submission, remove the penal restrictions under which the rebellious colonies then labored. His explanation of the government policy toward the commission contained a telltale phrase; he characterized it as "a door to retreat" for the Americans. It was not to be a negotiation between equals or near equals:

If they persist in their appeal to force, the force of this country must be exerted. The spirit of this country will go along with me in that idea, to suppress, to crush such rebellious resistance.[6]

Lord North supported Germain's interpretation of the commission, although he emphasized somewhat more strongly the inquiry into grievances.[7] A member of the House (Thomas Walpole) pointed out the total inadequacy of the government policy. After noting Germain's insistence upon submission as the first step, he remarked justly:

Very little, however, must His Lordship know of human nature, or of the people annexed to his department, if he thinks the motives which have induced them to associate, arm and fight in the defense of their supposed rights will not for ever prevent the return of peace, unless more adequate and just provision be made for obtaining it.[8]

The government policy stood, however, and Lord Howe was chosen to be commissioner. A promise was held out to him, contrary to the intent of the King's speech, that he should be sole commissioner.[9] Germain, Knox reported, had little liking for the commission and in particular was opposed to having Lord Howe as a sole commissioner. He insisted either that others should be joined in the commission with Lord Howe or that he should be rigidly bound down by instructions. Germain wished Eden and perhaps Knox to be included in the commission. Lord Howe turned this down flatly, although he made two concessions: he agreed to accept and be bound by any instructions it was thought proper to give him, and he agreed to have his brother, General Howe, put in the commission with him. He would not accept the command of the fleet alone, insisting that he must be both commissioner and commander. This was agreed to by the cabinet, but the government was finding that it had a rigid character in Lord Howe. Germain reported to Eden that he despaired of Lord Howe as a commissioner.[10]

The next problem related to the instructions which were to be given to the Howes. Germain insisted that the first requisite was to demand from the colonies the acknowledgment of "the supreme authority of the Legislature to make laws binding on the colonies in all cases whatsoever." [11] North believed that this was a necessary acknowledgment but he did not wish to insist upon it as a preliminary to all negotiation. It might come in later. Dartmouth was against its being required at all. Germain was suspicious that if he gave in on the point of the timing of the acknowledgment of legislative supremacy, North would forsake this principle entirely.

The debate then revolved around the point as to whether the declaration of the supremacy of the British Parliament should be "a preliminary or an ultimatum" to any negotiation which the commission might undertake. Knox proposed a middle way. He suggested that assemblies might be called by the governors and informed that they were empowered to appoint delegates to meet the commissioners after all illegal governments had been dissolved and legal governments formed and after all bodies of armed men had been disbanded. However, they were not to be declared at peace and the terms of the Prohibitory Act lifted until they had made the declaration.[12] This did not meet with approval; Germain insisted that no delegates might be sent until the declaration had been made. Both Dartmouth and North spoke of resigning their offices. Germain said that it would be more proper, as being less a blow to the King's government, if he should resign his office. Knox, who lived on terms of intimacy with Germain, and who, on the whole, approved his policy, made this comment: "The truth was, Lord George having now collected a vast force, and having a fair prospect of subduing the colonies, he wished to reduce them before he treated at all." He feared, as Knox saw it, that if peace were restored neither Parliament nor the government would reopen the war to obtain an acknowledgment of legislative supremacy. Knox sympathized to a degree with this position. He was not in favor of suspending hostilities against New England, but he thought this might be done in the south, both to divide the colonies and to draw supplies from that quarter.[13] Knox was by way of being a ferocious Tory himself.

In this severe conflict of views, Germain turned for advice to Suffolk and Wedderburn, the solicitor general. Suffolk was strongly against Germain's taking any hasty decision on the point of resignation. He assured Germain that he would never think of urging him to forsake principles which he had so sincerely adopted. If North had in mind any course of action derogatory to the dignity of Parliament, or if he aimed at getting out of the war as his chief object, he would find Suffolk unalterably opposed to him. But he was disposed not to press the formality of a preliminary declaration too far. He asked Germain to consider the substance of the matter. If submission— the laying down of arms, the dissolution of illegal governments, and the restoration of constitutional government—was obtained, was it worth while to insist upon and to carry to the length of resignation from office, the point of a declaration? Suffolk also made a very strong point of the fact that Germain had never publicly declared for more than North was then willing to accept. He reflected his own uneasiness by observing that North was not alone in his position and that many wise men believed the declaration was only "a matter of words." Real submission, and not extorted profession, must be the essential goal.[14]

Wedderburn leaned toward this view, but inclined to emphasize some tangible, outward mark of submission. "If the objection is only pointed at a *verbal declaration* as contrasted to *actual submission*, I feel disposed to adopt it." He suggested imposing a penalty on the colonies for their treason, which they might remove by subsequent evidence of the reality of their submission. Let them work their way home. He was sure on one point: ". . . to end the war without finishing the dispute, is much worse than to have given up the point without a struggle." In any case, he felt Germain ought to see Lord Mansfield, the chief justice, whose opinion, Wedderburn thought, would correspond closely to Germain's own. He urged Germain to give the matter cool and steady discussion and not to consider resignation, for that would be fatal to "the plan of coercion" which was the only possible solution for the problem presented by the rebellion.[15]

Both of these opinions weighed with Germain, and if he had ever seriously entertained the idea of retiring from his post, these opinions persuaded him to reconsider.

A cabinet meeting was set for Monday, 18 March, to thrash out the difficulties:

On Sunday Lord North proposed to Lord George to talk with Lord Mansfield next day and put off the Cabinet. Lord George would not go to Lord Mansfield on his own account and would have had Lord North to go, who on the other hand would not go alone. So they agreed to go together.[16]

This hardly appears to be the meeting of large minds, but a compromise resulted. The commissioners, instead of demanding the declaration of the colonies, were to wait for offers. If the colonists did not make the declaration, they were not to be restored to peace, unless upon further instructions from home. If the colonists offered to make the declaration, hostilities were to be suspended. There is some difference in emphasis between this and Germain's original position, but little change in substance. In view of the real character of the revolutionary struggle, this so-called compromise illustrates in a striking way the unreality of the whole discussion. Neither Germain's views nor those of Lord North had the slightest chance of being accepted by the Congress, or by any substantial number of the American people. It was a pointless discussion and served to indicate in the very beginning how little in the way of concession the commission would be able to offer.

This was the view of Lord Howe. In a letter to Germain of 26 March, he declared that he was unable to accept the commission and his instructions in their present form. He felt they offered no opportunity for success. The preliminary conditions were so severe as to discourage the very beginning of negotiation. He would, however, undertake the commission on the following basis:

If they will agree to offer a contribution in lieu of taxation, lay down their arms, restore the civil government, and by their assemblies declare their obedience to the authority of the British Legislature, and apply to be relieved from the restrictions upon their trade, in such manner as shall be deemed a satisfactory evidence of their future good intentions, they shall be declared at the King's peace, and any complaints made in a dutiful manner shall be received and favourably considered.[17]

Germain entered into some explanations with Lord Howe which seem, in part at least, to have mollified him.[18] But a few days later, apparently realizing that none of his original objections had been met, he wrote again to Germain. Three specific points were raised by this letter. *First:* that Rhode Island and Connecticut, being excluded by his instructions from the King's peace until their charters were amended, ought to be told what alterations were in prospect, and upon acceptance ought to be admitted into the general negotiation. *Second:* that the Prohibitory Act itself made obligatory the acceptance of Rhode Island and Connecticut upon their proper return to their duty. *Third:* that the only power the commissioners were given related to the declaration of peace and the granting of pardons. All other matters were contingent upon reference to the government in England. The commissioners ought to be able, on the point of taxation, to indicate what would be acceptable to King and Parliament.[19]

This letter gave Germain pause, and he again turned to Wedderburn for advice. These were legal matters and Wedderburn was one of the law officers of the Crown. Wedderburn first took up the case of Rhode Island and Connecticut. The desirable alterations in their charters should be appointive during pleasure; that the assembly should be forbidden from passing acts effective from the date of passage; and that the assembly should be prohibited from trying property cases, as was the situation in Rhode Island. The most important point, in Wedderburn's opinion, was to secure an appointive governor, at pleasure, equipped with the veto power. The idea that it was mandatory upon the government of Great Britain to extend the King's peace to any colony which desired to return to its duty, was a mistake and a dangerous one: "... of the two evils I know not but a precipitate peace would be worse than a lingering war." As far as taxation (contribution) was concerned, it ought to be placed upon a well-understood system, such as a proportion of tonnage in the northern colonies and upon the number of slaves in the southern colonies, or it might bear some fixed relation to the ordinary revenue in Great Britain.[20]

Having taken legal advice, Germain replied to Lord Howe on 2 April. He first made the point that, though he was glad to give verbal explanations, Lord Howe must understand that his constitutional position forbade him from making any alteration in instructions which had been passed by the cabinet. He had hoped that the alterations already made in this way would have been satisfactory. With respect to Rhode Island and Connecticut, Germain did not pass on to Howe the specific recommendations made by Wedderburn. He merely stated that if they agreed to "a proper alteration" and acknowledged the legislative supremacy of Great Britain, they might be treated in the same manner as the other colonies. In this case Lord Howe need not send to England for further powers. This could have given little comfort to the puzzled and dissatisfied commissioner. On taxation, Germain agreed with Lord Howe that he should know the expectations of the cabinet and particularly of Lord North. Germain contended strongly that it was a mistaken idea to suppose that the Prohibitory Act was mandatory on the point of the restoration of the King's peace. It empowered but did not require the commissioner to take such action.[21]

The whole letter appears to evade the objections raised by Lord Howe. It does not pass along any of the specific ideas put forth by Wedderburn and draws upon the latter's views most strongly in refuting the belief that the Prohibitory Act was compulsive in its operation. It is true that the constitutional position of Germain made it difficult, if not dangerous, for him to meddle with and interpret instructions which had been passed by all the ministers. This same consideration did not apply to any speculations in which Wedderburn might indulge himself. Today a minister of the Crown must be very careful in any advice he gives or ideas he sanctions, lest they be taken for the official governmental position. This collective responsibility had not become so clearly the custom of the constitution in Germain's day, but it was emerging. Nevertheless, there does seem to be a lack of frankness and a close-lipped attitude in Germain's reply.

Lord Howe must have sensed something of this because, after sleeping on the matter, he wrote to Germain the next morning in a cold and ironical manner. He was, he said, highly sensible of Germain's condescension [22] and aware of the trouble he was causing. He could not presume further to break in upon his time. He had been greatly honored by the "verbal ideas" Germain had thrown out, but he was unwilling to commit him to an expression of his private opinion.[23] For a time the matter rested here, with Lord Howe dissatisfied and the commission and the instructions in no final form.

The fact of the matter was that the government feared to break with Lord Howe. In particular, it feared to break with him on an untried question: the alteration of the charters of Rhode Island and Connecticut. It was impossible to know how opinion in the House and outside would react to this new aspect of the American question. If Lord Howe were passed by and other dispositions made with respect to the commission and the command of the fleet, it could be confidently predicted that he would make public the nature of the whole controversy. In addition, the cooperation between the general and admiral in America would be jeopardized if General Howe's brother were treated in this way. Altogether it was an awkward situation. There was one consolation in respect to Lord Howe, as Wedderburn pointed out, "he would not be very anxious about the terms of his Instructions, if he did not mean to be guided by them." [24]

Lord Howe was pressing for an additional instruction setting forth the precise alterations which the government expected in the charters of Rhode Island and Connecticut. He feared that without such an instruction the two colonies would have to be left out of any negotiations and that this, because of a feeling of solidarity among the colonies, would, at the very beginning, wreck the whole of the efforts of the commission. He also wanted a discretionary power with respect to Rhode Island and Connecticut, allowing him, in case of necessity, to bring them into the negotiations on an equal footing with the other colonies. Wedderburn presumed he "would admit that it would be improper to use that power in their favor, unless it should become of absolute necessity to the submission of the other colonies." [25] The solicitor general advised Germain to have a long, confidential talk (*"en ami"*) with Lord Howe and discover exactly what he wished to have covered in the additional instruction. "I really think the best security for the good execution of it will be the idea that he is confided in, which more than anything will induce him to endeavor to pursue your ideas." [26] He went on to remark sagely that, in original intent, the instructions had been drawn with a view of getting the business done, but that it was now necessary before they were signed and sealed that they should be revised, in the face of the evident possibility that the government might have, publicly, to defend them.

These were very troublesome and vexing matters and, in the meanwhile, the time of Lord Howe's departure for America was approaching. On 27 April, Germain wrote General Howe:

It was hoped and expected that Lord Howe would have proceeded with his embarkation; the necesssary arrangements respecting the very important commission of offer of pardon and negotiation in which he and you are joined, make that very doubtful.

The transports would proceed without Lord Howe, but he would probably not be detained many days, and, since he was to sail without convoy, he had every chance of arriving before the troops.[27]

It was under the compelling necessity that Lord Howe should sail for America with the reinforcements that his final instructions took form. Nothing illustrates better the two-fold policy of the British government: on the one hand, conciliation, on the other hand, coercion. It is to be noted that in the end coercion—the dispatch of the reinforcements—was the overriding consideration. The government, and this meant largely Germain, gave in to Lord Howe on what had seemed essential matters. The instructions to Lord Howe and General Howe and an additional instruction were dated 6 May.[28] The instructions set up the conditions upon which the rebel provinces might take up again their normal and legal place within the empire. All congresses were to be dissolved and constitutional governments re-established. All troops were to be disbanded and forts delivered to the proper authorities. General assemblies were to meet and apply for the removal of the restrictions of the Prohibitory Act. The commissioners were to examine strictly the sincerity of intention displayed. If any doubt arose as to the allegiance of a colony or its obedience to the authority of the British legislature, the matter was to be referred to the home government. An Act of Parliament of 20 February 1775 had provided that no tax would be levied on a colony except for the regulation of trade, provided that the colony would make a contribution, disposable by Parliament, for the costs of government and defense. This was the offer of the commission on the taxation point. Loyalists must be compensated. There must be no tax on British imports or on exports necessary for British manufacturers. There should be a general overhaul of the governments in the colonies, particularly with respect to Rhode Island and Connecticut. There would also, on the other hand, be a revision of those laws by which the colonists felt themselves aggrieved. There might be no discussion of the Quebec Act (1774). In the last analysis, everything was to be referred to the home government. The commissioners were forbidden to "pledge yourselves to any act of consent or acquiescence that may be construed to preclude Our Royal Determination."

The additional instruction set forth clearly enough the alterations which the British government expected in the charters of Rhode Island and Connecticut. The following laws were to be repealed: those which forbade an appeal to the Privy Council in civil cases; those which prevented the King from appointing the commander of the militia; and those which declared a right in the people to be exempt from acts of Parliament. The governor's office was to be appointive or, if elective, the tenure of office was to be contingent upon royal approval. Legislation was to be subject to a royal negative within a reasonable time. The commissioners were directed not to negotiate with Rhode Island and Connecticut unless they secured these alterations, unless failure to do so threatened to wreck the whole work of the commission. In that case, the commissioners were given discretionary power to include Rhode Island and Connecticut.

On these particular issues Lord Howe had gained his point. There was no explicit demand for a declaration in exact terms of the principles of the Declaratory Act of 1766, that is to say the right of the British Parliament to make laws binding upon the colonies "in all cases whatsoever." Germain had contended for this. Some indication, though a vague one, was given as to the expectations of the home government on taxation. The specific alterations desired in the charters of Rhode Island and Connecticut were itemized. These were victories for Lord Howe personally, but they added little to the general scope of the proposals. There was no largeness of vision here. There was convincing evidence of the failure of the British government to catch anything of the true character of the revolutionary movement in America.

II

Lord Howe sailed from England on board the "Eagle," 64 shortly after the instructions had been completed. He arrived off the coast of Massachusetts Bay on 20 June.[29] In the meantime, Sir William Howe, having evacuated Boston on 17 March, arrived in Halifax on 2 April.[30] He remained at Halifax until 10 June, when he sailed for New York in the frigate "Greyhound," arriving off Staten Island 25 June.[31] The correspondence between General Howe and Germain in the period from 2 April to 10 June reveals a good deal of the expectation each had formed with respect to the coming campaign.

Howe was anxious to impress upon the government in England that his seeming retreat to Halifax was only the prelude to vigorous action against the enemy at New York. He had begun to develop this idea as soon as he boarded ship to sail for Halifax. On 21 March, while still in Nantucket Road, he wrote Dartmouth that he intended to launch an offensive against New York from Halifax as soon as he secured provisions and transports for his army of 5,000.[32] This was a necessary measure to check the enthusiasm of the rebels which had mounted greatly due to what they considered to be the retrograde movement of the British army in its removal to Halifax. This morale problem, as it affected both his own troops and the rebel troops, was a constant worry to Howe. He was prepared to embark upon a campaign without waiting for reinforcements from Europe, as he considered delay highly injurious to his situation and advantageous to the rebel army. This was his view in March and it was reiterated again and again in his letters during this waiting period.

It was, however, necessary for him to reform his forces, make some arrangements for the Loyalists whom he had evacuated from Boston, and wait for provisions and transports. He had been in Halifax for three weeks before he wrote a dispatch to England—his first dispatch to Germain.[33] New York and Rhode Island were to be the major objectives, but, since the army was not in sufficient strength to make an attack on both, New York, as the greater object, would be attempted first. This offensive ought to be immediately undertaken "to check the spirit which the evacuation of Boston will naturally raise among the rebels." Howe had high hopes of success and even looked forward to an early decisive action with the enemy. In his opinion, such an action should be sought by the British army. The troops were in high spirits and good health. This first official letter was full of confidence and resolution.

Either this confidence and resolution were only of an official character or Howe was of a most mercurial temperament. For, a day later, in a private letter to Germain, he wrote of the "lowering aspect" of the whole situation in America. He represented himself as almost despairing of bringing the rebel army to a decisive action. Since the enemy had the whole country at his disposal, he could exchange space for time. Such strategy was calculated to defeat the whole British purpose. Howe expected no help from the loyal inhabitants until a decisive victory for the King's arms had created a situation in which loyalism might flourish.

Germain must have been puzzled and annoyed by two such disparate evaluations of the situation, written on consecutive days. He could not, however, fail to be flattered by the fulsome manner in which Howe wrote of his acceptance of office. At a time, Howe asserted, when most men would shrink from the conflict, Germain's high sense of public duty had led him to step forward and to accept the onerous responsibility of office. The army rejoiced at the idea of serving under Germain's direction, feeling sure that it would receive from him every possible assistance in the difficult task ahead. Howe also expressed his own appreciation of Germain's goodness to him, and his heartfelt wish that every success should attend the "noble effort" of the new secretary.[34]

News of the evacuation of Boston, contained in Howe's letter of 21 March, arrived in London on 3 May. Germain immediately took this letter to the King and wrote to Howe the same afternoon.[35] He gave full approval of the evacuation of Boston. Under the circumstances no other course was possible. Such considerable reinforcements were at that very time on the high seas, or on the point of leaving England, that the whole British situation in America would soon be greatly improved. The forces destined for Canada sailed on 7 and 8 April; the troops to reinforce Howe would sail on either 4 or 5 May. A part of the latter force, the Hessians, would proceed to Rhode Island and they would take post there if contrary orders were not waiting for them on their arrival. Germain reflected no urgent mood in this letter. He approved strongly of Howe's zeal in wishing to push forward the attack on New York, but, at the end of his letter, he complacently remarked that since such large reinforcements were being sent out, he hoped they would arrive before the attack took place. Such ideas, put on paper early in May, while these forces were still in British ports, certainly do not reflect any expectation that the campaign would begin early. However, this letter had no effect on Howe's plans, since he did not receive it until 27 July, when he was already on Long Island.

As Howe waited in Halifax during the early days of May, he had to make his plans in accordance with his own judgment and his directions from the government in London. His most recent dispatch from Germain was dated 5 January.[36] Germain had then informed Howe that in a separate dispatch he would deal more in detail with the plan of campaign for 1776. Since Howe had received no further word, he began to feel apprehensive that perhaps he was embarking upon a plan of operations which did not have the approval of the Home Government. He gave expression to this uneasiness in a letter to Germain of 7 May.[37] He was proceeding, he wrote, on the assumption that the King would approve of the attack upon New York and that that attack ought to be launched without the least delay. This latter consideration weighed heavily with him. Delay would increase the possibility of the summer fogs shutting in, and thus make naval operations hazardous and slow; it would give the enemy more time to entrench himself strongly in his positions; and it might mean that the reinforcements from Europe would arrive on the American coast before Lord Howe did. For all these reasons he was determined to push on with his plans and trust that they had the full approval of the King. Howe never did receive from Germain a dispatch which might be regarded as a separate to the one of 5 January. The substance of the plans evolved by both Howe and Germain from June of 1775 on to the end of the year was the plan of campaign for 1776. No comprehensive and authoritative document from London sums up and gives classic form to the over-all strategic concept. Germain, by implication, indicated that no such document was necessary, for, in answering Howe's letter of 7 May on 11 June, he declared:

It is not necessary for me to enter into the particulars contained in your letter of May 7; but as I feel myself perfectly satisfied with what you have already done and purpose to do, it would be ungenerous in me not to endeavor, in my turn to contribute to your happiness by assuring you that your actions and intentions are honored with the entire approbation of your sovereign.[38]

Howe received this letter on 12 August after having committed himself wholeheartedly to an attack upon New York.

An interesting sidelight upon Germain's conduct of the war comes out in Howe's letter of 7 May. At the beginning of the year, Germain had raised the question as to whether Admiral Graves was justified in destroying the town of Falmouth. If Graves had given his reasons for this drastic measure, Germain was unaware of that fact. Such action could be condoned only in the face of the complete intransigence of the inhabitants. He wanted an explanation. Howe (7 May) gave an account of the matter which made it appear that the expedition had been undertaken on orders from Gage [39] and that the officer detailed to the duty had carried out a bombardment of the town and later, landing a party of men, the town had been largely destroyed. The officer had decided upon this action only after an extensive parley with the townspeople who finally decided "to wait their fate." No more is heard of this incident of the war, but Germain's scrupulous inquiry ought to be recorded.

During the rest of May and the first ten days of June, Howe remained inactively at Halifax. In his letters to Germain, he registered his "most sensible mortification" at being so long detained by lack of provisions,[40] and his lively apprehension that the rebel army would take heart from the retreat from Boston and the subsequent immobility of the British forces.[41] In this trying situation he was still capable of paying a dutiful, if somewhat dubious, compliment to Germain. He felt that the secretary's indefatigable exertions and resources would still be equal to the contest and—"the foreigners willing"—his honor would be vindicated and the nation satisfied that the expenses incurred had been justified.

Howe was also preoccupied at this time with the problem of command, when, as he expected, the army from Canada would make contact with his own.[42] He recognized that Carleton was his senior and would take over the command, but he wished that the combined armies might have the character of allied armies, rather than the one absorbing the other. He wanted to retain his authority over promotions, and all the internal regulation of his army. He expected that the senior officer would not appropriate the troops of the junior without the latter's consent. He suggested that separate encampments be established.[43] It is interesting to speculate upon the degree to which these difficulties, thus early raised by Howe, might have influenced the Home Government in its decision to give the command of the northern army to Burgoyne, Howe's junior, in 1777. That decision was made by 22 August 1776 [44] and on that day Germain answered Howe's letter of 12 May. He wrote:

I herewith transmit you a copy of a dispatch sent to General Sir Guy Carleton, which I think makes it unnecessary for me to enter into a discussion of that part of your letter which relates to the difficulties that might arise upon a junction of your respective armies.

Carleton had been directed to devote his attention to the civil affairs of the province of Quebec, and Burgoyne was to make a junction with Howe and put himself under his orders.[45]

The provision ships for Howe arrived early in June and the reinforcement of Highlanders on 8 June.[46] On 10 June, Howe and the army set sail for New York. As the active part of the campaign of 1776 got under way Howe could not refrain from

expressing my utter amazement at the decisive and masterly strokes for carrying such extensive plans into immediate execution as have been effected since your Lordship has assumed the conducting of this war, which is already most happily experienced by those who have the honour of serving here under your auspices.[47]

Complete harmony and confidence existed between minister and commander, when, as far as the oncoming campaign was concerned, the former had largely performed his duties, and the latter was only beginning to undertake his.

While Howe waited in Halifax, stirring events were on foot in Canada. On 6 May the reinforcements from England arrived and the siege of Quebec was precipitately raised by the rebel army. Carleton, taking with him the forces aboard the first relief ships, immediately set off in pursuit of the rebels. Burgoyne himself arrived too late to take part in the early operations against the rebels in retreat. He believed that if the captain in charge of the convoy had allowed him to press on with fifteen or twenty of the fastest ships, not a single rebel would have escaped.[48]

Both he and Carleton had a second opportunity in the middle of June to achieve this same result. On 14 June General Sullivan and the major part of the rebel army had begun to retreat up the Richelieu. Burgoyne with a force of 4,000 was in pursuit. In order to cut off Sullivan's retreat, Carleton was to sail up the St. Lawrence to Longueil, and march overland to St. Johns. Arnold, having meanwhile evacuated Montreal, was marching with a small garrison toward St. Johns. Everything depended on Arnold's column and Sullivan's column reaching St. Johns and embarking for a retreat down the lake before the British forces came upon them. Burgoyne had instructions not to press the rebels too strongly so that Carleton might have time to cut off the retreat. Carleton was to have been at St. Johns on the morning of 16 June. On the afternoon of 15 June he was lying aboard ship, wind-bound at Varennes. He could have disembarked his troops and marched them overland by a good road to St. Johns. Arnold arrived at St. Johns on 16 June. There were no boats available at that time to receive his troops. Sullivan did not arrive at St. Johns until late on 17 June. On 18 June, the necessary boats arrived and the American troops embarked. Just as they rowed beyond the range of muskets, Burgoyne's forces entered St. Johns. Carleton came up next morning. A historian of this affair has summed up the situation in this way:

He could have captured the whole American army and all the American boats, which would have given him command of Lake Champlain, had he done his duty as a soldier. But the statesman had obscured the soldier. The Declaration of Independence was still in the future and he was reluctant to push 'the deluded people of the colonies' over the brink into an irreconcilable war. His deliberate delay ruined the campaign of 1776 and possibly altered the outcome of the war.[49]

Had Carleton seized control of Lake Champlain in the middle of June rather than at the beginning of October, when it was done at the cost of a severe naval engagement with Arnold, the course of events might have been radically changed. Mahan remarked upon the importance of Arnold's delaying action in opposing Carleton's naval force:

Whatever deductions may be made for blunders, and for circumstances of every character which made the British campaign of 1777 abortive and disastrous, thus leading directly to the American alliance with France in 1778, the delay with all that it involved, was obtained by the Lake campaign of 1776.[50]

But Arnold imposed, what, in Mahan's view, was a disastrous delay upon Carleton in October. To have seized command of the Lake in June, with no enemy naval force upon it, and with no substantial enemy land force at the other end of it, would have been a major stroke.

Although, in all probability, Germain, to the end of his days, never understood the situation as it developed in the first half of June 1776, Carleton, if the argument is sound, did. Later (1777), when Germain brought to Carleton's attention the effect his withdrawal from before Ticonderoga had upon the fortunes of Howe, through the release of American troops to serve with Washington in the successful thrust against Trenton, Carleton was touched upon a tender spot. It was, however, not the retreat across the lakes in November which was open to criticism, but the failure to act aggressively in June. "Whatever blame there may have been in Germain's own mind was attached to the right man but to the wrong action." [51] This whole situation had a most important bearing upon the subsequent relations between Germain and Carleton.

With the preparation and the dispatch from Britain of the reinforcements for Howe and Carleton, Germain had completed his major contribution to the campaign of 1776. He had been eager and efficient in marshaling the forces of coercion. Working with the means at hand, he had achieved a real measure of success, and Howe's compliments have the ring of sincerity. With the preparations of the instructions for the two Howes as peace commissioners and the dispatch of Lord Howe to America, Germain had completed, such as it was, his contribution to conciliation as an essential part of the campaign of 1776. Here his misconception of the whole revolutionary movement made it utterly impossible that this aspect of his policy should meet with any substantial measure of success. The British government tried both coercion and conciliation in the campaign of 1776. The former attained a limited objective; the latter attained no objective at all.

CHAPTER 6

THE PLANS FOR THE CAMPAIGN OF 1777

I

The campaign of 1777, culminating in the battle of Saratoga [1] (October) and followed within four months by the Franco-American alliance, was of decisive importance in the War for American Independence. It ended the colonial phase of the war and opened its international phase. After 1777, military and naval maneuvers and encounters in the West Indies, the English Channel, and the Mediterranean, as well as those on the coast and mainland of North America, became of determinative importance. Germain's career, too, divided at this point. From 1775 to 1778, with full control of the sea approaches to North America he was in charge of carrying forward a war against rebellious colonists. After 1778 he became virtually war minister in the British government, charged indeed still with the task of breaking the revolution, but a revolution now enormously strengthened by the support of the first-rate sea power of a rejuvenated French Navy.

No campaign of the war aroused a more heated controversy at the time, nor has one exerted a stronger fascination for politico-military historians down to our time. As a result of the campaign, the Howes demanded and were granted a parliamentary inquiry (1779). This provoked a flood of pamphlet material which ventilated the whole controversy before the public. The inquiry was completely inconclusive ending with no single resolution of the House.[2] The storm centers of the bitter controversy were the Howes, Burgoyne, and Germain; Carleton was an enigmatic figure in the background.[3]

The basic idea of the campaign of 1777 was not a new one. It consisted, in its essential objective, of taking hold of Albany by an attack from Canada. The natural route for such an attack was by way of the Richelieu and Lake Champlain. A chain of posts, St. Johns, Crown Point, Ticonderoga, and others would stretch back from Albany to Montreal. This operation would be reinforced by action up the Hudson from New York. In the end a cordon of power would extend from the Atlantic to the St. Lawrence. The geography of North America urgently suggested this strategy. As Gates wrote Hancock, it had been the uniform plan of France and England throughout their long struggle for supremacy in North America.[4]

The idea naturally came to the fore during the troubled times of the 1760's. Carleton had suggested, nine years before the Declaration of Independence, that the forts of Crown Point and Ticonderoga should be put in better condition for defense, and that New York and Quebec should be strengthened. He declared that such a chain of fortifications

will link these two provinces so strongly together as will add great security to both; they will facilitate the transport of ten or fifteen thousand men in the beginning of a war, from one to the other as the circumstances require.[5]

In April 1775, Dartmouth emphasized the importance of possessing the line of the Hudson to cut off New England from any aid she might draw from the middle colonies.[6] After the outbreak of hostilities in America, Carleton returned to his earlier suggestion. In the fall of 1775, he wrote to Dartmouth:

. . . I think that this war can not be carried on more advantageously than from hence, and that a body of ten or twelve thousand men here early next spring completely equipped with some frigates might greatly change the face of things on this continent.[7]

Such a force was sent to Canada in the spring of 1776 with the twofold objective of driving the American armies from Canada, and, by pursuing the enemy beyond the borders of Canada, of cooperating with the army under Howe at New York.[8] Carleton succeeded in the first objective but failed in the second.[9]

In the meantime, the government in London, through the prodding of Howe, had decided upon a solution of the problem in command presented by the expected junction in the fall of 1776 of the army under Carleton—the senior officer—and the army under Howe. It was the duty of Germain to convey the decision of the government to Carleton. This he did in the middle of August 1776. He began by paying Carleton a handsome compliment on his success in driving the rebel forces from Canada. But he drew the general's attention to another important part of his task, that relating to his responsibilities in the province of Canada. That province must be pacified, the loyal inhabitants rewarded, the disloyal punished, and good order and legal government established:

It is an object of the greatest importance to the country; the difficulties attending it are immense; but His Majesty depends upon your zeal and upon your experience for carrying it into execution.

Carleton was therefore to return to Canada and

detaching Lt. Gen. Burgoyne, or such other officer as you should think most proper . . . direct the officer so detached to communicate with and put himself under the command of Sir William Howe.[10]

The problem emerged clearly at this point. At the beginning of the campaign, with a similar operation in view, Carleton had been ordered merely to pass the lakes and "contribute to the success of the army under General Howe." [11] The government in London considered Howe in the role of commander in chief; he was operating at the center of the conflict and in that area the decisive action of the war would occur. Nevertheless, it would be impossible to direct Carleton to put himself under the orders of Howe. Howe's suggestion that the two armies, upon junction, should be treated as allied armies seemed a makeshift solution, and a solution which would almost inevitably give rise to friction and misunderstanding. In this situation, the government decided to resolve the difficulty by the simple expedient of ordering Carleton back to Canada and Burgoyne forward to New York. Burgoyne was regarded as a competent and vigorous soldier, and now, after a year's experience, familiar with the position of affairs in America. The vexing problem was to make Carleton see the situation as one in no wise derogatory to him. Germain did his best. He began his dispatch with praise and he concluded it in the same vein:

I cannot finish this dispatch without repeating to you the confidence which H. M. places in your duty, your zeal and your attachment to his service and that you cannot more effectually recommend yourself to his royal approbation and favor than by exerting yourself as successfully in your civil capacity as you have already done in your military command.

Already, half way through the campaign of 1776, it had been determined that Carleton would not command the northern army beyond the frontier of Canada. Burgoyne had been named in 1776; but in that year the advance had not been made beyond Ticonderoga. It was very natural that in 1777—the continuation of the operations of 1776—Burgoyne should be considered for the command. However, Germain's dispatch of 22 August never reached Carleton; it was taken by Captain Le Maitre who was in the mouth of the St. Lawrence three times in the fall of 1776, but was forced back to England.[12] Essentially, the same instructions were contained in Germain's letter to Carleton of 26 March 1777, but the results of Carleton's military operations in 1776 were known by Germain when he wrote the later dispatch, and this introduced new asperities into the relations between the two men. Looking back upon the matter in July 1777, the King was of the opinion that the measure of ordering Carleton back to Canada was necessary and proper. He remarked:

...I think as things were situated [i.e. in August] 1776 the ordering him to remain in the province was a necessary measure, yet it must be owned to be mortifying to a soldier.[13]

Indeed, tensions had already developed. In addition to dealing with the problem of command on 22 August, Germain wrote another letter to Carleton touching civil appointments in the province of Quebec.[14] He thus involved himself in the matter of the internal administration of that province, a preserve which Carleton regarded as peculiarly his own, and one in which, because of his tortuous maneuvers, it was dangerous for an outsider to meddle. This was trouble for the future. Already difficulties had arisen between Germain and Carleton over the appointment of a quartermaster general in the northern army. Carleton had been authorized prior to Germain's taking office to appoint a quartermaster general in Canada, and before there was any thought of sending a large army to Canada he had made the appointment. Germain, in England, knew nothing of Carleton's appointment, and, needing the assistance of an officer in this capacity during the raising and fitting out of the large reinforcements for 1776, he had appointed Lieutenant Colonel Christie. Christie arrived in Canada on 1 June 1776 and presented his commission to Carleton. Carleton thus had two quartermasters general: one, his own appointee, Thomas Carleton, his brother, and the other Germain's appointee. Carleton refused to install Christie in his office, and Germain acquiesced in this arrangement quietly and with no apparent ill will.[15] Had he been vindictive he might have indulged in some edged comment upon Carleton's obvious nepotism.

In private, however, Germain gave evidence that he was nettled. He wrote Burgoyne on 23 August:

Lieut. Col. Christie has met the treatment I expected. His experience in the department of the Quarter-Master-General was of great use to me when I was making preparations for the recovery of the province. As he is disagreeable to the general, it is impossible they should remain together, but when an officer has been employed by me for the benefit of the public, I cannot consent to his disgrace to gratify the humour of any individual, and the King is too just to condemn upon accusation only.

He went on to say that Christie would be given a battalion in the Royal Americans. This letter also provided further evidence of Germain's developing attitudes:

Every attention will be shown to General Carleton, and his services will be amply rewarded, but the settling of Canada will require all his application. The Red Ribbon which the King conferred upon him was against my opinion. My wish was that such a mark of favor should have been deferred till the province of Canada had been regained. I then imagined it would have done the general more honour, but I suppose the King could not forbear granting so agreeable a commission to Lady Maria as the carrying such a mark of his royal approbation to her husband.[16]

Howe was informed of the change in command of the northern army on 23 October.[17] The campaign of the Howes in 1776 extended from the middle of August to early December. In this period they had won the Battle of Long Island and extended the British outposts as far as the Delaware River. Taken all in all these operations of the Howes constituted probably the most successful British campaign of the war. But they came far short of being decisive; the Revolution as an idea and as an organized force remained vigorous and formidable. The Howes had conducted a neat, cautious campaign for limited, though substantial, objectives. The end of the campaign saw Clinton safely established at Rhode Island (December). During the year, Carleton, missing an opportunity in June, was checked at the head of Lake Champlain until October for lack of water transport. When this was available, he was checked again by Arnold at the Battle of Valcour Island (11 October). Arnold had impeded Carleton's progress, but with his inferior force he could not hold him up permanently. Carleton advanced and took Crown Point. He hesitated before Ticonderoga but, deciding that the place was too strong and the season too late, he evacuated Crown Point on 2 November, and retreated toward Canada.[18]

The stage was now set for the preparation of detailed military plans for 1777. By December 1776 there were four basic sources on which to build an over-all strategic concept for the next year. *First:* The old idea, dating back at least a century, of drawing a cordon of power from the St. Lawrence to the Atlantic by Lake Champlain and the Hudson. *Second:* The impetus of the campaign of 1776 shaped the plans for 1777; operations would be carried on in the spring from the point where the forward impulse had been arrested in the fall. *Third:* A working over of these ideas with variations by Howe in a letter to Germain of 30 November 1776.[19] *Fourth:* A memorandum containing Carleton's ideas brought back to England by Burgoyne in early December 1776.[20] These sources, together with the additions later of Burgoyne, the King, Germain, and two second thoughts by Howe, are the essential bases upon which our analysis must be founded.

On 30 November, Howe, on the point of going into winter quarters, wrote Germain to outline what he hoped yet to do in 1776 and what he had in mind for 1777. Not much was left for 1776: Clinton was under orders to sail with 6,000 troops against Rhode Island with the first fair wind, and Cornwallis was to be stationed in command of a string of posts across the Jerseys. Carleton was in retreat from Crown Point and, because of this action, it might be confidently predicted that the northern army would not reach Albany before September of the next year.

With this assessment of the situation in mind, Howe put forth a specific detail of forces and objectives for 1777. *First:* An offensive army of 10,000, after taking possession of Providence, should penetrate into the country toward Boston, and, if possible, take possession of that town. Under the protection of the shipping, 2,000 men should be left in Rhode Island and should make small incursions into Connecticut. This operation would be undertaken by Clinton. *Second:* An army of 10,000 should move up the North River from New York and seize Albany; 5,000 should be left for the defense of New York and the nearby posts. *Third:* A defensive army of 8,000 should hold Jersey in order to check Washington's army and threaten Philadelphia. This city would be attacked in the fall and Virginia as well, provided that the success of the other operations would permit the release of the necessary troops. South Carolina and Georgia would be the objects of a winter campaign.

A campaign on this scale would require an army under his command of 35,000 to oppose a contemplated 50,000 in the rebel army. This would mean an over-all reinforcement for 1777 of 15,000 rank and file. Howe was well aware that so large a reinforcement was unobtainable in the British Isles, and he suggested that troops be sought in Russia, Hanover, and the other German states. He expressed a preference for Hanoverian chasseurs. In addition, a naval force of at least ten ships of the line must be sent to America.

The setbacks suffered by the revolutionary forces in 1776 had led many to wonder whether success would ever be possible. Hopes were kept alive, however, by the assurances held out by the leaders of the Revolution that foreign aid would soon support the cause. Dr. Franklin had gone to France to make an attempt to secure the essential outside assistance. Howe regarded this as a serious matter. He declared:

I do not presume to point out a way of counteracting him, but were this effected, and the force I mentioned sent out, it would strike such terror through the country that little resistance would be made to the progress of His Majesty's arms in the provinces of New England, New York, the Jersies, and Pennsylvania, after the junction of the northern and southern armies.[21]

This was an ambitious plan, calling for a reinforcement of 15,000 men for Howe's army alone. The Home Government had scoured the British Isles in 1776 for recruits and had engaged 17,000 foreign levies. It was expected that the large force thus formed, together with the troops already in America, would constitute an armed force capable of crushing the rebellion with only minor reinforcement. This force had achieved limited success around New York, in the Jerseys, at Rhode Island, and had driven the forces of the Revolution out of Canada. But the revolutionary army was still very much in being, and Howe estimated that it would take the field in 1777 with a strength of 50,000. Must Germain each year raise, equip, and send beyond the Atlantic a force in the neighborhood of 20,000? This was a staggering prospect: the British had never before faced such heavy military responsibilities. Howe's request was bound to make the government pause and examine the future prospect.

Howe's plan also raised the main problem of the campaign of 1777; the degree to which the northern and southern armies were expected to cooperate. In the section of his letter in which he set forth, in an orderly manner, the forces required and the objectives of each, he made no mention of a junction of the forces under his command with those operating from Canada. He merely earmarked 10,000 troops for the purpose of taking Albany by an advance up the North River. This, it would appear, would be a self-contained operation, depending in no way for support from an outside source. But later in his letter, in a very offhand manner, he spoke of "the junction of the northern and southern armies." Was the junction to be an actual junction or a "junction of cooperation"? [22] Did Howe think of the campaign in terms of two columns advancing from opposite directions upon a single point—Albany—and the fate of each depending upon the ability of the other to get to that point so that, by mutual support, the two might survive?

Howe had set forth the needs of the southern army. His dispatch arrived in England on 30 December. In the meantime, Burgoyne had returned to England, arriving in London on 9 December.[23] He carried with him Carleton's ideas for the next campaign. Before leaving Canada, in a letter to Clinton, Burgoyne had made a very frank analysis of the operations of 1776.[24] He had been against allowing the whole of the British force to remain inactive from June until October while the naval force was being prepared for transport across Lake Champlain. He had urged Carleton to dispatch him at the head of three British battalions, a corps of artillery, some Canadians and a large body of Indians, by Lake Ontario, Oswego, and Fort Stanwix to the Mohawk River.

This plan I formed after many conversations with Sir John Johnson who was in person with our army and gave me minute intelligence both of the country and disposition of the people ... I think he and I together should have raised a combustion in that country of great effect—a powerful diversion in regard to your army and a yet more positive assistance to that of General Carleton, when ready to cross Lake Champlain for I cannot suppose any general would have remained at Ticonderoga, Fort

Edward or any other post above the junction of the Mohawk and Hudson Rivers. This idea and reasoning upon my plan was approved. It failed for want of sufficient *store of provision*.[25]

After this plan failed of adoption, Burgoyne suggested that a corps of the army should go along with the fleet when it set off across Lake Champlain in order to take sudden advantage of any military opportunity. Carleton first adopted, then rejected, this plan, and the naval force proceeded with Carleton in charge, leaving the army at the head of the lake. Burgoyne was cautious in drawing any conclusions. He observed of this conduct on the part of Carleton:

I should be unjust to General Carleton, if I denied that odd and misplaced as his part may appear at the head of the naval department only, he had reasons to justify that proceeding. They would carry me too far, nor is the occasion proper to open them to you now.

Carleton's dilatory conduct, subsequent to his failure to press the attack against Sullivan and Arnold in June, fits into the picture of Carleton as a man who was being guided by political rather than by military considerations. This is the charitable construction; otherwise he was not only "cold" and inactive, but verging upon neglect of duty. Both Burgoyne and Major General Phillips acquiesced in Carleton's decision not to attack Ticonderoga after having taken Crown Point. Burgoyne thought that a feint might have been tried "to feel their pulse." He had, however, been convinced of the utility of keeping possession of Crown Point through the winter. He had left Carleton there to return to England. On the way down to Quebec he had arranged for a service of supply for that post. But after Burgoyne's departure, Carleton decided to abandon Crown Point. Burgoyne could see no justification for such action.[26]

It may be urged that Burgoyne was unfriendly toward Carleton. This does not appear to be the case either at this time or later. After having raised these serious doubts about Carleton's conduct, he still declared:

I must honor Carleton's abilities and judgment, I have lived with him upon the best terms and bear him friendship. I am therefore doubly hurt that he has taken a step in which I can be no otherwise serviceable to him than by silence.[27]

But Burgoyne was an ambitious man. He did not relish a "secondary station in a secondary command." He was returning to England partly because of this, partly because his constitution was not proof against the severity of a Canadian winter, and partly to perform some duties still remaining to the memory of his wife, Lady Charlotte, who had died a few weeks after he left for America in the spring of 1776.[28] As he waited for passage to England, he represented himself as "an unconnected cipher in the world—the partner lost which made prosperity an object of solicitude—my prospects are closed. Interest, ambition, the animation of life is over." [29]

Before leaving Canada, Burgoyne had discussed with Carleton the general military situation and the needs of the army designed to operate from Canada.[30] Carleton had put some of his own ideas on paper in a letter to Burgoyne of 22 October.[31] However, he instructed Burgoyne to draw up a memorandum in writing for presentation to the government on his arrival in England. This memorandum was to include Carleton's ideas as Burgoyne had collected them, and, specifically, was to demand a reinforcement of 4,000 men for the Canadian army.[32]

II

Burgoyne arrived in England on 9 December and the next day had an interview with Germain. He immediately voiced his strong objection against the abandonment of Crown Point.[33] There was a general feeling in governmental circles that the Canadian campaign had fallen short of expectations, and Germain characterized it as "operations conducted without sense or vigor." [34] As a participant, Burgoyne was not in favor.[35] Germain wished to report to the King the results of his interview with Burgoyne before the latter was granted an audience.[36] Burgoyne did not see the King until late in December.[37] In the meantime, he had given his ideas to Germain and had submitted the written memorandum desired by Carleton.[38] This document did not call for reinforcements on the scale of Howe's demand of 30 November,[39] nor were the objectives sought so precisely defined. Reinforcements to the number of 4,000 regulars, together with the completion of the establishment of the army in Canada, were declared necessary. After an active campaign the raising of the army to its establishment would in all probability require a substantial replacement. The army from Canada, after passing Lake

Ontario, would be employed in operations on the Mohawk River. Another corps would penetrate southward to the Connecticut River. Albany and the Hudson were not mentioned in the memorandum. Provisions for 20,000 men for six months, together with a corps of boatmen, were requisitioned. Certainly, Carleton had felt the lack of water transport in the previous campaign.

The memorandum is very puzzling. There is no hint in it of either an actual junction or of cooperation with the southern army. Indeed, the objectives set for the army, which Carleton still thought would operate under his command, were very limited and very ambiguously stated. What is to be understood by "operations on the Mohawk River" and penetration "to the Connecticut River"? Does this mean the taking of Albany and large-scale operations in New England? Certainly, the latter was not seriously proposed, as the memorandum spoke of it as a possible operation only. The limited character of the objectives set, together with the vagueness with respect to operations, was not calculated to impress the government in London with the vigor and aggressiveness of Carleton's conceptions. When this is considered against the background of the abandonment of Crown Point in November, it is not surprising that the King should observe that "perhaps Carleton may be too cold and not so active as might be wished." [40]

The King was not disposed, however, to go so far as to recall Carleton. He felt that this would be cruel and that the situation did not require such drastic action. Some of the criticism of Carleton he was inclined to attribute to personal animus: "... that there is great prejudice, perhaps not unaccompanied with rancour in a certain breast against Governor Carleton is so manifest to whoever has heard the subject mentioned, that it would be idle to say more than that it is a fact...." [41] It has been commonly assumed, and there seems no reason to question the assumption, that "the certain breast" was a direct reference to Germain. [42] The rancor has been variously explained: it arose from differences over politics—Germain was a Tory, Carleton a Whig; [43] Carleton had testified against Germain at his court-martial in 1760. [44] The confusion in British politics at this time makes the former explanation seem strained; [45] Carleton was in Canada at the time that the battle of Minden was fought. [46] He could scarcely testify to the events of that day when he was more than three thousand miles distant from the scene. The real explanation of Germain's growing irritation with Carleton by December 1776 arose from differences between the two subsequent to Germain's taking office in 1775. These frictions resulted from the appointment of Christie as quartermaster general and certain civil appointments in the province of Quebec. The source of these difficulties was not so much in any defect in Germain's temper as in a defect in Carleton's. The trouble lay in Quebec, not London.[47]

Wherever the fault lay, the King had come to the conclusion that some other officer must command the Canadian Army in 1777. He had seen Carleton's memorandum as drawn up by Burgoyne and was disposed to agree that a force of 4,000 must be sent to Canada.[48] He saw the operations of 1777 from Canada as comprising two forces, one proceeding by the lakes and Ticonderoga and the other by the Mohawk. The object was the taking hold of Albany. This significant command might be given to Burgoyne; Phillips was to remain in Canada with Carleton. It should be emphasized that Burgoyne was spoken of as a possible commander for the Canadian Army in 1777; he was not definitely chosen.

In any case, Burgoyne could scarcely have been ignorant of the fact that he was being considered for the northern command. He was active in giving advice to the government. To supplement, explain, and add force to the memorandum he had already prepared of Carleton's ideas, he submitted a further memorandum. The latter document took as a text the earlier and presented a gloss upon it.[49] Little new was added, but the whole impression created was one of brisk decision and minute knowledge. Detailed information as to the numbers of troops in Canada and the number needed make this requisition much more forceful than the original. Going beyond Carleton's memorandum he added a demand for gunboats which had been so badly needed in 1776.

Toward the end of December, Burgoyne had an audience with the King, and at this time he "laid himself at His Majesty's feet for such active service as he might think him worthy of; . . ." [50] On 1 January 1777, just before leaving for Bath on his physician's orders, he wrote a letter to Germain. Conscious as he was at this time of Germain's favor, he sought his support for an appointment to active service. He declared that he was available on a day's notice and that he left in Germain's office copies of Carleton's memorandum and his own demand for gunboats. He told Germain of his audience with the King and of his request for active North American service, and, in a fulsome manner, he presented Germain with his request for that service.[51] He later described the conclusion of this letter as containing acknowledgments and professions "as were natural to flow from a warm and unsuspicious heart impressed with the sense of another's favour." [52]

A problem still remains as to whether Burgoyne sought to use his presence in England during the winter of 1776–77, together with the unpopularity of Carleton with the ministry, to attempt to supplant that commander in the next campaign. On the one hand there is clear evidence of Burgoyne's unfavorable opinion of the manner in which Carleton had conducted operations in 1776 given in confidence to his friend Clinton as well as in a more or less public manner to Germain. There is the fact that he first wrote the memorandum of Carleton's ideas, brief and sketchy, and then filled it in with fuller observations of his own. He sought from the King and Germain an active command in America. On the other hand, he believed that Carleton was to be superseded in any event as evidenced by Germain's dispatch to Carleton of 22 August. He believed that the decision to supplant Carleton had been made, not only upon the political reasoning which appeared in that dispatch, but also upon great law opinions, that Carleton could not, with the commission he then held under the great seal, pass the frontiers of his province.[53] These were fair considerations for any man to take into account, and, coupled with Burgoyne's ambition and dislike for a "secondary station in a secondary army," they put his conduct in a reasonable light. As the man on the ground when an important post was to be filled, he took Clinton's place in 1776 and Carleton's in 1777.

Burgoyne spent the month of December in London in consultation with the government on the plans for 1777. At the beginning of the new year he went down to Bath to take the waters.

III

Howe had, in the meantime, shifted his attention to Philadelphia as a major objective for the next campaign. He had received what he regarded as dependable information to the effect that the capital of the rebellion might be taken by a modest British force.[54] He had determined to make the attempt. This radical change in his plans was outlined to Germain in a letter of 20 December. He proposed that 2,000 troops should remain at Rhode Island, 4,000 at New York and adjacent posts, 3,000 for service on the Hudson, and 10,000 for the expedition against Philadelphia. This could be undertaken with the force Howe then had in America (20,000). It meant that all other operations would be contingent upon reinforcements from Europe and, in particular, that the offensive plan against Boston would be deferred, and the major operation up the Hudson to Albany, originally reckoned to require 10,000 troops, would be reduced to 3,000, "to act defensively upon the lower part of Hudson's river to cover Jersey on that side, as well as to facilitate in some degree the approach of the army from Canada." [55] At a single stroke, the whole concept of the character of the campaign had changed. On 30 November [56] Howe had suggested a force of 8,000 to act defensively in Jersey and give a "jealousy" to Philadelphia. He now proposed that the principal army under his command should act offensively against that city. If the government in London wished other operations carried out, it must supply the necessary reinforcements. In particular, any substantial effort to open the way to Albany must depend upon further reinforcements, unless Howe completed his campaign in Pennsylvania in time to turn northward. This was a distinct possibility, because Howe did not expect the army from Canada to reach Albany before September,[57] and "the subsequent operations of that corps will depend upon the state of things at that time." [58] That the move against Philadelphia was not regarded as incompatible with support of, and cooperation with, the northern army can be demonstrated from both contemporary and more recent opinion. Germain later wrote:

It was certainly expected that Sir William Howe would not have been detained so long in the Jersey's and the King's expectations of his having finished his operations towards Philadelphia in time enough to cooperate with the Northern Army is sufficiently explained in the letter of the 18th of May laid before the House.[59]

Charles Francis Adams, writing in 1911, remarked:

If he [Howe] had pressed Washington, it was said, and inflicted a crushing defeat, he might have left part of his force to occupy Philadelphia, and marched the rest of the assistance to Burgoyne. This is what the ministry expected.[60]

Further two points should be stressed: Howe makes no mention of going to Philadelphia by sea, and the clear design is that a British force will be between Washington and the Hudson; the campaign, being planned in December, would presumably begin early. These two elements of a land campaign across the Jersies into Pennsylvania, and a campaign which should begin early were part and parcel of Germain's concept that Howe could cooperate with the northern army in September or October.

Howe's original demand for a reinforcement of 15,000 (30 November) arriving in London in late December had struck Germain with dismay. He took two weeks to think the matter over and his answer shows ingenuity rather than a frank appraisal of the situation. He told Howe that:

When I first read your requisition of a reinforcement of 15,000 rank and file, I must own to you that I was really alarmed, because I could not see the least chance of my being able to supply you with the Hanoverians, or even the Russians in time." [61]

But he was reassured when he checked over Howe's army returns. These he interpreted in a way which would indicate that a reinforcement of 7,800 would bring Howe's total strength to very nearly 35,000. This reinforcement, he felt, could be procured. In addition he blandly pointed out to Howe that he could rely "for particular parts of the service" upon provincials for whom clothing and equipment would be provided from England. Howe, in his opinion, because of the recent British successes, would be faced by a greatly weakened and dispirited enemy. A further factor in the situation which ought to give encouragement to Howe lay in the fact that whatever support the rebels had counted upon Franklin procuring them would not materialize. In view of this situation, Germain concluded that a reinforcement of 7,800 would prove to be sufficient. Howe, during the parliamentary inquiry (1779), remarked sourly:

This misconceived calculation can no otherwise be accounted for, as I apprehend, than by his lordship's computing the sick and the prisoners with the rebels as a part of the real effective strength of the army.[62]

Germain did not dispute the details of the charge at that time; he merely asserted that the force sent out had been adequate "not to the reduction of America united against us, for such a reduction would be impossible, but to the reduction of the rebellion." [63] Germain was also under the necessity of disappointing Howe in his requisition for artillery, and, in addition, he cut down from 300 to 100 Howe's estimate of the number of horses he needed. Taking all things into consideration, this represented a British withdrawal. In 1776 Germain had substantially met the demands of the field officers. In 1777 he did not. Disappointment over performance in America, severe opposition at home, and the staggering, and, as it seemed, continuous demands of the American war, combined to bring about this decision. It was the beginning of Howe's disgruntlement and talk of a starved offensive which culminated in his resignation.

Germain did not comment in January upon Howe's plan of operations contained in his dispatch of 30 November beyond remarking that it was well digested and had been laid before the King. He promised Howe a full consideration of these matters when the King had given them the careful study they deserved. In the meantime, Howe's letter containing his radical change of plans (20 December) was received on 23 February and a further letter from Howe of 20 January was received on 3 March.[64] In the latter, Howe emphasized that his chief effort would be against Philadelphia and that other efforts would be strictly in proportion to the reinforcements he received. No mention at all was made of cooperation with the northern army. Howe asked, without much conviction, for a reinforcement of 15,000 to 20,000 troops. If this large reinforcement were available: "Philadelphia being now the principal object, by the greater number we should be enabled to detach a corps to enter the Delaware by sea, and the main body to penetrate Pennsylvania by way of Jersey; there would also in that case be a sufficient corps to act from Rhode Island." It is to be observed carefully that the first mention of a sea invasion of Pennsylvania is brought forward here, but only if 15,000 to 20,000 new troops are available, and even then the main thrust would be by land through the Jersies. A British army would stand between Washington and the Hudson. Both of Howe's letters stating in very plain terms that the main effort of his army would be against Pennsylvania were received in England long before Burgoyne left for Canada. Clearly, that general must have known Howe's intentions.

Howe's first plan of operations, entailing a reinforcement of 15,000, was never the subject of consideration in an official dispatch. His second suggestion, so drastically modifying the earlier one, arrived in England before Germain was ready to comment on the first plan. In a way, the later suggestion must have been a relief in London; operations could be begun along the lines laid down there with the forces presently available in America. The hearty manner in which Germain endorsed Howe's changes (3 March) gave some evidence of this. Germain declared:

I am now commanded to acquaint you that the King entirely approves of your proposed deviation from the plan which you formerly suggested, being of opinion that the reasons which have induced you to recommend this change in your operations are solid and decisive.[65]

But he declared that the King was of the opinion that a diversion ought to be made against Massachusetts Bay and New Hampshire. Howe was further informed that in place of a reinforcement of 7,800, he might now expect only 2,900. This was not a fifth part of the number he had originally required.

Howe had already given some thought to his second in command for the next campaign. He felt that since Clinton was senior to Burgoyne and had been considered for the Canadian command in 1776 he would, in all probability, be given that post in 1777. If that were to be the case, he wished Burgoyne to serve under him in the operations from the Atlantic side.[66] This met with Germain's approval and he sent Howe's request to the King immediately upon its receipt.[67] The King entirely approved of this idea and it appeared by the end of February that the command of the Canadian army had been settled.[68]

This, however, was to reckon without Burgoyne who had not been idle as he took the waters at Bath. He had turned over in his mind the various essentials for operations in the coming year and had thrown his ideas together in a document he entitled "Thoughts for Conducting the War from the Side of Canada." [69] This document was dated 28 February. Early in March it had been decided that Burgoyne would be given the Canadian command.[70] The deciding factor seems clearly to have been the favorable impression created by Burgoyne's memorandum.

This critical memorandum contained three alternative plans of

campaign for the coming year with remarks upon each: *First:* That
the northern army was to effect a junction with General Howe "or
after cooperating so far as to get possession of Albany and open communications to New York, to remain upon the Hudson's River and
thereby enable that general to act with his whole force to the southward." *Second:* That the northern army should move to the Connecticut River and there join the Rhode Island army. If such a junction were effected, "it is not too sanguine an expectation that all the
New England provinces will be reduced by these operations." To
facilitate either of the foregoing plans, Burgoyne suggested an expedition at the beginning of the campaign by Lake Ontario and Oswego to the Mohawk River. This was a very essential service if the
forces available would permit it. *Third:* That the northern army
should be transported by sea to join forces with General Howe or
"to be employed separately to cooperate with the main designs." The
last, Burgoyne declared, should not be considered except upon a clear
demonstration of its necessity. It would require a larger number of
troops to be left in Canada than would be the case if a British army
was beyond the lakes, and, in any case, he felt that no operation
would be as formidable to the enemy and effectual to end the war
as an invasion from Canada by Ticonderoga.

The force necessary for a campaign by land would be 8,000 regulars, artillery as required in Carleton's memorandum,[71] a corps of
watermen, 2,000 Canadians, and approximately 1,000 Indians. This
force ought to arrive in Canada by 20 May and Ticonderoga should
be in British hands by early summer. "The next measures must depend upon those taken by the enemy and upon the general plan of
campaign concerted at home."

This was an invitation to the government to select one from among
the three plans Burgoyne had suggested. There is ample evidence to
show that Burgoyne's memorandum was given careful scrutiny before the government made its decision. There are three documents
extant which are largely made up of observations, suggestions, and
reasonings upon Burgoyne's "Thoughts." Two of these are in an unknown hand: "Remarks on the Conduct of the War—from Canada,"
and "Remarks on the Requisitions and Observations." [72] The third
document entitled "Remarks on 'the Conduct of the War from Can-

ada'" is in the King's hand. It is clear that George III's "Remarks" are based upon the other two documents.[73]

Some mystery has developed over the authorship of the two memoranda in the unknown hand.[74] The only method of establishing a probable authorship is through internal evidence. These ideas occur in the two documents: that the numbers of troops which are to be left in Canada should be particularly ordered; that it was a mistaken idea of humanity not to employ Indians, for, if the British did not employ them, the rebels would; that instructions should be sent to the respective commanders "to put them out of doubt" on this point; [75] that strong instructions should be sent to Carleton to assist the general who commanded the army with as many Canadians as possible; that General Howe "seems to think" that he cannot act in Massachusetts from Rhode Island. These ideas form familiar categories in Germain's thinking. The occurrence of these ideas in the documents under question constitutes fairly high presumptive evidence that Germain was their author or inspirer. The evidence, however, is not determinative.

The net result of the critical analysis of Burgoyne's "Thoughts" came to this: the plan to transport the army by sea was vetoed; the plan for a junction with the Rhode Island army on the Connecticut River met a similar fate; and, in the affirmative, an advance to Albany and a diversion down the Mohawk were approved. This was the plan of campaign for 1777. No one person was the author of the plan. The essentials came from many sources and the plan in its simple outline was very old. The "responsibility" for the plan was a collective responsibility resting squarely upon the King and his ministers. Since the King "can do no wrong" is good constitutional doctrine, the ministers stand forward to bear the traditional burden of collective ministerial responsibility.

The Burgoyne plan has been the object of elaborate analysis and exegesis and interpretations of it have varied rather widely. Van Tyne made these observations on the plan:

The plan which Burgoyne was sent to execute is not so simple as has always been supposed. Since to march an army down from Canada, and get control of the Champlain–Hudson line would separate New England from the other colonies, and leave it to be conquered unaided by them, military experts have assumed that this was the aim of the British Government and its generals. In all the available correspondence as to the aims of the campaign, not a sentence makes any such proposal. All the logic of the situation and military custom point to that as the object, but for this idea there is no contemporary document. . . . Burgoyne's plan . . . had just one aim—to bring aid to Howe so that his army could go against the entire army of Washington. Of course while doing that the invading army would have to engage part of Washington's army to the northward, and that would prevent its going against Howe.[76]

This statement needs some modification in view of at least two contemporary documents. One of these is a memorandum submitted to Germain in 1776 which stated in part:

By our having the entire command of the communications between Canada and New York, which is both convenient and easy, being almost altogether by water, the troops from both these provinces will have it in their power to act in conjunction, as occasion or necessity may require. In consequence whereof, the provinces of New England will be surrounded on all sides, whether by His Majesty's troops or navy, and liable to be attacked from every quarter, which will oblige them to divide their force for the protection of their frontier settlements, while at the same time all intercourse between them and the colonies to the southward of Hudson's River will be entirely cut off.[77]

Germain came very close to this idea in a memorandum which he prepared himself after the failure of the campaign of 1777, and at a time when he was under attack for not directing Howe specifically to make the junction and accomplish the scission of the colonies. It would appear at this time that he had every personal motive to deny that scission was an object of the operations in 1777. Yet he wrote:

The possessing the Hudson's River was of the utmost consequence as it divided the southern from the northern provinces and no measure could so effectually answer that purpose as the forces from Albany and New York cooperating to that point. No man either civil or military doubted of the expediency or the practicality of the measure and those who remembered the late war best knew the alarm which was spread in New England, upon the movement of a French army toward Albany.[78]

These documents, and particularly the latter, seem clearly to indicate that the ultimate division of the northern from the southern colonies was a prime object of the campaign of 1777. The confusion in interpretation in recent studies has arisen from the attempt to disprove the violent contemporary criticism of the British plan in

1777. That criticism was based on two assumptions: that scission was not only the prime object in 1777 but the immediate and all-embracing one, that Burgoyne's army would plunge in a desperate thrust toward Albany, and that Howe would advance under strict orders up the Hudson River to succor and support an extended salient. Both of these assumptions are demonstrably false, and recent scholarship has performed a real service in displaying the evidence of their falsity. The junction of Howe and Burgoyne at Albany, though not the first and breathless move outlined in the plans for 1777, was nevertheless an essential object of that campaign. The plan did not preclude Howe going to Philadelphia, as Burgoyne was expected independently and securely to make his way to Albany and establish himself there. The plan did not look forward, however, to the establishment before the end of operations in 1777 of a cordon of power from the St. Lawrence to the Atlantic. This would effectually separate New England from the southern colonies.

At the beginning of March 1777 the decision had been made to give Burgoyne the command of the Canadian army over the head of Clinton. Clinton had been considered prominently for that post up until the very end of February.[79] He arrived in England in March, having been given permission by Howe to return home after the taking of Rhode Island.[80] When Germain received the news that Clinton was coming to England, he was not enthusiastic. He remarked to Knox: "I am surprised at Clinton's coming home. Burgoyne will not be sorry to see that he is not the only general, second in command, who takes liberty without the King's leave." [81] When Clinton arrived in England, he must have been even more unwelcome to Germain. In 1776 he had been sent off on the fruitless and inglorious campaign against Charleston and was thus disappointed in the northern command which, according to Germain, would have been offered to him if he had not already been assigned to the Charleston command.[82] Again in 1777 he had failed to secure the same northern command. In both cases Burgoyne had taken his place. In addition, he was most unhappy in his position as second in command to Sir William Howe. He was determined not to serve another campaign under the conditions of 1776.[83]

It is related that Clinton had still another grievance.[84] He is said to have returned to England in 1777 to seek satisfaction from Germain because the latter had published a mutilated copy of a letter Clinton had written describing the unfortunate attack he had made upon Sullivan's Island in 1776. The story continues that Clinton returned to England in a ferocious mood and that Germain sent a messenger to Portsmouth to meet the abused general with a mollifying letter. But Clinton could not be put by thus easily for he knew his man. He had observed him on the day of Minden. Germain had to devise other expedients to avoid the dreaded duel. He offered Clinton the Order of the Bath and an address of thanks from both Houses of Parliament. "Though Clinton was not to be bullied or coaxed, his ambition was flattered." So he was made a Knight of the Bath, received the thanks of Parliament, and made friends with Germain. He then returned contentedly to America.

This is a superb story and it appears to be little more. The available documents reveal only that Clinton returned to England, that he asked permission to resign, that he was offered Carleton's position as commander in chief in Canada,[85] that he had a number of warily friendly interviews with Germain in which he advised against an attack upon Philadelphia,[86] that he was given the Red Ribbon,[87] and that he returned to New York, arriving there on 5 July. The story would not be worth recounting if it did not illustrate so graphically the tendency to embellish, and to point up with picturesque detail, stories relating to Germain. It has also the common denominator of the reference to Minden. Germain had become, even contemporaneously, a stereotype. He made his mark in the crude cartoons of the day, as always in flight, and in poetry he figured as "All pale and trembling on the Gallic shore," etc.[88] Subsequent writers have tended to accept this legend and the "genre" story above is a typical source.[89]

By late March plans for the next year had been as well digested as it seemed likely they would ever be and commanders had been allocated to their appointed tasks. It was the time to give solid form to these decisions in an official directive. Germain set himself to this task in a dispatch to Carleton of 26 March.[90] This dispatch included in part the directions given in Germain's letter of the previous August which had failed to reach Quebec in the fall of 1776. Carleton had been directed at that time to return to his civil duties in the province of Quebec and to order Burgoyne to push the offensive forward into the rebellious colonies and put himself under the command of

Sir William Howe.[91] The same orders were repeated in the March letter.

But between August and March events had occurred which made Carleton appear to be even more ineligible for the northern command. He had failed to attack Ticonderoga, he had given up the post at Crown Point and retreated to Canada, and as a result of these actions and the consequent reinforcement of Washington, Cornwallis had suffered the humiliating defeat at Trenton in December. This was the cause-and-effect relationship which Germain perceived, and, without attaching blame to Carleton, he pointed to the facts:

> Since I wrote that letter [22 August] I have had the mortification to learn that, upon your repassing Lake Champlain, a very considerable number of the insurgents, finding their presence no longer necessary near Ticonderoga, immediately marched from thence and joined the rebel forces in the provinces of New York and Jersey. That unexpected reinforcement was more particularly unfortunate for us, as it enabled the rebels to break in with some degree of success upon parts of the winter quarters that were taken up by the army under the command of Sir William Howe.

This passage in Germain's letter has been widely cited as an example of perverse and malignant criticism of an able officer. It was certainly not that, but Carleton reacted as though it had been. He was conscious of the effect of his dilatory tactics in June 1776 [92] and took it for granted that Germain, under cover of the Trenton affair, was probing that issue.[93] This excited his strong temper and drove him to angry and defensive retaliation. Ill feeling had been smoldering since the previous summer, but it was this paragraph in Germain's letter which provoked Carleton into writing a series of letters to Germain, which, for venom, involved rhetoric, and ill-concealed insult, must be nearly unique at the official level in the long history of the relations of responsible officers in the field with any of His Majesty's principal secretaries of state. Germain later remarked, rather mildly, of these letters that their "style and manner were improper to have passed between one gentleman and another." [94]

A hitherto unknown letter in the Knox Papers raises a most puzzling problem at this point.[95] It is an undated letter from Germain to Knox. The pertinent passage reads:

> I did not want the papers if Lord North had not done with them. You will return them and make copies of them for Lord Suffolk when you are

at leisure. In the copies you will leave out that paragraph in the letter to Sir G. Carleton relating to the affair at Trenton.

There are two possible interpretations of this passage. Either Germain wished the paragraph in his letter of 26 March relating to Trenton deleted in the copies which his cabinet colleague would see and allowed to stand in the copy sent to Carleton, or he wished it deleted in all the copies including that sent to Carleton. The former is a tortuous interpretation and involves a deception dangerously open to exposure, and the latter interpretation is the clear and simple one. It may be urged, however, that since the passage did remain in the letter which went out to Carleton, this was Germain's intent. In a situation of this kind the possibilities of clerical error are enormous, and it may well be that the fatal paragraph remained in Carleton's letter through a mistake attributable to Germain's office staff. Shelburne, in commenting upon another supposed error on the part of Germain's office, which he characterized as "a very idle one," remarked:

It requires as much experience in business to comprehend the very trifling causes which have produced the greatest events, as it does strength of reason to develop the deepest design.[96]

This may be the heart of the matter.

The remainder of the important March letter was devoted to the plans for 1777. Carleton was to keep in Canada a force of 3,770, Burgoyne was to be dispatched on his mission at the head of 7,173 troops, and a diversion was to be made down the Mohawk River to Albany under Lieutenant Colonel St. Leger with a force of 675. Both Burgoyne and St. Leger were to be supplied with a sufficient number of Canadians and Indians. Not only did Germain particularize by name and number the units to be kept by Carleton in Canada, but he itemized the posts these troops were to garrison.[97]

After Carleton had provided Burgoyne and St. Leger with everything necessary for their forces, he was to order Burgoyne

to proceed forthwith to and down the Mohawk River to Albany and put himself under the command of Sir William Howe.

Germain promised that he would write to Howe by the first packet, but, in the meantime, Carleton, Burgoyne, and St. Leger were to neglect no opportunity to correspond with that general. In order to give some latitude of action to Burgoyne and St. Leger, Carleton was commanded to

inform them that until they shall have received orders from Sir William Howe, it is His Majesty's pleasure that they act as exigencies may require and in such manner as they shall judge most proper for making an impression on the rebels, and bringing them to obedience, but that in so doing they must never lose view of their intended junction with Sir William Howe as their principal objects.

This passage was later to be interpreted in a variety of ways: by Burgoyne that it constituted a peremptory command to force his way to Albany at all costs; and by the government that it gave Burgoyne the right to exercise his own judgment when exigencies arose, setting only the goal of Albany if it were a practical objective.

The British plan of campaign was complete by 26 March. In its bold outline the design was clear. Carleton was to hold Canada. Burgoyne was to penetrate by Ticonderoga and Lake George to Albany. He was to establish himself there. St. Leger was to push down the Mohawk River and join Burgoyne at Albany. Both Burgoyne and St. Leger upon reaching Albany were to put themselves under the command of Howe. Howe, believing in 1777 that Pennsylvania was a stronghold of Loyalism, as in 1776 he had believed New York was, had determined upon an attempt to capture the capital of rebellion—Philadelphia. The home government had approved this move. So far everything was clear.

The great problem was the degree to which there should be cooperation and junction, real or virtual, between Howe's forces and those of Burgoyne. Germain expected that Howe, after completing the capture of Philadelphia, which was not envisaged as a serious or prolonged military task, would reach out his lines to join Burgoyne. This would be at the end of the campaign. Burgoyne expected to reach Albany "on the high road to glory," put himself under Howe's command, and contribute to the latter's success. Howe expected, in some undefined way, to cooperate with Burgoyne at the end of the campaign. There was a good deal of vagueness on all sides as to the precise meaning in terms of troop dispositions, establishments, and the like of the terms "cooperation" and "junction." There was a general disposition to allow events to give clarity to these terms.

Events did clarify the situation. Disastrous defeat for Burgoyne and a limited, late, and barren victory for Howe made mockery of hopes of cooperation or junction, real or virtual. Then the soldiers and civilians who had borne the major responsibilities in the planning and the execution of this campaign began to examine the genesis of the design and its lamentable failure, each with the view of exonerating himself and, as an almost inevitable corollary, blaming someone else. It was in this atmosphere that the "problems" of the critical year of the Revolution had their birth.

CHAPTER 7

THE CRITICAL YEAR
OF THE REVOLUTION, 1777

I

Minden and Saratoga taken together have traditionally been accepted as *prima facie* evidence of Germain's cowardice and abysmal incompetence. At Minden he proved himself unworthy to lead troops in the field; Saratoga demonstrated that his leadership was equally fatal to success even though he was three thousand miles distant from the field of combat. The two actions were separated in time by eighteen years, but in any account, however fragmentary, of Germain's career, they are commonly coupled as uniform evidence of his disastrous influence upon the destiny of the First British Empire. That empire survived and enlarged itself in despite of Minden; Saratoga was its death knell. In consequence, Saratoga has remained the larger item in the bill of particulars against Germain. In his career and in the history of the American Revolution, the year 1777 was the critical year.

Burgoyne left London on 27 March and arrived at Quebec on 6 May.[1] By the middle of June he had collected his forces at the head of Lake Champlain and a few days later the colorful army had embarked and Burgoyne had set forth on his "high road to glory." [2] Clinton arrived at New York on 5 July and Howe embarked for Philadelphia on 23 July.[3] The campaign of 1777 had been launched and from this point on its destiny was in the hands of Burgoyne and Howe. However, between April and July Germain was still in a position to alter the course of events from London. The great problem raised in respect to this period is the degree to which Burgoyne, Howe, and Germain understood the common objectives of the operations to be undertaken. Much confusion was later created by charges and countercharges, by second and even by third thoughts. The contemporary record is available and is capable of a plain reading.

On 2 April Howe wrote to Germain [4] and on 5 April he wrote to Carleton.[5] He enclosed a copy of his letter to Carleton in his letter to Germain. That letter was received by Germain on 18 May, and it showed very clearly Howe's conception of the plan for 1777. It was based upon the troops he had available in America. The main object was to be an invasion of Pennsylvania by sea with a force of 11,000. New York was to be held by 4,700 regular troops and the provincials under Governor Tryon (3,000) were to be employed on the Hudson River or in Connecticut "as circumstances may point out." He was obliged because of lack of reinforcements to cut down the force to be employed at Rhode Island to 2,400. He proposed to abandon the Jersies. He made a single reference to the northern army.

Still I think it probable that by the latter end of the campaign we shall be in possession of the provinces of New York, the Jersies and Pennsylvania, though this in some measure must depend upon the success of the northern army.

There is no single word of cooperation of any kind. He declared that his hopes of completing the campaign that year had totally vanished, and he complained throughout his letter of his lack of reinforcement. In his view, the forces in 1776 had been adequate to the operation, but in 1777 this situation did not exist. The government at home, measuring the success of operations in 1776 when the army had been judged adequate to its task, must have formed the most dismal picture of what might be expected in 1777 when the forces were judged not adequate.[6]

All of this was depressing enough, but not to be considered singular in view of its source. Germain must, however, have been brought up with a start by two separated paragraphs of this dispatch. In the first, with seeming complacency, Howe changed again the whole nature of the campaign: "From the difficulties and delays that would attend the passage of the Delaware by a march through Jersey, I propose to invade Pennsylvania by sea and from this arrangement we must probably abandon the Jerseys which by the former plan would not have been the case. On the contrary the enemy's western and principal army would have been between the two corps destined for this service and we should then have had the communication open for the Seneca Indians to have joined us." What was more important than keeping open a communication with the Seneca Indians was withdrawing the British force between Washington and the Hudson and sending it off on a long sea voyage at the height of the campaign when not only would it cease to be a strategic consideration for a long period, but it could not even be communicated with. In the other paragraph Howe, remarking upon delays which would occur in the evacuation of the Jersies, declared, with great truth, that: "... it is probable the campaign will not commence so soon as your Lordship may expect." Howe sailed from New York for Philadelphia on 23 July. Thus, two disturbing new elements entered the picture: a "sea invasion" and a "late invasion."

Howe's letter to Carleton (5 April), which Burgoyne saw before setting out upon his expedition, contained a statement in the most categorical form of the degree to which Howe expected to cooperate with Burgoyne. The relevant paragraph deserves full quotation:

Having little expectation that I shall be able, from the want of sufficient strength in this army, to detach a corps in the beginning of the campaign to act upon the Hudson's River consistent with the operations already determined upon, the force your Excellency may deem expedient to advance beyond your frontiers after taking Ticonderoga will, I fear, have little assistance from hence to facilitate their approach, and as I shall probably be in Pennsylvania when that corps is ready to advance into this province, it will not be in my power to communicate with the officer commanding it so soon as I could wish; he must therefore pursue such measures as may from circumstances be judged most conducive to the advancement of his Majesty's service consistently with your Excellency's orders for his conduct.[7]

Howe undertook, however, to leave sufficient forces at New York to open shipping on the lower Hudson River by clearing out the enemy's posts in the Highlands. The corps which was to accomplish this task might subsequently "act in favor of the northern army." But Howe did not even mention in this letter that he was proceeding by sea to Pennsylvania.

This letter was taken to Canada by Sir John Johnson [8] and was carried by Carleton to Montreal before Burgoyne's departure.[9] Carleton gave the letter to Burgoyne.[10] A copy of this letter was received by Germain on 18 May together with the one from Howe of 2 April which he answered on the day of its receipt.[11] It would appear that Howe's letters of early April, received by both Germain and Burgoyne before actual operations were undertaken, ought to have made his position perfectly clear. However, Germain in his dispatch to Carleton of 26 March had said that he would write to Howe by the first packet. In the meantime, the responsible officers in Canada were to neglect no opportunity to communicate with that general.[12] This has led to the supposition that Germain intended to write a specific letter of instruction to Howe ordering him to consider as his major responsibility operations up the Hudson to cooperate with Burgoyne. It has been asserted that:

> A subsequent dispatch containing full and explicit instructions to Sir William Howe as to his cooperation with Burgoyne was written, but by one of those shameful acts of official neglect, of which our history unfortunately affords but too many examples, this document was suffered to be pigeon-holed in London, where it was found after the convention of Saratoga, carefully docketed, and only wanting the signature of the minister [i.e., Germain].[13]

Burgoyne later said that he had seen Howe's letter to Carleton of 5 April but that it had not weighed with him because it had been written before Howe could have received his specific instructions from Germain.[14] This introduces the problem of the pigeon-holed dispatch which has given rise to what seems now a truly formidable misinterpretation of history.

Lord Shelburne supplied an explanation of the supposed lack of specific instructions for Howe which satisfied many who believed that such instructions must have been framed.[15] He declared that when Germain, on his way to the country, called at his office to sign the dispatches to Burgoyne and Howe, he found that the dispatch to Howe had not been fair copied. Since Germain could not bear to have his timetable upset, he was in a temper because his office had not properly expedited the paper work. The clerks, to mollify him, suggested that the dispatch, after it had been completed, would be sent to him in the country. It was thought this could be accomplished before the packet sailed with Burgoyne's instructions. However, the dispatch containing these went to America and "the wind detained the vessel which was ordered to carry the rest. Hence came General Burgoyne's defeat, the French declaration, and the loss of thirteen colonies." Shelburne declared he had this story from Germain's secretary—seemingly a direct reference to Knox.

Trevelyan pointed out the essential improbabilities of this story and warned against its acceptance.[16] When the Historical Manuscripts Commission published its *Report* on the Knox Papers (1909) a memorandum of Knox's came to light which seemed to clarify the situation. Knox gave this account:

When all was prepared, and I had them to compare and make up, Lord Sackville came down to the office to sign the letters on his way to Stoneland, when I observed to him that there was no letter to Howe to acquaint him with the plan or what was expected of him in consequence of it. His Lordship started, and D'Oyley stared, but said he would in a moment write a few lines. 'So,' says Lord Sackville, 'my poor horses must stand in the street all the time, and I shan't be to my time anywhere.' D'Oyley then said he had better go, and he would write from himself to Howe and enclose copies of Burgoyne's Instructions, which would tell him all that he would want to know; and with this his Lordship was satisfied, as it enabled him to keep his time, for he could never bear delay or disappointment; and D'Oyley sat down and writ a letter to Howe but he neither shew'd it to me or gave a copy of it for the office, and if Howe had not acknowledged the receipt of it, with the copy of the Instructions to Burgoyne, we could not have proved that he ever saw them. I applied upon this occasion to D'Oyley for a copy of his letter, but he said he kept none. I then desired he would get one from Howe, who had the original, but he would not ask for it, and Lord Sackville did not call upon Howe for it. Thurlow would, however, have called for it if the inquiry had gone on, as I had told him all the circumstances.[17]

Christian D'Oyley was undersecretary in the American Department from May 1776 to February 1778. He had had considerable experience in the drafting of military correspondence, having filled the post of deputy secretary of war.[18] He was a particular friend of Sir William Howe, and a pamphleteer of the time described the letters he drafted to Howe for Germain's signature as "D'Oyley's love letters." [19] It is, therefore, not surprising that Germain should have entrusted to him the drawing up of a letter to Howe. The problem centers around the contents of such a letter. Was it understood that D'Oyley's letter would contain specific instructions for Howe to take his forces up the Hudson for a junction with Burgoyne at Albany? Did Germain expect D'Oyley to enshrine the classic concept of the convergence upon Albany of two strong military forces as the sole object of the campaign of 1777? Certainly, nothing that Germain said or wrote subsequently indicated such an expectation and much which he later said and wrote indicated that he had no such expectation.

It is definitely established that D'Oyley did write Howe and that he enclosed a copy of Germain's letter to Carleton of 26 March. This letter contained the entire plan of campaign of 1777 for the northern army. Howe received D'Oyley's letter and its enclosure. The endorsement on Germain's letter to Carleton of 26 March is to this effect:

Copy of this letter was sent to Sir William Howe in a letter from Mr. D'Oyley, (which has not been entered) by the 'Somerset' man-of-war which arrived at New York the 24th May. Sir William Howe acknowledged receipt of it in his letter of the 5th July, No. 9.[20]

On 3 June Howe mentioned in a dispatch the arrival of the "Somerset," [21] and on 5 June he wrote: "Observing by your Lordship's dispatch to Sir Guy Carleton, received this day by the Somerset under cover from Mr. D'Oyley that Lt. Col. Fraser of the 26th regiment is serving in that army . . . ," he went on to consider the problem presented by conflicting ranks. Fraser was one of the few officers mentioned in Germain's letter to Carleton of 26 March, thus establishing that it was the letter of this date that Howe received on 5 June. In this letter, too, Howe remarked: "I trust your Lordship may expect a successful campaign to the southward; yet I fear little can be done to the northward more than to give security to this province . . ." [22] On 5 July, Howe again acknowledged receipt of copies of the letter to Carleton "transmitted by Mr. D'Oyley." [23]

It is indisputably clear that D'Oyley wrote a letter to Howe and enclosed a copy of Burgoyne's instructions for 1777. The letter which D'Oyley wrote was probably only a formal note informing Howe of the fact that there was an enclosure which would be self-explanatory. That D'Oyley's letter contained nothing which would have affected Howe's intention of proceeding against Philadelphia is made abundantly clear in Howe's acknowledgment written on the day of receipt. He told Germain he hoped that the expedition to the southward might secure a solid success but that to the northward he could do little beyond guaranteeing the security of New York. He could not have written in this manner if he had just received orders to abandon the expedition to the south and proceed up the Hudson River.

As we have already observed Clinton was in London during April. He had several interviews with Germain and explained to him his objections to Howe's Pennsylvania strategy. Germain argued that Howe would finish the Pennsylvania business in time and would be in a position to support Burgoyne in the autumn. Clinton disagreed entirely.[24] The whole argument between the two men was based upon the assumption that the invasion of Pennsylvania would be a land invasion and that it would be launched in good time. On 29 April Clinton left London to take ship for New York. On 18 May, Howe's letter of 2 April arrived in Whitehall. This was the concept of the "sea invasion" and the "late invasion" of Pennsylvania. This put a different face upon the whole matter.

Professor Willcox in his recent article writes concerning the failure of Germain to send "a word to Howe about the northern army. He did send him a copy of his dispatch to Carleton of March 26, which said that Burgoyne had orders to force his way to Albany and put himself under Sir William's command; but during the crucial weeks Germain did not raise the subject with Sir William himself. Between March 3 and April 19 he wrote him no less than eight letters, and in none of them did he refer to it. At last, on May 18, when he had learned that Howe was going by sea, he urged him to do just what Clinton had said could not be done—finish the campaign in time to co-operate with Burgoyne. By then it was too late. Howe did not receive the dispatch until mid-August, when he was irretrievably committed to Pennsylvania. If he had, he might not have complained in July—as, it will be seen, he did—that he failed to understand the purpose of the invasion from Canada." [25]

This criticism of Germain is something very different from the pigeon-holed dispatch criticism. It goes to the heart of the matter, and I give it very serious consideration. I would, however, advance these counterconsiderations. As soon as Germain learned that a "sea invasion" and a "late invasion" of Pennsylvania were what Howe had in mind, he wrote on that same day (18 May) drawing Howe's attention to the need to cooperate with the northern army.[26] This was the new element in the situation, which elicited the response historians have looked for. There is an argument to be made, perhaps with difficulty, that had Howe carried through the original concept of proceeding toward Philadelphia early in the campaign by land, clearing the Jersies as he proceeded, he might have been able to co-operate effectively in late autumn with Burgoyne. When Clinton evacuated Philadelphia in the summer of 1778, proceeding across the Jersies, fighting the Battle of Monmouth against Washington, and suffering cruel heat, he accomplished his march from Philadelphia to New York in the space of seventeen days. Howe's dilatory campaign against Philadelphia from New York by sea took sixty-five days. Certainly, a campaign of this sort made illusory any idea of cooperation with the northern army. But Germain had not counted upon that.

There was still a further chance, as Willcox points out, to dissuade Howe from his overseas adventures.[27] Clinton arrived in New York in early July to find that Howe had spent June in maneuvers with Washington in New Jersey and was wasting further time in embarking his troops, and also to discover, with even greater alarm, that Howe was taking with him almost the whole of the British forces *by sea* for Philadelphia. If Clinton believed, as he urged upon Germain in London, that a land operation against Pennsylvania was incompatible with the northern campaign, how much more did he believe that Howe's present intention would wreck any possibility of Germain's ideas of cooperation. Clinton knew from recent talks what Germain's ideas were. Howe told Clinton that he would consider as a good campaign the fall of Philadelphia and the conquest of New Jersey. Clinton declared: "I told him government did not seem to hold that language, but [I] declared freely—too freely—I thought this must finish it. He stared." [28] But Howe's answer was that "I have sent my plan home, and it has been approved." [29] But it had not, for the approval he had was for an overland invasion; the approval for a sea invasion, tied to cooperation with the northern army, "was received by Sir William Howe on the 16th August on his passage up Chespeake Bay being numbered 11—" [30]

Germain gave Howe great latitude and freedom of action, trusting that his knowledge of the local situation and good judgment would secure a maximum British advantage. A good example of the cavalier way in which Howe dismissed the serious instructions of Germain and the King is provided in the case of the proposed attack on New England in 1777. Germain had recommended to Howe, on insistence of the King, that a diversion should be made on the coasts of Massachusetts and New Hampshire.[31] Howe reported in the coolest way that he and his brother, the admiral, had decided against such an operation because it was not practicable.[32] Germain probably gave Howe too much latitude and the general became careless, even negligent, in his correspondence with the minister. During the critical month of June 1777, Germain often complained of his ignorance of Howe's intentions and movements: "... perhaps Sir Wm. Howe may acquaint us in what manner and when he intends to begin his operations ...," [33] and again: "I cannot guess by Sir Wm. Howe's letters when he will begin his operations or where he proposes carrying them on." [34] Howe became even more taciturn as the campaign developed. During the parliamentary inquiry into the conduct of the Howes, Germain pointed out that he had not had a single line from the general between 22 August and 28 October 1777, a space of two months and six days. Germain declared that during this time he knew no more of the whereabouts of the general or his actions than the man in the street.[35]

But, despite the inadequacy of Howe as a correspondent, Germain was informed of Howe's plan to open the campaign with an attack upon Washington in Pennsylvania. He had approved that plan and saw no objection to it on the grounds that it conflicted with Burgoyne's operations. It is true that he expected Howe to have begun his operations earlier,[36] that he expected Howe to invade Pennsylvania by land, and that he expected, on Howe's assurances, an easy victory. With these expectations—perhaps great expectations—he harbored still another—that Howe would cooperate with Burgoyne at the end of the campaign.

No criticism can be made of Germain on the ground that he intended and then failed to send Howe explicit orders to rescue Burgoyne at Albany. There is the highest presumptive evidence that no such dispatch was either written or considered. The valid criticism which can be made of Germain is that he overestimated the vigor and aggressiveness of Howe and underestimated the character of the resistance which that general would meet in Pennsylvania. But a campaign to the south, begun late, launched by sea, and carried forward in a languid manner, meant no great decisive action against Washington's army, with the consequent drawing off of the revolutionary forces from the north and the resulting support for Burgoyne. Howe's tendency toward accepting limited success also meant his containment in Philadelphia and his complete inability to give support of any kind to Burgoyne in September and October. As a result of this, Burgoyne's enemies multiplied and Saratoga resulted. Germain had misconceived the relationship between the southern campaign and the northern, or at least he had misconceived the relationship between the kind of southern campaign which Howe carried out and a northern campaign of any kind.

II

As the relations between Howe and Germain, so cordial in 1776, began to deteriorate during the summer of 1777, the relations between Carleton and Germain came to open rupture. Germain had little doubt but that his letter of 26 March, relieving Carleton of his command, would provoke the bitter anger of that general. There is some evidence to indicate that Germain had decided to delete from that dispatch the provocative paragraph relating to Trenton.[37] The paragraph, however, remained, whether because of a clerical error or by design, it is impossible now to establish. Carleton received this dispatch together with two of 22 August 1776 on 6 May.[38]

On 1 July, Germain remarked to Knox: "I shall wait with impatience for Carleton's dispatches. I do not wonder he is displeased at receiving such particular directions from hence as he must see they proceed from the inactivity of the last campaign." [39] Germain did not have long to wait for Carleton's dispatches. They arrived in London shortly after Germain wrote Knox. On 2 July, Lord North reported to the King that he had received a dispatch from Carleton, asking for permission to resign his command

which, indeed, it could hardly be supposed that he ever meant to hold when he wrote Lord George Germain the letters which are brought by the same conveyance.[40]

The King felt that Carleton's action in asking to resign was necessary if he wished to preserve his dignity. He still believed that the ordering of Carleton back to Canada had been a proper measure even if it must have been mortifying to a soldier.[41]

Germain received three dispatches from Carleton early in July. They were dated on 20,[42] 22,[43] 23 [44] May 1777. The first contained a bitter, rambling, and insulting commentary upon Germain's dispatches of 22 August and 26 March, together with a defense of his own conduct drawn from his interpretation of the campaign of 1776, and the history of the Seven Year's War. The second, among a variety of other things, accused Germain of striking at the very basis of the King's government in Canada because of his dislike for Carleton. The third was a comprehensive, confusing, and angry criticism of Germain's interference in the internal affairs of the province of Quebec.

Germain had declared before he received Carleton's dispatches that he would be glad of the opportunity to applaud that general's conduct during the campaign.[45] The general gave him little opportunity. His letter of 20 May was quite unprecedented.[46] He began by saying that he had not been surprised in not receiving instructions from Germain in the fall of 1776. He had expected none since he believed the opinion was pretty general that the officer on the ground ought to be the best judge of the proper measures to be pursued rather than "a great general at three thousand miles distance." Since his demand for the workmen and the material necessary for building a naval force on Lake Champlain had been largely disregarded by Germain and since the workmen who were sent came late and were few in numbers,[47] he had been forced to accept one of two conclusions: either "your Lordship had taken your measures with such great wisdom that the rebels must immediately be compelled to lay down their arms and implore the King's mercy without our assistance" or "your Lordship might not wish I should have the power, least with an indiscreet advance, I should push on so as not to be able to return, as might become necessary for the defence of Canada." This note of heavy and sullen irony, bordering on insult, is most striking.

Carleton then went on to point out that had Germain's dispatch of 22 August reached him rather than being returned to England, he would in all probability have received it in November. He would then have been faced with the necessity of ordering Burgoyne forward into the enemy country in the face of an oncoming Canadian winter. This, in Carleton's opinion, would have been to hazard the whole force to the climate or to the enemy. In view of this he considered it "as a particular blessing your Lordship's dispatch did not arrive in due time." This was merely a play on words and dates. No eighteenth-century soldier or statesman considered carrying forward a winter campaign and least of all so conventional and orthodox a man as Germain. He always was anxious that the army in America should go into winter quarters early and was solicitous of the comfort of the soldiers.

Carleton then came to consider the part of Germain's letter of 26 March which rankled with him most: the notice which Germain had taken of the relationship between the affair at Trenton and Carleton's retreat to Canada. He declared that the strength of Howe's army was such that it ought easily to have been able to defend itself "though all the rebels from Ticonderoga had reinforced Mr. Washington." Carleton declared:

His [Howe's] winter quarters, I confess, I never thought of covering; it was supposed 'tis true, that was the army favoured by your Lordship, and in which you put your trust, yet I never could imagine, while an army to the southward found it necessary to finish their campaign and go into winter quarters, your Lordship could possibly expect troops so far north should continue their operations, lest Mr. Howe should be disturbed during the winter.

Yet, Carleton declared, it was upon this ground that the command of the northern army was taken from him and given to Burgoyne. A large part of the dispatch was devoted to an analogy between his conduct and Lord Amherst's conduct in 1759. The lesson drawn was that Amherst had done much the same thing that Carleton had done and had drawn no censure from the Home Government.

What conclusions may be drawn from this amazing document? The main point Carleton labored throughout the whole letter related to the utter folly of Germain in ordering a corps of the northern army to penetrate to Albany in the middle of a Canadian winter. Carleton himself could not have seriously thought that Germain had any such idea in mind. He must merely have affected to believe that Germain had proposed such a plan of action and then used this concept as a point upon which to exercise his dialectic. He protested too much. He felt keenly the censure implied in relieving him from his command. He may have been conscious that his conduct of the military operations in 1776 was open to censure. The best defense was in offense and the best offense was to attribute absurd ideas to Germain. He said that the main reason why the ministry had taken the command from him was because he had turned back to Canada in

November 1776. The ministry had decided upon this course in August. If there had been anything in his military conduct which had led the ministry to come to this decision, it must have related to conduct prior to August. Carleton, in his probable consciousness that there was a fault in his conduct in June in not pressing the attack against Sullivan and Arnold, confused cause and effect. He had an excellent case for the retreat to Canada in November; he had little defense, on the military side, for his dilatory tactics in June. The best course, then, was to affect to believe that he was being superseded in the command for conduct which he could defend successfully, even though he had to fly in the face of the clearest chronology. Carleton was not without skill in his attempt to confuse the issue. His long, disjointed, ill-written dispatch must be read very carefully in order to detect inconsistencies. First things do not come first nor second things second, but the whole, breathing impatience and self-righteousness, has the appearance of proceeding from a much-wronged man.

His letter to Germain of 22 May is even more difficult to assess.[48] He declared that it was rumored, as soon as Germain's appointment to the American secretaryship was known in Canada, that it was the intention of the new secretary to dismiss Carleton and that in the meantime his position would be made as difficult as possible. This would be accomplished

by every kind of slight, disregard, and censure, occasion and events might render plausible. The removal I thought probable, but expected it would come with candour to myself and safety to the Crown, and in this shape it might have taken place without public evil or private regret, but the latter system strikes not at me, for I am nothing, but immediately at the King's government.[49]

Germain, in Carleton's view, was capable of attempting to undermine the King's government in Canada at this critical juncture of the war in an effort to satisfy a personal grudge.[50]

These letters made a deep impression on Germain, and, down to the end of his time in office, he felt they stood as a bar against his acting in concert with Carleton in any public undertaking.[51] Germain gave serious consideration to the problem of composing a suitable reply. He drew up a draft in his own hand, which is much mutilated by revision and marginalia. The draft was shown to the King and approved by him before being sent out to Carleton.[52] He began his letter by taking notice of the very extraordinary way in which Carleton had thought it proper to express himself in his letters of 20 May and 22 May. Carleton could only have permitted himself the use of such unusual expressions because he believed that the orders for the operations in Canada proceeded from Germain alone and upon his mere authority. Germain then delivered Carleton a solemn, heavy, but perfectly good-tempered lecture upon the relations which existed, under the British Constitution, between the King and his responsible ministers:

Affairs of such importance receive the fullest consideration from His Majesty's most confidential servants, and they are then submitted with their humble opinion, to the King, who, after mature deliberation, gives such commands there upon as His Majesty judges most proper.

The execution of any matters touching America was his (Germain's) proper responsibility. If he had given an improper form to the royal orders, he stood ready to accept full and complete responsibility. Germain went further. He told Carleton that as far as the dispatch relating to Burgoyne's taking over Carleton's command and setting forth a distribution of troops in Canada (26 March) was concerned, the King had given "particular direction for every part of it." It had only remained for Germain to put the King's ideas in the form of a dispatch. He declared, however, that he had agreed with every part of the orders sent out.

It would appear at this point that Germain was thrusting the King somewhat too much to the fore. Later, Fox checked him on a similar point. Germain had spoken in the House of an order originating not from the cabinet but from the King. Fox arose immediately to declare that he

would never sit silent in that House and hear such unparliamentary language pass unnoticed. The King could do no act proper for the discussion of that House. The constitution knows no such individual power and he hoped never would. He would not, he said, suffer even an idea to go forth that the King transacted anything relative to government without advice; and those only were amenable to that House who dared to advise his Majesty improperly.

Germain accepted Fox's lecture, declaring that he supposed the King was advised but that he had had nothing to do with the advice proffered.[53] Germain was on sound enough ground in his first statement to Carleton of the King's position as acting on responsible advice but, in his later elaboration, he appeared to imply that the King was acting on his own mere motion. Even upon the consideration of remnants of prerogative authority in the sphere of military operations, this probably did not constitute a proper exposition of eighteenth-century constitutional practice.

Having attempted to set Carleton straight on constitutional matters, Germain explained certain aspects of the policy considerations which had led the Home Government to supersede Carleton in his command. Since it had been determined to appoint only Lord Howe and Sir William Howe to the commission to restore peace in 1776, it had seemed impossible to vest in Carleton the command of an army in which Sir William Howe was to serve. Carleton had been relieved of his command for reasons of public policy and not because of any personal animosity on the part of Germain.

On individual points of criticism in Carleton's letter, Germain took high ground. It would, he declared,

ill become my situation to enter into an ill humoured altercation with you upon various parts of your letter respecting the operations of the last campaign.

Every exertion had been made to send out to Carleton the forces necessary to conduct a successful campaign. It had been considered by the ablest officers who had served in America that a campaign to drive the rebels out of Canada and penetrate to Albany had been an entirely practicable project. Germain could not resist the temptation to indulge in a further reference to Carleton's retreat from before Ticonderoga:

... if the intelligence we have since received be true, the rebels intended to have abandoned their post at Ticonderoga, had you marched your army toward it.

As far as Carleton's bitter allegations with respect to Germain's supposed personal dislike were concerned, Germain dismissed them as hardly worthy of serious consideration. He had never received any "disobligation" from Carleton. If Carleton had been his worst enemy, his own principles would have forbidden him from acting in any way except one which should contribute, in the maximum degree, to

Carleton's success. Even upon the supposition that he could be expected to act from reasons of personal animosity, his own great stake in the success of the war in America put such a construction of his conduct out of the question. He concluded by noticing with utter amazement Carleton's charge that he had encouraged "faction and cabal" in the government in Canada. "I trust you did not so lightly give credit to intelligence when you were to decide upon measures relating to the public service."

This was a rather substantial reply to the many serious and dark charges which Carleton had laid at Germain's door. On the whole it has the ring of sincerity. Years later when the question arose as to whether he could approve of the appointment of Carleton as commander in chief in America, he insisted that before he could ever again act with Carleton, some explanation of that general's letters in 1777 must be made. At that time he asked the King to re-examine them in the light of the situation as it then existed and decide whether or not he had deserved the harsh opinions and expressions Carleton had used. If he did, he was not fit to hold office. If he did not merit that treatment, he ought to stand acquitted. Carleton's charges had never been modified and at that hour the allegations were still "perfectly unexplained." He did not ask for

any submission which it would be unbecoming for G.[uy] C.[arleton], as a gentleman to make, but as a debt due only to that justice which Ld. G.[eorge] thinks he has a right to expect—and he confesses himself injured.

If an explanation, honorable in its character, was made, Germain assured the King that he would act on all occasions "with that implicit confidence and cordiality with Sir G.[uy] which should always follow forgotten injuries. . . ." [54] This was years later, but a few days after Germain had written his reply to Carleton, he confided to the King:

The ill-humour of the General continues in its full force, and Lord George is not conscious of deserving any of the imputations laid to his charge, and therefore bears them with great indifference; . . .[55]

There is some evidence at this time of a general feeling in ministerial circles that Carleton had gone too far. On 4 August Germain wrote to Knox: "I am glad Lord North's letter to Sir Guy Carleton has so good a chance of being sent." [56] If Germain was prepared to welcome a letter from North to Carleton at this time, it must have been a letter which supported him. We have no evidence that such a letter was ever sent, but at least it was under consideration and indicates some solidarity between the prime minister and his American secretary.

Despite the bitter anger Carleton felt toward Germain at this time, and despite his chagrin at having been relieved of the command of the northern army, he vigorously supported Burgoyne's preparations. Burgoyne remarked that it was easy to see that Carleton sensibly felt his supersession but that "his zeal to give effect to his measures in my hands are equally manifest, exemplary and satisfactory." [57] After the defeat at Saratoga, when Carleton's support meant a good deal to Burgoyne, he expressed himself in a still warmer manner:

Had that officer been acting for himself or for his brother, he could not have shown more indefatigable zeal than he did, to comply with and expedite my requisitions and desires.[58]

News of Burgoyne's capture of Ticonderoga (6 July), reached England through an unofficial channel around the first of August.[59] Germain confided to Knox that, if this news were authentic, there was every reason to exepect a glorious campaign "from that quarter." Burgoyne's own account ought to arrive in a few days and if it proved to substantiate the unofficial report, Germain declared he was ready to speculate upon a winter's campaign in the south.[60] The possibility of victory in the north under Burgoyne put Germain in high good humor and served to compose his temper, irritated by his receipt of Carleton's choleric letters. He toned down an asperity in one of Knox's letters [61] and permitted himself a certain gaiety in his personal correspondence.[62] But uncertainty with respect to what had happened at Ticonderoga continued, and, on 22 August, Germain directed Knox to insert in the *Gazette* a letter from Burgoyne, forwarded by Howe, which described the preparations being undertaken for the assault on Ticonderoga. This was something of an anticlimax, and in order to "give some satisfaction to the public," Knox was also directed to insert Howe's confident prediction that Ticonderoga was in Burgoyne's hands.[63]

III

On the day before Burgoyne took Ticonderoga, Clinton arrived in New York from England.[64] Howe sailed from New York for his campaign in Pennsylvania on 23 July.[65] The period from 5 July to 23 July was, at New York, an important period in the campaign of 1777. There was still time for Howe to change his mind about the southern campaign. He received intelligence of Burgoyne's movements while still in New York, and he carried on important conversations with Clinton. After Howe sailed the die had been cast. For a month he was at sea and completely out of touch with developments either at New York or to the north.

Before he sailed he had news of Burgoyne's steady advance.[66] Burgoyne's report of his situation breathed confidence and the highest spirits. He reported that, after taking Ticonderoga, he would garrison it with troops from Canada, and his own force would be full and complete for further operations. He would then push forward to Albany. This report gave Howe no alarm with respect to the safety of Burgoyne. He therefore wrote Burgoyne on 17 July that he intended to proceed with his campaign in Pennsylvania and that, after Burgoyne's arrival at Albany, the movement of the enemy must regulate his operations. Clinton would remain at New York and would act as circumstances should direct.[67]

The day before Howe wrote this letter to Burgoyne he had made a clear analysis of his view of the situation for Germain.[68] There is nowhere a better exposition of Howe's over-all strategy with respect to the southern expedition. Washington's army was on the move in the Jerseys, and it was impossible to predict its objective. It appeared that General Washington might be going to cross the North River with a view to preventing any possibility of a junction between the northern and the southern army. Since there was no certainty, however, Howe made three suppositions as to Washington's possible moves with the countermoves he would make in each case. *First:* Suppose Washington crossed the North River. Howe would immediately proceed against Philadelphia, leaving Clinton a force sufficiently large to act defensively against the whole rebel army. If

Washington were engaged at New York, it would leave Howe a clear path for a quick and telling blow in Pennsylvania. *Second:* Suppose Washington moved into Pennsylvania for the defense of that province. Howe would then take with him his full complement of troops. In this case Burgoyne would have little interruption in his campaign, except that due to the difficulties in the transport of stores and provisions. *Third:* Suppose Washington should march against Burgoyne. The strength of Burgoyne's army was such as to "leave me no room to dread the event." But if Washington should make Burgoyne his sole objective "he may soon find himself exposed to an attack from this quarter and from General Burgoyne at the same time, from both of which, he would find it difficult to escape." It appears from this that there were no moves which Washington might possibly have made, except taking his full force against Burgoyne, which would have changed Howe's determination to attempt the conquest of Pennsylvania. Nowhere did he take account of a rebel army separate from Washington's or the rise of the New England militia.

While Howe was still at New York, Clinton did his best to dissuade him from the southern campaign. In his opinion Howe's best move was to go up the North River and make a junction with Burgoyne.[69] He pointed out all the advantages of a move to join Burgoyne and all the disadvantages of a move to the southward. Nothing would prevail upon Sir William, and he had the last word by pointing out to Clinton that his Pennsylvania campaign had been approved by the Home Government. Howe, of course, did not have at this time the approval of the Home Government for a campaign against Philadelphia by sea.

The next point canvassed by Clinton related to the distribution of Howe's forces as between New York and the army he would take to the southward. Howe took with him well over 13,000 troops and left Clinton 8,306 at New York.[70] Clinton called this "a D . . . d starved deffencive" and could not believe Howe really meant to move against Philadelphia. He told Howe "tho' he was pleased to say he was going to sea with the present Northerly Wind," Clinton believed he would "see him return with the first Southerly Blast and run up the North River." [71]

Howe sailed for Philadelphia with well over 2,000 more troops than he had specified for that campaign.[72] In addition he later ordered

Clinton to send him five additional battalions and he returned only two of these to New York.[73] Had he taken with him only the 11,000 he originally stipulated for that service, Clinton would have had a sufficient force at New York, after his reinforcements reached him from England in September, to have carried forward a more substantial operation on the Hudson in the fall of 1777. This might have altered the outcome of the campaign. Germain expected Howe to leave with Clinton all forces in excess of those Sir William had pronounced necessary for a successful campaign in Pennsylvania. It was partly upon this supposition that Germain had approved that campaign.[74] However, Germain's letter of 18 May containing the royal assent to the proposed southern expedition, with the reservation that it should be completed in time to cooperate with the northern army, did not reach Howe until 16 August when he was on his passage up Chesapeake Bay.[75] He had taken this route to Philadelphia, rather than the Delaware, on the advice of naval officers, but this had added two weeks to the length of his voyage and he was now separated from Burgoyne by 350 miles. The receipt of Germain's letter gave the general pause. He saw little chance of cooperating with Burgoyne and apparently had given it little thought. He had brushed aside Clinton's expostulations of a month earlier. Now he was confronted with the expectations of the Home Government. His reply clearly revealed both trepidation and a defensive attitude. He had not found loyalism flourishing in Pennsylvania. It was the old disappointment. The inhabitants, he reported,

excepting a few individuals are strongly in enemity against us; many having taken up arms, and by far the greater number deserted their dwellings, driving off at the same time their stock of cattle and horses.

He was faced by the enemy's principal army. His forces were insufficient for the task in hand. He expressed real concern about the expectation entertained in London that he would complete his operations in time to cooperate with Burgoyne:

It is with much concern that I am to answer that I cannot flatter myself that I shall be able to act up to the King's expectations in this particular . . .[76]

At almost the same time Germain was writing him from London:

I shall have a very sincere pleasure in congratulating you upon the expected success of the army under your command. In the meantime you will give me leave to partake of the joy which you must have derived from the accounts of General Burgoyne's rapid progress and the fair prospect which you now have of an earlier junction than you lately supposed likely to be effected.[77]

Sir William Howe and Germain clearly did not understand each other. Events and irrevocable action had now gone so far as to make impossible any lessening of the disastrous consequences of this misunderstanding. It had grown and developed through a readiness on the part of Germain to entrust a large latitude of action to Howe on the presumption that Sir William entertained, on essential matters, the same over-all strategic concept that he did. This concept could be gathered from no single dispatch; it must be drawn from a concordance of ideas going back at least to mid-summer 1776. Howe either had never viewed the campaign of 1777 as in any sense a joint operation with the northern army or had found himself, through dilatory tactics, in a position where it was impossible for him to act in this sense, and upon reconsideration had to believe, or at least to assert, that he had never had a conjoint operation in mind.

Burgoyne, too, as the summer progressed and as his difficulties multiplied, began to re-examine his position. The set-back at Bennington (16 August) was the turning point. Up to that time Burgoyne had been uniformly confident.[78] He had only regretted that he could not, because of his instructions, carry the war into New England:

Your Lordship will pardon me if I a little lament that my orders do not give me the latitude I ventured to propose in my original project for the campaign, to make a real effort instead of a feint toward New England.[79]

He reiterated this same theme to Howe [80] and, up to the middle of August, he was all confidence. Bennington was a real check. After that time his correspondence emphasized strongly the peremptory character of his orders. Less than a week later, this tendency was perfectly clear. He had determined to push on and to pass the Hudson. In a letter to Germain, he represented Albany as his mandatory goal:

Had I a latitude in my orders, I should think it my duty to wait in this position, or perhaps as far back as Fort Edward, where my communications with Lake George would be perfectly secure, till some event happened to assist my movement forward; but my orders being positive to 'force a junction with Sir William Howe,' I apprehend I am not at liberty to remain inactive longer than shall be necessary to collect about twenty-five days provision, and to receive the reinforcement of the additional companies, the German drafts and recruits *now* (and unfortunately *only now*) on Lake Champlain. The waiting the arrival of this reinforcement is indispensably necessary, because from the hour I pass the Hudson's river, and proceed toward Albany, all safety of communication ceases.

To push forward was so dangerous as to be justified only by "orders from the State." [81] Before he wrote this letter, Burgoyne had received Howe's letter of 17 July, informing him that he (Howe) was setting out for his campaign in Pennsylvania.[82] He could, therefore, have expected little help from Howe's main army, though he knew that Clinton had been left at New York with a force to act as circumstances should direct.

On 13 September, Burgoyne crossed the Hudson River and hazarded his expedition. A little more than a month later (17 October) he surrendered his whole army to Gates at Saratoga. From the crossing of the Hudson to the surrender at Saratoga, Burgoyne's progress was one long tale of mounting disaster. He had given up his communications with Canada, the terrain was formidable, the populace hostile, and the mobile New England militia gathered in strength. Burgoyne, during this period, was revising not only his ideas about his orders but also his ideas about the character of the rebel army. After the event of Saratoga, he wrote Germain:

I should now hold myself unjustifiable if I did not confess to your Lordship my opinion, upon a near inspection of the rebel troops. I do not hazard the term, but apply it to the great fundamental points of military institution—sobriety, regularity, and courage. The militia are inferior in method and movement, but not a jot less serviceable in the woods. My conjectures were very different after Ticonderoga; but I am convinced that they were delusive, and it is a duty to the state to confess it.[83]

Little help came from New York though Clinton did his best. At the end of September 3,000 reinforcements from England arrived at New York, of whom 1,700 were fit for duty.[84] Clinton determined upon an effort on a limited scale against the forts in the Highlands. He had a small but brilliant success in the capture of Forts Montgomery and Clinton on the right bank of the Hudson. He wrote Burgoyne: *"Nous y voilà* and nothing between us but Gates; I sincerely hope this little success may facilitate your operations." [85] In his desperation Burgoyne had sent a message by Captain Campbell asking Clinton for orders. The message was dated 28 September and was received 5 October. Clinton very properly sent back by Captain Campbell the following answer:

That not having received any instructions from the Commander-in-Chief relative to the Northern Army, and unacquainted even of his intentions concerning the operations of that army, excepting his wishes that they should get to Albany, Sir Henry Clinton cannot presume to give any orders to General Burgoyne. General Burgoyne could not suppose that Sir Henry Clinton had an idea of penetrating to Albany with the small force he mentioned in his last letter.[86]

Clinton's forces went up the Hudson as far as Kingston, but at that point they were eighty miles from Saratoga. This was the sum total of cooperation of the forces under Howe with those under Burgoyne, and it procured, not a junction at Albany, but a mitigation of the terms of surrender at Saratoga. The Convention of Saratoga was accepted by Burgoyne on 17 October and his troops laid down their arms. In the meantime Howe had captured Philadelphia and did nothing more that year. The campaign of 1777 was over.

From Bennington to Saratoga Burgoyne had been constructing his defense against possible charges of having mismanaged the campaign. Three days after the surrender, in two private letters, he gave this defense classic form. Through all the long years of subsequent controversy, he brought forward only variations upon the theme that the positive and peremptory orders of the Home Government had driven him to Saratoga and disastrous defeat. He wrote Germain:

I rest my confidence in the justice of the King and his councils, to support the General they thought proper to appoint to as arduous an undertaking, and under as positive a direction, as perhaps a cabinet ever framed. It will, I am sure, be remembered, my Lord, that a preference of exertions was the only latitude given me, and that to force a junction with Sir William Howe, or at least a passage to Albany, was the principle, the letter, and the spirit of my orders.[87]

On the same day in a letter to his friend Colonel Phillipson, anticipating "ministerial ingratitude," he attempted to arm his friend with arguments to use in his defense at home:

It was the will of the State to risk a corps of troops to assist the great and general arrangement of the campaign. If the State thought it necessary to devote a corps of troops for general purposes, it was no more within the General's duty to decline proceeding upon motives of prudence, and upon speculation of consequences, than it would be justifiable in a sergeant who heads a forlorn hope at the storm of a breach to recede because his destruction was probable—mine was a forlorn hope with this difference that it was not supported.[88]

Early in December, Germain received Burgoyne's dispatches giving the details of the Saratoga disaster and containing his defense of positive orders. Germain immediately repudiated this interpretation and never retreated from that position. He declared:

it was never understood that at such a distance any order could be positive, in the present case the words of the order will not bear the strict construction, the General put upon them.[89]

The nub of the controversy then came down to the so-called "saving clause" in Burgoyne's instructions. That clause read as follows:

You [Carleton] will at the same time inform them [Burgoyne and St. Leger] that until they shall have received orders from Sir William Howe, it is his Majesty's pleasure that they act as exigencies may require and in such a manner as they shall judge most proper for making an impression on the rebels, and bringing them to obedience, but that in so doing they must never lose view of their intended junctions with Sir William Howe as their principal objects.[90]

Burgoyne utterly rejected the idea that this section of his instruction gave him any discretion. He held that if any discretionary authority was granted, it applied only to operations undertaken after he was in possession of Albany.[91] Germain contended that Burgoyne's instructions had been largely drawn up by himself and that he had seen them and approved them before they were sent out to Carleton.[92] He also contended that the instructions were in no sense mandatory and, in his most forceful exposition of his view, he asserted:

Positive orders were the only excuse or reason assign'd in the public letters for the resolution he took of passing the Hudson's river under such circumstances. How far the orders were positive the Instructions show, but had they been worded in the most peremptory style any officer knows the first principle of his profession, every man of common understanding must see that orders given at such a distance presuppose a discretionary power in the commanding officer, but when circumstances change, there can be no doubt that a General when he cannot apply for fresh instructions that he must act for the good of the service, but when his instructions give him discretionary power and he is directed to correspond with and obey Sir Wm. Howe, how is it possible General Burgoyne could endeavor to shelter himself under the pretext of being bound by positive orders from the Secretary of State.[93]

It is difficult not to sympathize with a secretary of state who is brought under fierce criticism on the one hand (Howe) for not giving positive orders and on the other hand (Burgoyne) for having done so.

IV

In the first days of December the news of Saratoga arrived in London. It led immediately to an almost unbelievably bitter attack upon Germain in the House by an Opposition which, though small in numbers, was brilliantly articulate. On 2 December, when news of a military disaster was only a rumor, Fox attacked Germain with ringing invective:

For the two years that a certain noble lord (G. Germain) has presided over American affairs, the most violent, scalping, tomahawk measures have been pursued:—bleeding has been his only prescription. If a people deprived of their ancient rights are grown tumultuous—bleed them! If they are attacked by a spirit of insurrection—bleed them! If their fever should rise into rebellion bleed them, cries this state physician! More blood! More blood! Still more blood! When Dr. Sangrado had persevered in a similar practice of bleeding his patients—killing by the very means which he adopted as a cure—his man took the liberty to remonstrate upon the necessity of relaxing in a practice to which thousands of their patients had fallen sacrifices, and which was beginning to bring their names into disrepute. The doctor answered, 'I believe we have indeed carried the matter a little too far, but you must know I have written upon the efficacy of this practice, therefore though every patient should die by it, we must continue the bleeding for the credit of my book.' [94]

Fox concluded his attack by calling on Germain to say what he thought of the courage of Americans after he had read "the accounts arrived that very day." Rumor of defeat had provoked Fox's attack; Germain was left to conjecture what he must bear when the fact of defeat had to be announced.

Governor Pownall followed Fox in the debate. He declared that British sovereignty in America had vanished forever, that the Navigation System was annihilated. The only thing which Britain might still salvage from the wreck of Empire was a federal relationship—and that probably only a commercial federalism.[95] Germain rose in his place to defend himself and the government policy. He confessed that, despite the great strength of Britain, he had begun to despair of success in the face of a people united in revolution. But he would regard himself as criminal if he advised, or even cooperated in measures "for entering into a foederal union with rebels." He had rather part company with America completely. It was clear to him that America had been aiming at independence from the beginning; Parliament must either acquiesce in this or continue the struggle with the greatest exertion "upon the mere principle of self-defence." The hope of victory lay in convincing the people at large that their leaders were aiming at a permanent separation from Great Britain rather than, as the people imagined, a guarantee of the security of their rights and a modification of British claims. If numbers could be detached from the cause in this way, and a means could be found to cut off the secret assistance which the revolutionary cause received from abroad, Germain still believed that Americans might "return to their duty." Turning to Fox's dreadful attack, he said:

The hon. gentleman who spoke last but one had represented him as delighting in blood: he begged leave to assure him, he was entirely mistaken; he had always abhorred the effusion of blood could it have been possibly avoided.

He also asserted that Fox had misrepresented him with respect to his alleged insistence upon unconditional surrender. He did not demand that; he was ready to compromise on many subjects; indeed, he was even ready to tolerate many American prejudices. But he insisted on one thing as the proper foundation of any treaty—the acknowledgment by Americans of their position as subjects of the British Crown. "This was his decided opinion before he came into office; he had been uniform in his language." [96] Two years in office, limited and disappointing success in 1776, and humiliating defeat in 1777 had not served to change Germain's views of the constitution. He was still a "man of principle."

The public acknowledgment of the defeat at Saratoga had to come the next day. Colonel Barré called upon Germain in the most direct way to tell the House as

a man of honour, what was become of general Burgoyne and his brave troops; and whether or not he had not received expresses from Quebec, informing him of his having surrendered himself with his whole army prisoners of war? [97]

This was a heavy hour for Germain. During his life he had the unenviable distinction of being injured, in his personal reputation, equally by British victories and defeats—Minden, Saratoga, Yorktown. As he stood before the House, challenged as a man of honor to say the truth about the fate of a British army, he could not strike an heroic attitude, nor yet did he cry shame upon others. He followed the only course open to him, a cold recital of the facts as he knew them—facts still unauthenticated by any official communication.[98] He informed the House that he had had news from Quebec. The news had come to Ticonderoga by deserters and had been relayed from there to Quebec and on to London. Burgoyne had surrendered a British army to the rebels. It was not an unconditional surrender. The army was not to serve again in America, but it was to have safe passage to a port and leave to return to England.

It was a most unfortunate affair; but he hoped the House would not be over anxious in condemnation, nor decide upon the propriety or impropriety of the concerted plan that led to this unhappy event. He hoped they would suspend their judgement both on the conduct of the general and of the minister on this occasion. He hoped the conduct of both would appear free from guilt. For his part, he declared he was ready to submit his conduct in planning the expedition to the judgement of the House. If it appeared impotent, weak, and injurious, let the censure of the House fall upon him. He was ready to abide it; as every minister, who regarded the welfare of his country, ought at all times to have his conduct scrutinized by his country.

Barré, Luttrell, Burke, and Fox immediately fell upon Germain. They used every art of rhetoric, every appeal to emotion, every advantage resulting from the defeat of a line of action which they had criticized from its inception. They laid under heavy contribution the device of peroration. To lend force to their ringing phillipics, both Burke and Fox represented themselves as being under great restraint. Burke thanked the two speakers who had preceded him for allowing

him time "to calm the tumult and perturbation in his breast." [99]
Fox declared that he was happy

at being prevented from speaking immediately after the fatal tidings of
our disgrace had been communicated to the House: rage and indignation
so swayed his breast at that time, that if he attempted to speak, his words
must have been unintelligible.[100]

The Opposition at this time included a group of able orators which
the Government could not match. They had, in the circumstances
of the unsuccessful American War, an ideal target for declamation.
They had, in the great concepts of liberty and freedom as opposed
to tyranny and repression, a theme to stir the hearts of men, British
and American, in the eighteenth as in the twentieth century. The
attacks of the Opposition upon the Government in wartime, and the
open espousal of the cause of the enemy, seem strange when viewed
by a generation grown used to the doctrine of total war. Lecky has
pointed out that during the struggle with America, as during the
French Revolutionary War, that when Fox differed from the policy
of the government "he never appeared to have the smallest leaning
or bias in favor of his country." [101]

Barré declared:

The minister alone who concerted the scheme was obnoxious to repre-
hension for its failure. It was an inconsistent scheme, an impractical one,
unworthy of a British minister, and rather absurd for an Indian Chief.
... we find them [the rebels], by experience to be men of the most ex-
alted sentiments; inspired by that genius of liberty which is the noblest
emotion of the heart, which it is impossible to conquer, impractical to
dismiss.[102]

Luttrell followed:

We had employed the savages to butcher them, their wives, their aged
parents, and their children; and yet generous to the last degree, they gave
our men leave to depart on their parole, never more to bear arms against
North America.[103]

Burke followed and enlarged upon the difficulties under which
Americans labored in the present war,

but he could also have informed them, that men fighting for liberty, were
not influenced by such particulars; that these affected only the body,
but that the souls of the Americans were unreduced.[104]

Fox concluded the attack of the Opposition:

He inveighed most bitterly against Lord George Germain; looked upon him as solely responsible in the first degree; and next expressed his opinion, that all those who had concurred in the measures of the war, by giving their vote in support of it, were likewise criminals in an inferior degree.[105]

Lord North had the last word:

As to the noble lord in the American department, he trusted he had acted on the soundest principles of candour and deliberation. He could not possibly make any objection to the inquiry into that noble lord's conduct as he made no doubt but he would acquit himself before that House.[106]

So ended the impact of the first news of Saratoga upon the Parliament of Great Britain. It was not the last, however, that would be heard of that great defeat in Parliament and outside. Saratoga took its place alongside Minden as the common topic of reproach for Germain.[107]

The subsequent desultory inquiry into the campaign of 1777, culminating in the Howe Inquiry (1779), was thoroughly political in character. In this respect it resembled Germain's trial after Minden. On the day that the news of Saratoga was announced to the House, Burke declared that no fault was to be found with the general and his troops, "it could be traced nowhere but to the noble lord, whose ignorance was not brought as an extenuation but as a justification for his crime." [108] This was long before any informed judgment on the campaign could have been matured. No study had been, or indeed could have been, made of the documents. They were not available. But the Opposition saw the finest opportunity they had had since the opening of the controversy to attack the minister through his generals. There was no need to examine too closely the details of the campaign. The facts known then, and later, the facts made available through documents placed before the House, could be read in a variety of ways. If a thesis was accepted, evidence could be found to support it. The Opposition had a thesis: Germain was responsible for the failure of the campaign. Hutchinson in his *Diary* gives a good example of the relationship between the generals and the politicians: "At Lord Townsend's. It is said that when Burgoyne arrived [14 May 1778], Charles F[ox] asked him his plan? To charge Howe with leaving him to be sacrificed. 'If thats your plan we must forsake you: we are determined to support H(owe).' The next news—that Ministry is chargeable; and his speech in the H(ouse), and his new publication are conformable to this account." [109]

This combination of a disgruntled general (Howe), a defeated general (Burgoyne), and an intensely political Opposition ranged against an embattled ministry, made for anything but a proper legislative inquiry. It did, however, provide an excellent opportunity for the display of forensic ability, and, on the whole, the generals and the Opposition far excelled the ministry. The contest of wit and eloquence, however, did little to illuminate the issues at stake, and this is strikingly illustrated by the entry in the *Parliamentary History* at the end of the Howe Inquiry: "...the Enquiry was put an end to, without coming to a single Resolution upon any part of the business" [110] Inconclusive in its own day, the Howe Inquiry has left its mark upon the writing of the history of the American Revolution. Burke [111] and Fox, men of liberal sentiments, elevated ideals in politics, and consummate oratory in Parliament, spoke for Howe and Burgoyne and against Germain. Historians have read the record spread across the pages of eighteenth-century biography, collections of letters, and in the sober columns of the *Parliamentary History* and *Parliamentary Register*. They have been caught up by the lofty language and the well-turned phrase. Thinking in terms of subsequent constitutional development in the British Empire, they have been repelled by Germain's ideas. Condemned for a constitutional position which history has rejected, but which, in his day, despite its unattractive character, was tenable in logic and even respectable, Germain has had a rough handling from historians, whether Tory or Whig, British or American. His position has tended to be fixed not by a cool and steady examination of his policy from month to month as he executed the duties of American secretary, but rather in terms of the daring and brilliant attacks made upon him in Parliament, in terms of the derisive and bitter stories told about him, and in terms of the British defeat in America.[112]

A study of the critical year of that war (1777) is a case in point. The British failure was not due to a dispatch pigeon-holed because of Germain's eagerness to keep an appointment in the country; it was not due to an intolerable defect in his temper which made it utterly impossible for him to work harmoniously with Carleton, Burgoyne, and Howe; it was not even due to his supposed ignorance of American forests, winds, and rebels.[113] There was almost certainly no pigeon-holed dispatch; Burgoyne had a latitude in his orders; the miscarriage of great projects has commonly been the occasion for the falling out of those who laid the plans and those who attempted to carry them through. If Germain was ignorant of American conditions, he was abetted in this ignorance by Burgoyne's ideas of the feasibility of a campaign from Canada and Howe's notions of loyalism. Germain bears no unique responsibility for the failure of the British effort in 1777; upon closer examination it will appear that he ought to bear a rather more modest share of that responsibility than it has been customary to assign to him.

CHAPTER 8

CONCILIATION AGAIN:
THE CARLISLE COMMISSION, 1778

During the first six months of 1778 the character of the war in America changed entirely. Saratoga was the key. As John Adams remarked:

It determined the wavering counsels of France to an alliance which in its turn baffled Lord North's last scheme of conciliation by sending commissioners, and filled him with despair.[1]

The first half of 1778 partook of the character of the old and the new: the old in the shape of another effort at conciliation, the new in the revolutionary and decisive fact of the conclusion of the Franco-American Alliance and the open participation of France in the war. The old expedient of conciliation, though on a broad enough base probably to have been effective at the beginning of the struggle, failed as completely as the earlier, meager effort had done. It was born of a major military defeat and applied at a time when the revolutionary struggle was broadening into a great international war. The major factor in this new phase of the war was naval power. Naval power in the form of a rejuvenated French Navy made its first appearance on the coasts of North America in the summer of 1778. In the fall of 1781, off the capes of the Chesapeake, it played the decisive role in the securing of American independence.

Up to this point in the war, the British Navy had been used for little aside from transport and blockade. Its supremacy had been undisputed, except for the activities of privateers. The depredations of these vessels had been a constant source of annoyance, but had in no essential way threatened the British control of the sea approaches and coastal waters of North America. As a factor in warfare, the British had had the free and unfettered use of sea power. It had not, in the early phase of the struggle, proved to be a decisive factor. This was partly because British sea power had no great single objective in the form of an enemy naval force. It was not possible, in the classic form of maritime warfare, to deal a fatal blow through a unique and annihilating victory at sea. On the other hand, under the conditions of eighteenth-century naval warfare, it was not possible to establish a really effective blockade of the long sea coasts of North America. The British never used, in its full form, the navy as a terror weapon. Full-scale depredations up and down the seaboard might or might not have been effective to break the will to resist. If victory had resulted in this manner, it would scarcely have healed the schism in the Empire. The relations between subject and sovereign would have been irretrievably embittered for generations to come. This was not attempted by the British. Of the three possible forms of naval warfare, two were impossible for the British and one was not tried. The entrance of France into the war, however, presented equally a threat and an opportunity to British sea power. It opened up a possible avenue to the successful conclusion of the war through a victory at sea as, on the other hand, it posed the threat of a disastrous conclusion of the war through a defeat at sea.

In the two major developments of 1778—North's conciliation effort and the beginning of the naval phase of the war—Germain played unequal parts. He had little share in initiating or carrying through conciliation. He played a conspicuous, and, as it appears now, an intelligent part in the opening moves of the naval war with France.

The beginning of the new year was for Germain privately, a time of personal sorrow, and publicly a time of frustration and bitterness. Burgoyne's defeat at Saratoga, and Howe's barren success in Pennsylvania, had left their legacy of ill-will. Burgoyne was a prisoner of war, disgruntled, and in the process of constructing a defense of his conduct by throwing the blame on others. Howe, blaming the limited character of his success upon lack of reinforcement from home, had requested permission to resign his command.[2] Carleton, before the campaign began, had asked to be relieved of his command,[3] and on 1 September, Haldimand had been appointed in his place.[4] These three generals were due to arrive in England during the course of 1778, and Germain must have been depressed, regardless of the merits of the case, by the prospect of the recriminations which were bound to ensue between himself and this assortment of embittered and defeated generals.

On 15 January, his wife died.[5] On the next day he wrote Knox that if his absence from his office and Parliament

should be prejudicial to publick business, that no personal consideration for me should prevent the Seals being put into other hands; for I really feel so little able to return to business with the activity our present situation requires, that I should act unfairly by those with whom I have served if I did not wish and advise their adopting the best measures for publick service. I do forsee that there may be difficulties in prevailing upon any proper person to undertake so responsible an office in such times; all I can say to that is, that when I came in there was little appearance of success, and as I never had any view but the giving every assistance in my power, so that if my being permitted to retire answers any publick end, I shall rejoice in having proposed it. A man at my time of life, depress'd by misfortune, will make a bad figure in an office that requires vigor of mind, activity and diligence.[6]

His friends urged him to rise above personal sorrow and return to his public duties. Suffolk declared that some little progress might be made without Germain, but the whole of the execution depended upon him.[7] The best treatment for private woe was public "busyness." [8] Another friend declared that "every man's eyes are upon you, and every man's voice in your favor." [9] Lord Milton exhorted him, in spite of personal sorrows, to carry on the beneficial work of subduing America.[10] By 26 January, Germain was back in London and had taken up his duties.[11]

The first item of business to be undertaken related to Howe's request to resign his command. On 11 December 1777, Germain had informed Howe in a rather cold manner that the request had been received and would be acted upon in due time.[12] D'Oyley, the friend of the Howes, felt that after the letters which had been written to the "Brothers," it would be difficult to persuade them to keep their commands, even if it was desired to do so.[13] Lord Amherst was considered for the post of commander in chief in America but he would not accept.[14] Germain was indignant at Amherst's refusal:

How he or any officers can decline service when so honourably and so directly offered by his Sovereign is beyond all conception.[15]

While Germain was away from his office due to the last illness of his wife, Amherst, at a cabinet council, gave his ideas of how the war must now be carried forward.[16] He declared that the principal operations must be naval—to distress the rebel trade and prevent them from receiving aid from Europe. Canada, Nova Scotia, Rhode Island, New York, the Floridas, and, if possible, Philadelphia, should be retained. This would entail a force in America of 44,000. The retention of Philadelphia was pointed out by Amherst as contingent, and he earmarked 12,000 men for that service. If it was given up, a material reduction of manpower in America was possible.

The cabinet discussed Amherst's opinion but came to no decision. North reported that the business was put over until Germain could be back in town and could be acquainted with the whole project.[17] The King had declared that as soon as the manner of carrying on the war should have been decided upon, a general must be selected. He foresaw difficulties:

...it will be difficult to get Sir W. Howe to remain and not less so to get Lord G. Germain to act in such a manner toward him as will make the efforts of others not prove abortive on that head.[18]

Early in February the King had come to regard the recall of Howe as "a measure settled"; [19] on 4 February Germain in a short letter informed Howe that his request to resign his command had been granted and that Sir Henry Clinton had been appointed in his place.[20]

This precipitated a minor cabinet crisis. The Chancellor, Lord Bathurst, on 16 February, because of the resignation of Howe, requested the King to allow him to resign his post.[21] He also wrote Germain that he no longer wished dispatches sent to his home.[22] The King, however, took a hand in the matter, and Bathurst was persuaded to remain in the ministry. He declared that he had "great esteem" for all the members of the cabinet except Germain. The King asked North to see Germain

and settle with him a proper account of the propositions to America, and a suitable letter to Sir W. Howe that may encourage him to act with spirit until the arrival of his successor.[23]

The "propositions" referred to in this letter were North's proposals for conciliation. Before the news of Saratoga had reached England, the King, in his speech at the opening of the session (18 November 1777), had declared that he would "ever be watchful for an opportunity of putting a stop to the effusion of the blood of my subjects

...." [24] After the news of the great defeat had reached England, North was disposed to consider another effort at conciliation. He promised the House that, after the Christmas recess, he would bring the matter up again in an effort to secure a treaty on the basis of concessions on the part of Great Britain.[25] Parliament was adjourned to 20 January.

Germain was scarcely consulted on this second attempt at conciliation. He later wrote of his part in the project:

> You will know how little I was consulted either about the Act of Parliament or the appointment of the Commissioners, or the powers to be trusted to them. My part in all that transaction was merely official . . .[26]

This may have been partly due to his unsympathetic attitude toward the Howe Commission in 1776 and partly due to the fact that he had come to symbolize the advocacy of strong measures toward America. He was ignored to the degree that the King felt he ought to warn North that it was essential that he should inform himself of Lord George's opinions on the proposed negotiations with America. To be sure, Germain's views as gathered by the King did not reach very far. Germain had told the King that the repeal of the Boston Charter Act would not be a sufficient concession to bring America to an accommodation; that the Declaratory Act, though a piece of "waste paper," was what aggravated the colonists most; that nevertheless "he should not like nominally to be drove to repealing it," and that in consequence

> if any step was to be taken at this hour, he would wish it might be such as might not require any further concessions, he therefore wished all Acts might be repealed subsequent to 1763.

Gloomily, Germain confessed that he could not be at all sure whether a measure of conciliation would be apt to hurry America into a French alliance or tend to prevent such a development.[27]

His attitude was negative, and it reflected the resentment he felt. This is made clear by a letter he wrote early in February to his old friend Irwin:

> . . . when I consider that this whole measure of conciliation, the choice of commissioners, etc., has been carried on not only without consulting with me but without the smallest degree of communication, and when I reflect upon the Chancellor's [Bathurst's] conduct towards me, which must have arisen from finding that he might without offense, vent his

ill-humour upon me, and in short, from various little circumstances, I cannot doubt but that my services are no longer acceptable.[28]

On 17 February, North introduced his conciliatory propositions in the House.[29] One was to put at rest forever the problem of taxation and in particular to repeal the tax on tea. The government was prepared to give up any claim to impose taxation in the colonies except in the way of regulation of trade. A concession of this character would probably have led to a solution of the difficulties between Great Britain and her colonies if it had been offered in 1774 and 1775. The second piece of legislation was to authorize the King to appoint commissioners with large powers to treat upon the matters in dispute. The commissioners might treat with the Congress as a legal body and also with provincial assemblies and individuals. The powers granted to the Howe Commission were limited; the powers to be granted to the new commission would be ample in form and content. Specific concessions would not be named, as they would be taken by the rebels as the irreducible minimum and no room would be left for negotiation.

The conciliatory bills were passed by the Commons on 2 March,[30] and by the Lords on 5 March.[31] Germain did not once speak during the debates. His participation in the initiation of these measures had been so limited as to be negligible and his execution of them, as lying within his department, was formal and by direction. The Cabinet felt that copies of the bills and a circular letter to the responsible officers in America ought to be dispatched before the legislation passed. Germain passed this information on to Knox [32] and a circular letter, dated 19 February, was prepared.[33] Copies of the conciliatory bills were enclosed, with instructions that they should be printed and widely distributed in America so that the people might understand them before they were misinterpreted and condemned by "interested leaders."

On 18 February, Germain wrote Howe a letter which treated of both conciliation and coercion.[34] He spoke of the "salutary measure" under the consideration of Parliament but looked forward to the possible "obstinacy of the Colonies in rejecting the generous terms now held out to them. . . ." In this case the war would be continued. In an attempt to mollify Howe and to stimulate him to continue his efforts against the rebels so long as he retained his command,

Germain referred to the great store the King set upon Howe's zeal-ous attachment, and the full confidence he had that Howe would exert every effort to insure "submission to legal government by a due exertion of the force under your orders." He gave point and direction to this by informing Howe that it was the King's intention that opera-tions should be undertaken as early as possible against the seaports of Massachusetts Bay, Connecticut, and New Hampshire. This letter was written at the direction of the King who wished that Germain should inform Howe of the new effort toward conciliation and also encourage him to act vigorously while he still retained his com-mand.[35]

By the beginning of March, Germain was thoroughly dissatisfied with his position. His ample means, his age, and the recent death of his wife, combined to give him adequate personal reasons for retire-ment from public life. The failure of North to consult him upon the new commission indicated the small confidence he enjoyed in the cabinet. The quarrel with Bathurst over the resignation of Howe had been added evidence that he could expect no support from his col-leagues. The disastrous defeat at Saratoga and his embittered rela-tions with Carleton, Burgoyne, and Howe made his position in Parlia-ment and in his own department most difficult. Added to this, there came the news early in March that the King had given Carleton a lucrative office under the Crown. This brought Germain to the point of resignation. It has been traditional to attribute Germain's offer of resignation in early March to his petty anger over the King's generos-ity to his old enemy Carleton:

The ground of his displeasure was that the King, anxious to reward the past services of a most deserving officer, bestowed on Sir Guy Carleton the sinecure Government of Charlemont, which Lord George chose to construe as an insult to himself.[36]

This is a very partial explanation of his position and behavior. Earlier, when the rumor was abroad that the King was going to bestow some mark of his favor upon Carleton, Germain had confided to a friend that if this did occur it would not be the decisive factor in influencing his judgment with respect to remaining in or quitting his office.[37] It would only serve, when added to many other considerations, to indi-cate that he no longer possessed the King's confidence. When a man in public office has come, for a variety of reasons, to believe that his position is unsound, he may fasten upon some unique, and what appears to him to be provocative situation, to determine his conduct. This seems clearly to have been the position of Germain. The appointment of Carleton was only the last in a series of provocations which determined him to offer his resignation.

The King was not disturbed by the news of Germain's defection. He called it

a most favourable event, he has so many enemies that would have made him an heavy load whenever the failure of the expedition under Lt. G. Burgoyne came to be canvassed in Parliament, yet I never would have recommended his removal unless with his own good will. Now he will save us all trouble, the laying it on the bequeathing the Government of Charlemont on Carleton is quite absurd and shews the malevolence of his mind.[38]

He further declared that Carleton had been in the wrong in allowing himself to write such bitter letters to a secretary of state and had in consequence been recalled from his command. But he did not conceive that this prevented him from granting an office to a meritorious soldier.[39]

The whole matter dragged on, however, and no decisive action was taken. In the meantime, the members of the commission had been selected. Lord Carlisle was to head the commission, and William Eden and a Mr. Jackson [40] were joined with him. It was by no manner of means a distinguished group of men who were to attempt the momentous task of bringing about an accommodation between Great Britain and America. Carlisle was a young man, not yet thirty, who had been a friend of Fox and was principally known in London as a man of fashion.[41] William Eden, a lawyer, had been befriended by Lord Suffolk and had come to occupy an important, though uncertain, position in public life. He was very ambitious and the strongest man on the commission.[42] He knew Germain and wrote to him before accepting a place in the commission.[43]

On 13 March, the commissioners, together with Germain, Thurlow, the attorney general, and Wedderburn, the solicitor-general, met at Lord North's. The purpose of the meeting was to discuss the general business of the commission. The ministers were inattentive and preoccupied throughout the meeting. Carlisle reported:

Little passed of any real importance, and I confess I came away shocked at the slovenly manner with which an affair so serious in its nature had been dismissed.[44]

There was reason for ministerial preoccupation and inattention. The commission had been designed, in part, to head off an alliance between France and America. Saratoga had greatly increased the probability of such an alliance and, under the stimulus of this threat and the weight of defeat, Lord North had been moved to action. Yet it was anything but prompt and decisive action. Conciliation, hinted at before Christmas 1777, had not taken form until February 1778. The effort was altogether too late. As North and Germain sat down to discuss the aims of the commission, they already knew that the chief aim—to block the Franco-American alliance—had already been defeated. Earlier that day, the French ambassador had announced to the British government the conclusion, on 6 February, of treaties of amity and commerce between France and America. This portentous development thrust the commission into the background and merged differences in the cabinet.[45] Germain, who was identified with the forceful prosecution of the war, became a valuable man.[46] A civil war within the British Empire had now broadened out into a great international war. The historic rivalry between England and France now stood beside, and perhaps overshadowed, the issues of the American Revolution. It unified British resistance and challenged British strength. The challenge, too, was of the most provocative type—a challenge upon the high seas.

CHAPTER 9

THE ANGLO-FRENCH NAVAL CRISIS, MARCH–JULY 1778

The naval operations resulting from the conclusion of the Franco-American alliance have been the object of careful study and expert criticism on the part of naval historians.[1] However, the formation of the naval strategy which gave direction and authority to these operations has been neglected. The problems presented by the entrance of France into the war were, nevertheless, the main preoccupation of the British cabinet during the spring of 1778.[2] Differences of opinion within the cabinet as to the most effective disposition and employment of the naval forces available developed early and continued throughout the spring and early summer of 1778. Germain was deeply involved in this conflict and, characteristically, developed a strong position of his own from which he never wavered. As a result of divided counsel within the cabinet, British naval strategy was ineffective in meeting the first challenge of French sea power in the war. The timidity and uncertainty which characterized British naval policy should not be attributed, however, to the formulation of wrong policy, but rather to the failure to formulate any policy which could command general agreement within the cabinet. It is now necessary to examine the cabinet disagreements which developed, to put the opposing views on the record, and to place in its proper perspective the "unpardonable fault" of the ministry in allowing the British Navy, on the American station, to be faced in July 1778 with the greatly superior French sea power under D'Estaing.[3]

On 8 March 1778, five days before the announcement by the French ambassador of the American alliance, Germain wrote Clinton his instructions for the coming campaign.[4] He informed Clinton of the desire on the part of King and Parliament to open negotiations with the revolted colonists with a view to conciliating the issues in dispute.[5] If, happily, the negotiations thus set on foot should be successful, it might well make unnecessary a further campaign. How-

ever, such a result could not be confidently counted upon, and therefore the King was determined to lay all requisite plans for the
vigorous prosecution of the war and every effort would be made to
send reinforcements to America.[6] It had, however, been determined
that the manner of carrying on the war must be materially changed.
Two objectives were set for the campaign of 1778–79: *First:* the
coasts of the revolted colonies from New York north to Nova Scotia
were to be subjected to a series of raids with a view to destroying
shipping, wharves, shipyards, and stores, and thus to prevent the
rebels from continuing their damaging raids upon British trade, as
well as to make it impossible for them further to build and equip a
naval force. This operation it was anticipated would be concluded
by the month of October. *Second:* an attack was to be launched during, or immediately following, the month of October on the southern
colonies. These tasks were entrusted to Clinton with the forces he
would have available after having dispatched 3,000 men to Canada, a
detachment of artillery to Newfoundland, three regiments to Halifax,
and two regiments to St. Augustine and Pensacola. Of the reinforcements planned for the North American service, over and above these
detachments, Clinton would have for his own immediate command
five new Highland regiments together with the Edinburgh and Glas-
gow regiments composed of 1,000 men each.

Clinton was given discretionary authority to evacuate Philadelphia.
He was to avail himself of this authority if, in his view, and in the
view of the naval commander, Lord Howe, the objectives outlined
in his instructions were impossible of achievement without the employment of the troops now necessary for the retention of that
city.[7] If the two commanders did decide upon the evacuation of
Philadelphia, they were to establish a post upon the Delaware, capable of being defended by a small force, to block the evacuated port
and to give protection to ships which might have to be stationed in
the river. The reluctance with which Germain granted this authority and the tendency even at the last moment to suggest the
retention of Philadelphia may be judged by Germain's final word on
the subject:

I would not, however, be understood to convey it to you as his Majesty's
opinion that the possession of Philadelphia is an object of small importance; on the contrary, his Majesty conceives the possession of it may

be attended with many advantages and that the abandoning of it may be productive of some ill consequences, and therefore it is his Majesty's wish that you may be able to retain it, and he consents to your withdrawing from it only upon the supposition that the service I have been pointing out to you cannot, in your opinion be effected while it is retained.[8]

Germain concluded his dispatch by observing that it was not too much to hope that the success of the southern campaign might mean that all of the revolted colonies south of the Susquehanna would be recovered, and that, in this case, the northern colonies might well be left to contemplate their wretched condition with their supplies cut off and their ports blocked.

Since these instructions were framed before the British government was informed officially of the conclusion of the Franco-American treaty of 6 February 1778, they envisaged the continuation of war against the colonies alone. However, the government was aware that negotiations looking toward a treaty between the colonies and France were on foot and that the official announcement of the treaty might come at any time. Lord Stormont, the British ambassador in Paris, in his year-end letter for 1777 predicted almost certain war on the part of France and Spain against Great Britain.[9] Neither Suffolk, North, nor the King was disposed to take his intelligence too seriously. They contented themselves with observing that he had added little to the information they already had and that, in any case, preparations for such an exigency were well in hand.[10]

Germain had been in touch with the progress of the negotiation of the Franco-American treaty through his secret agent, James Hutton, in Paris.[11] He had received reports during the first half of January which indicated that the French and Americans were having difficulty in coming to a general agreement on the terms of the proposed treaty and that there was a good deal of mutual suspicion and distrust. In particular it was reported that the French demands had become exorbitant and that, after the news of Burgoyne's defeat at Saratoga had reached Paris, the American negotiators were inclined to adopt a firmer and more independent attitude.[12] It is also clear that, up to the end, the American delegates were attempting to play upon French fears that an accommodation between Great Britain and the revolted colonies was possible and even imminent.

Germain's agent reported that he was approached by one of the American delegates with the proposition that he (Hutton) should go immediately to England and procure there a "sign manual" from the King declaring the independence of the colonies. If this were done, the delegate declared himself to be willing to go back to America and use his every effort to secure from Congress such an alliance between Great Britain and America as might satisfy all parties. This whole transaction must be accomplished in ten days.[13] Hutton made the journey from Paris to London in seventy-three hours, and placed the proposition before Germain, with the opinion that "there is a treaty on the carpet," but that Great Britain could still prevent it.[14] There is no indication that this precipitate and radical proposal, looking very much like an ultimatum with a time limit, received any serious consideration by Germain or by the cabinet. However, the urgency with which this proposal was put forth, whether or not it was prompted by good faith, must have been a clear indication that such substantial progress toward agreement had been made that the conclusion of the treaty was in sight.[15]

Further warnings of the warlike preparations on foot in France during February and the early days of March came from Lord Stormont as well as Lord North's agents in Paris and made it still clearer that war between Great Britain and France was almost a certainty.[16] Therefore, the instructions to Clinton drawn up on 8 March 1778 and envisaging a further prosecution of the war against the revolted colonies alone, were formed with the clear knowledge that their whole character and intent might be changed on a day's notice.[17] There is clear evidence that the British government was ready, immediately upon being informed on 13 March 1778 of the fact of the Franco-American treaty, to change overnight its whole strategical concept of the war, involving as it did additional commitments in other theaters of operations—notably in home waters and in the West Indies. In addition, the cabinet had now to face the problems raised by warfare against a first-rate naval power, whereas up to the time of the entrance of France into the war, the British had enjoyed an easy naval superiority. That these problems had all been faced in advance and that a policy designed to meet them had been agreed upon is proved by the precise and detailed decisions resulting from an unusually full cabinet meeting at Lord Weymouth's on 14 March 1778.[18] The minute of advice to the King resulting from this cabinet represented an almost complete change of policy with respect to the conduct of the war: measures were put forth in it which widened the field of military and naval operations from those underway on the continent and sea coasts of North America, to the West Indies, to home waters, to the Mediterranean, and to the defense of the kingdom.[19] Another cabinet meeting was held on 18 March and advice similar in character, differing indeed only in the number and strength of the military and naval forces sought to be deployed, was given to the King in the form of a further cabinet minute.[20]

The final intent of these two cabinet meetings, as far as the North American and West Indian theaters of operation were concerned, and the explicit orders to the appropriate commanders necessary to implement that intent, were embodied in secret instructions to Sir H. Clinton 21 March 1778,[21] and in a letter from Germain to Clinton of the same date.[22] The secret instructions to Clinton were mandatory in three respects and contingent in one. He was directed without option to send a force of 5,000 against the French island of St. Lucia in the West Indies,[23] to send a force of 3,000 against Florida, and to evacuate Philadelphia. If necessary, he was to evacuate his remaining forces from New York either to Rhode Island or to Halifax. New York, however, was to be retained if possible in order to give dignity and an appearance of power, and thus to help to create the conditions necessary for a successful conclusion of the peace commission under the Earl of Carlisle.[24]

Included in the secret instructions of 21 March was a letter from Germain to Clinton,[25] which contained little that was new. It did, however, emphasize the hope that New York might be retained, and enjoined on Clinton that the utmost secrecy should be maintained with respect to the destination of the fleet and troops which Clinton was to dispatch for the attack on St. Lucia. Germain told Clinton that it had been given out at home that the troops were being embarked for Great Britain. Clinton should see that the same story circulated in America so that the French commanders in the West Indies might be deceived. In addition, Clinton was told that he could not expect further reinforcements than the three regiments destined for Nova Scotia. The recruits which had been raised in

Great Britain to bring some of Clinton's regiments up to strength had had to be diverted to other services, and hence Clinton was directed to incorporate these understrength regiments into other corps and send home the commissioned and noncommissioned officers.

Up to this point, there had been essential agreement within the cabinet as to necessary measures to be adopted in consequence of the virtual entry of France into the war. However, during the month of April there developed a serious difference of opinion between Germain and Sandwich with respect to the proper disposition of the naval forces of the Crown. In order properly to assess the divergent views of these two ministers, it is necessary to outline briefly the naval problem presented by French sea power, and to analyze in some detail the character, weight, and availability of British sea power which could be mobilized at a given point and at a given time to meet this challenge.

At the beginning of April 1778, according to the best intelligence available to the cabinet, French naval strength was divided between the ports of Brest and Toulon.[26] There was some uncertainty as to the actual strength of the two forces, but of the fact of its location and of its general character and striking power there was no doubt.[27] Estimates of the Brest force ranged from 21 to 25 ships of the line, of the Toulon force from 12 to 18 ships of the line. The total French force must then be reckoned between 33 and 43 ships of the line. To what degree this force had been equipped, manned, and put ready for sea was a problem, but by the first week in May, it was reported as "in commission and fit for sea." [28] During April it constituted the threat of a "navy in being."

British naval strength in home waters was represented by Lord Sandwich on 15 March 1778 as follows:

Our whole force at home at present in commission consists of 55 line of battle and 46 frigates, including sloops, cutters and 8 armed ships of 20 guns. Of these 40 of the line may be considered as applicable to immediate service, the other 15 are getting forward, and if men can be had, (upon which the whole depends) may also soon be ready.

There are besides 8 ships under orders to be got ready for receiving men, and several others in succession which may be in proper forwardness to be commissioned before men will be procured for them. 2 fire ships and 2 bomb vessels are also under the same orders . . . there are in foreign ports 9 line of battleships.[29]

From this "state of the force" it is clear that the British sea power "as applicable to immediate service," amounted, at the beginning of April, to 40 ships of the line. Of this force, 20 ships of the line were to be put immediately under Admiral Keppel for the protection of the home seas, and the remaining 20 ships of the line were designed for "the immediate protection of our distant possessions." [30] Of these latter ships, 5 were in need of repairs, 4 were at sea, 7 were earmarked for definite foreign assignment, and 4 were unassigned.[31] On 7 April 1778, 5 further ships were added to the list of those ready for foreign service, bringing the total up to 26 ships of the line. The ships not marked for foreign service were available and would be ready for sea in six weeks.[32] The ships marked for foreign service might also, at the discretion of the cabinet and on the basis of greater urgency, have been diverted elsewhere. In addition, if all hands at the naval yards had been put to work refitting, rather than building, the six weeks thought necessary to ready ships for sea might have been cut to three.[33]

It is therefore a clear conclusion that a naval force, for the purposes of a highly important and significant operation, was available to the British in the latter part of April. On the basis of the acceptance of a calculated war risk such a force was available at the first of April.

As we have noted above,[34] French naval power was divided between the ports of Brest and Toulon. D'Estaing [35] was the commander of the Toulon squadron; D'Orvilliers was in command of the squadron fitting out at Brest. It was known that D'Estaing was preparing his squadron for sea. The problem presented was whether D'Estaing was destined for America, whether he was under orders to make a junction with D'Orvilliers at Brest, or whether he was bound for Cadiz and a junction with the Spanish fleet, as the first move toward Spain's entry into the war. The situation was complex, involving as it did both political and strategical considerations. It required for its proper solution that rare judgment which is capable of keeping in balance these diverse factors. A realistic appraisal of the situation had to be made and a decision taken in the face of the serious, and perhaps fatal, war risks involved. If, after sober consideration, and on the basis of the fullest information available, a war risk is accepted, a steady policy must be rigorously followed. The over-all strategic concept cannot be altered in the face of daily, and perhaps hourly, rumors, alarms, and fragmentary bits of intelligence.

At this early stage in the naval war, with D'Estaing still at Toulon, the problem of his possible junction either with D'Orvilliers at Brest or with the Spanish fleet at Cadiz, was, in reality, no problem. It was not necessary to come to a decision as to what junctions D'Estaing might have in view; it was quite possible to prevent him from making any junction at all. This could be accomplished by sending a British naval force to intercept and to engage him before he passed the Straits of Gibraltar. This would, of course, have involved weakening the home fleet, but it was known that D'Orvilliers was not ready for sea. The dispatch of a naval force to the Mediterranean would have obviated completely the great element of uncertainty in the whole situation—the intended destination and purpose of D'Estaing.[36] Once let him get beyond the Straits and at sea and he became twice as dangerous. Double defensive dispositions were then involved, because to play safe it was necessary to deploy forces to meet him both at home and on the American station. While at Toulon or in the Mediterranean, he was a stable, accountable menace.

In the face of this situation, we have evidence as to the policy which was urged in the cabinet by Sandwich and Germain. On 4 April 1778, Sandwich was of the opinion

that it will be very unsafe to leave England and Ireland without a much larger force than Admiral Keppel's 20 ships of the line for this defence. The additional force that I think necessary must be determined by the force that France and Spain have ready for sea, as our principal object must be our defence at home; when that is secured, detachments may be made as exigencies require. I think it will be very dangerous to divide our naval force till we have more ships of the line ready for sea.[37]

Two days later at a cabinet meeting at which Germain, Weymouth, North, and Amherst were present, Sandwich brought this general conclusion to bear upon the specific case raised by the possibility of sending a fleet to intercept and to engage D'Estaing at the

Straits of Gibraltar or to seek him out and to engage him in the Mediterranean:

> It is my opinion that there are not ships enough as yet in readiness to form a squadron fit to meet the Toulon fleet under Monsieur D'Estaing, unless we were to sacrifice every other intended service to this object; or to send out Admiral Keppel with a proper force to try to meet Monsieur D'Estaing which however, seems to me a very dangerous measure, as our own coast and Ireland should then be subject to alarms, as the Brest fleet (without considering the fleet of Spain) would be superior to anything we should have ready for sea till Admiral Keppel's return.[38]

This view of the naval situation, however, did not go unchallenged. Germain strongly urged that a fleet should be sent out to intercept the French fleet. He argued that a vigorous and aggressive use of British sea power thus early against France, while involving risks, also gave the prospect of material advantages of such a character as to justify the risks involved. He said later of his position:

> I never can sufficiently lament the not having sent a fleet to Gibraltar to prevent the Toulon squadron passing the Straits, the risk of that measure was trifling in comparison of what we may suffer by leaving such a fleet at liberty to attack us in North America, the West Indies, or Newfoundland; but having done all in my power that our fleet might be so employed, and Lord Sandwich not thinking it either advisable or practicable, I must content myself with having given my opinion according to the best of my poor judgement....[39]

This was clearly the opportunity to have dispatched a fleet against D'Estaing, when there was no need to take into consideration his probable destination. After D'Estaing had sailed, the problem became immensely more complex but still capable of a better solution than the one offered by complete inactivity. But in the first week of April 1778 a sufficient force could have been sent against D'Estaing with, as Germain phrased it, "trifling risk" and with such effect that the ministry might well have been relieved of that charge of an "unpardonable fault" which Mahan so warmly urged.[40] It would appear that Germain was correct in his estimate of the realities of the naval situation [41] and that, had his advice been acted upon in those critical first weeks of the naval war against France, certainly a different, and, as it would seem, probably more effective disposition of British naval forces would have been determined upon. However, this was only the beginning of Germain's differences of opinion with Sandwich. These differences became more clearly defined and were brought more into the open as the month progressed.

Sandwich's position was determined in part by Admiral Keppel, though Sandwich himself was a man of considerable naval experience. Keppel in politics was an adherent of Lord Rockingham and bitterly opposed to the American war. He had refused to serve earlier, when the war had had the character of a civil war, and was brought in only when, with the Franco-American alliance, the struggle took on the color of a great patriotic war.[42] His scruples against serving being no longer valid, he was given the command of the Home Fleet.[43] With no sympathy for the American war and, being charged with the naval aspect of the war in home waters, he always regretted the large land and sea forces tied up in America.[44]

Keppel, from the time he took command of the Home Fleet, had one fixed idea: he was against separation and dispersal. The main consideration as far as he was concerned—and from the direct responsibility of his command quite naturally so—was the protection of the home islands. In a survey of the situation for the King, written shortly after he had taken over the command, he summed up the matter in this way:

And now in regard to the great fleet, the consideration of its being the bulwark and real safety of these dominions, I cannot but think that in every view of it, it should be *preserved in force* superior to the enemies if possible, and depend upon good intelligence for adopting any separation. . . . I must repeat that it would be unwise to separate the great fleet by detachment.[45]

He gave the same advice to Sandwich in very strong terms.[46] There can be no doubt but that Sandwich was influenced by this advice.

It is not difficult to see why these divergent views with respect to naval strategy developed. Sandwich and Keppel were primarily concerned and primarily responsible for the safety of the British Isles. Sandwich and, to a far greater degree, Keppel were willing to put to hazard the fortunes of the war in America, if the needs of the service there seemed to conflict in any material degree with the needs of the service at home. This is not to argue bad faith, but it is a reasonable conclusion that they both would err on the side of overcaution when a risk to home defenses was involved. Germain, on the other hand, was primarily responsible for the vigorous prosecution of the war in America. To all intents and purposes during the years of the War for American Independence, Germain was secretary at war. He shared of course, as secretary of state, an over-all responsibility for the war in all theaters, nevertheless he was so closely identified with the policy of rigorously pushing forward the offensive against the revolted colonists—and in this connection he had accepted the lead—that he was naturally prepared to accept risks for the ends he had in view. These are general considerations which should be stated, and they may help to explain the positions taken by Sandwich, Keppel, and Germain. They do not, however, excuse or even satisfactorily explain a timid and dilatory naval policy on the one hand, nor, on the other, a reckless and misguided one. It is submitted that Germain's policy was neither reckless nor misguided but was, in fact, in line with the realities of the naval situation as it existed in the first ten days of April 1778.

Sandwich's view of the situation, as expressed in his "opinion" of 6 April,[47] was the one accepted by the government, and no squadron was dispatched to the Mediterranean. It was not long, however, before disquieting news began to be received in England with respect to the possible intentions and destination of the Toulon fleet under D'Estaing. It became clearer that, once out of the Mediterranean, this squadron would become an unaccountable factor. On 15 April, Lord North wrote to the King:

It appears now to be lamented that we cannot send out a squadron to meet the Toulon fleet while in the Mediterranean, as their destination is uncertain; and they may perhaps sail to the East or West Indies instead of joining or endeavoring to join the Brest squadron.[48]

The information upon which North had formed this opinion was enclosed for the King's study. On the next day, the King replied:

The papers transmitted . . . are if true very material, and confirm me in the wish of beating the Fleet commanded by d'Estaing, and I will this day see whether Lord Sandwich cannot encourage Keppel on a promise of sending out additional ships to the reinforcement of his squadron, to detach a sufficient force to beat this Frenchman before he passes the Fort of Gibraltar.[49]

D'Estaing with a force of 12 ships of the line and 5 frigates sailed from Toulon on 13 April, but he did not pass the Straits of Gibraltar until 16 May.[50] There was still time to send a force to meet him.

There is no evidence, however, that the King had any success in his efforts "to encourage" Keppel to send a force against D'Estaing, and another week was allowed to slip by with no decision taken. On 23 April, North wrote to Sandwich that he had learned, on good authority, that either D'Estaing had already sailed with six ships of the line or that he was waiting to be joined by six other ships of the line. In the latter case, he was still at Toulon.[51] North's information was good as to the force under D'Estaing but faulty with respect to the date of his sailing. Lord North expressed in this letter his apprehensions as to the destination of D'Estaing's fleet, but he had now come to believe that it was bound for North America, and that "if he arrives there unmolested, he will do a great deal of mischief even with six ships." [52] Taking up the line of thought he had suggested in his letter of 15 April to the King, he now suggested to Sandwich with characteristic uncertainty:

There has been such pains taken to conceal M. d'Estaing's destination, and the success of his expedition is apparently so much at heart, that I do not think it probable he will be inclined to strike any stroke in European seas unless attacked. It may therefore be less dangerous to send out a squadron of seven or eight ships of the line to watch his motions, and to attack him only in case they think themselves superior or equal. This is a nice point. I am rather inclined to run the risk and wish you would consider it. . . .

North and the King were changing their minds and were coming around to the policy Germain had advocated at the beginning of April.

All speculation as to the size of D'Estaing's fleet was put to rest by the receipt of a cipher dispatch from the British *chargé d'affaires* at Turin. This dispatch was written on 12 April and was received in London on 25 April.[53] It contained authoritative information that there were in the Toulon roads nine ships of the line and six frigates and that these were to be joined immediately by three other ships of the line which were then taking on their water and provisions. D'Estaing had arrived at Toulon a few days before and it was believed he would hoist his flag and sail on 20 April. Other intelligence at this time from The Hague gave further details of the sailing of the Toulon squadron. Taken together, these reports precipitated a cabinet crisis and gave Germain the lead in formulating naval strategy.

Germain was not slow, in his downright manner, forcefully and perhaps untactfully, to urge his position. He wrote to North on 27 April:

I have this instant seen the dispatches from the Hague which bring so very particular and interesting an account of the sailing of the Toulon squadron, and of the manner of its equipment with stores, clothing, seamen, etc. etc., and convinces me that the destination of that fleet must be North America, where it will be joined by all the marine force of the rebellious provinces, and in that case will be able to attack and destroy our fleet in those seas and possess themselves either of Halifax, Philadelphia, or Quebec, if some immediate step be not taken by sending a strong squadron to reinforce Lord Howe and prevent the fatal consequence which may follow from the French having an avowed superiority at sea upon the coast of North America.[54]

He then went on to point out with precision and warmth that he had advocated earlier that a force should be sent out to intercept D'Estaing before he passed the Straits of Gibraltar but that he had been overborne by Sandwich. He then continued:

I must now only entreat your Lordship maturely to consider of the very alarming situation of this country, and to lose no time in advising His Majesty immediately to employ such a part of the fleet now at Spithead as may probably prevent the disgrace of this Kingdom, and not leave your Lordship and the other Ministers liable to be accused of inactivity in not endeavoring to avert those dangers which do immediately threaten us.[55]

This strong letter had its effect. On the same day (27 April) North wrote to Sandwich that further advices made it certain that D'Estaing's destination was North America and that in all probability he would begin his operations by an attack on the fleet in the harbor of New York or against the army at Philadelphia. In consequence of this grave situation, he had asked Lord Weymouth to call a cabinet meeting for Wednesday, 29 April.[56]

Sandwich, now faced with an extremely uncertain and puzzling situation, yet one which his decision of 6 April [57] had made almost inevitable, was in a painfully awkward position. He wrote Keppel on 28 April that there seemed every reason to believe that D'Estaing had indeed sailed for North America and that it appeared likely that he would either attack Nova Scotia and Canada or that he would engage Lord Howe and thus cut off the British Army.[58] Faced with a cabinet meeting the next day called for the express purpose of taking a decision on a naval situation which had been aggravated by the stand taken by Sandwich and Keppel earlier, there was little further that the first lord could say to his admiral, beyond underlining the complexity of the situation. He wrote:

However, we cannot say where he is going and therefore our dilemma is very great, particularly as we are not able to make any detachments from home consistent with the security of this island. Whether this situation of affairs will occasion any alteration in your instructions, I cannot yet say; but you may be assured that you will have the earliest information from me of everything in which I think you are in the least degree interested.[59]

The day before the critical cabinet meeting of 29 April, Sandwich was still against any detachment from the Home Fleet.

The King now took a hand in the proceedings. On 28 April, he wrote North enclosing a copy of the letter Keppel had written him on the policy of separation.[60] In this letter, after a long argument against separation, Keppel had remarked in his final sentence: "If the destination of the Toulon fleet can be ascertained, suppose West or East, equal force will on [*sic*] course be sent close upon them...." [61] The King, knowing of the cabinet meeting, and aware of the division of opinion which was likely to be reflected there, thought it wise thus to fortify North. On the morning of the day of the cabinet meeting, at 9 o'clock he wrote to Sandwich:

I have not the smallest doubt that d'Estaing's fleet is gone with Deane and Gerard [de Rayneval] [62] to attack either Philadelphia or New York. I think this so very material that without loss of time I transmit this intelligence unto you. Keppel in his own papers, mentions that if certain intelligence arrives, he must be authorized to detach.[63]

The stage was now set for the final showdown between Germain and Sandwich on the question of naval strategy. Germain's position on this vital issue has never been presented, and the most important document in the whole series leading up to the cabinet crisis of 29 April 1778 has never been published.[64] This document, "A Protest from Lord George Germain," was written by Germain on 29 April. It is couched in the conventional phraseology of a cabinet minister, as though addressed directly to the King, but was in all probability presented to the cabinet on that day. It is the strongest and most eloquent expression of Germain's opinion on naval matters and it deserves to be placed fully on the record:

The fate of the country evidently depends upon the preventing the Toulon Squadron from acting with success against our Fleet and Army and our possessions in North America; and there is every reason to believe it can have no other destination. If we are not able to resist France in this its first offensive operation, what have we not to dread when it shall be joined by the land and sea forces of the revolted provinces? What security can we then give our fisheries; what protection can we grant Jamaica and the Leeward Islands? I must therefore humbly submit my opinion to His Majesty (after lamenting that a fleet was not sent to stop Monsr. d'Estaing passing the Straits of Gibraltar) that at least twelve ships of the line should be now immediately detached to Halifax; and if the enemy should not be at that port to pursue and attack them in whatever station they may have taken, and even to follow them to the West Indies, if they should have proceeded thither after having complied with their orders upon the coast of North America. A frigate should be immediately dispatched advising the Commanders-in-Chief of the attack they are to expect and of the detachment made for their defense. The remainder of the fleet under Admiral Keppel, with the reinforcements preparing to join him, it is presumed will be sufficient for the protection of this country: but in all military operations of importance some risk must be run, and it is more meritorious to suffer in a vigorous and necessary exertion of our forces, than to remain inactive and tamely to submit to the loss of our detached fleets, armies and distant possessions, which must infallibly draw after it the absolute ruin of Great Britain.—I must therefore in discharge of the duty I owe to the King, and in vindication of my own conduct on this occasion protest against the measures now adopted; trusting that H. M. will duly weigh and consider them before he finally determines upon them. If I err in judgement, I hope H. M. will look upon the opinion I offer as proceeding solely from an anxious zeal for maintaining the honour of the Crown by preventing if possible a national disgrace.[65]

Judging from the result of the cabinet meeting of 29 April, Germain's protest had decisive results. With Sandwich, North, Amherst, Weymouth, and Germain present, a cabinet minute was drawn up advising the King to send a fleet of thirteen ships of the line to North America immediately.[66]

Germain at once set to work to draw up the necessary letter of instructions to the Admiralty to implement the policy adopted by the cabinet. This letter was finished and sent to the King for his approval before 8 P.M. on the night of 29 April.[67] The Admiralty was instructed to send thirteen ships of the line to Halifax. This force was to seek out D'Estaing on the American coast and, taking with him any British naval craft he encountered, the commander was to attack D'Estaing whenever the opportunity offered. If the French force had gone to the West Indies, the British force was to follow. If D'Estaing was not on the North American coast, and if it was ascertained that he was not in the West Indies, the British fleet was to return to England.[68] After some hesitation, Admiral Byron was selected as the commander of the fleet to be dispatched to North America.[69] It would appear, up to this point, that decision and energy had replaced the indecision and inactivity characteristic of the preceding three weeks: that indeed a definite risk was being accepted on the basis of a worthwhile advantage to be gained. It was perhaps not the "Nelson touch," but it resembled it far more nearly than the muddle which had followed Sandwich's opinion of 6 April. However, the newfound unanimity and vigor were early undermined by objections developed by Sandwich.

Sandwich now took the position that it was dangerous and difficult to have the fleet winter abroad. There was nothing in the letter which Germain had sent to the Admiralty which indicated that the fleet was to winter abroad, though by implication it might if its mission demanded it. Sandwich asked Stephens, his secretary, to represent his opinions on this subject to Germain. Stephens did this but to little effect. Germain refused to alter his letter pointing out that:

The motions of this squadron must be so much influenced by the motion of the French, that his Lordship does not think himself authorized to fix a time for the return of the former without being even able to guess what may be the intention of the latter.[70]

Again, Sandwich, writing from Portsmouth with the concurrence of Lord Mulgrave and Sir Hugh Palliser, commanded Stephens to put as strongly as possible before Germain their combined objections to having the fleet winter abroad.[71] This second attempt to limit the operations of the British naval force under Byron met with no success. Germain laid Sandwich's arguments before the cabinet, and it was unanimously agreed to make no change in the instructions already issued.[72] It was, however, abundantly clear that Sandwich, Keppel, and influential members of the Admiralty Board were by no means convinced that the decision of 29 April to dispatch immediately a naval reinforcement to North America was a wise decision. Further obstruction on their part was to nullify the effect of that decision and when, tardily, it was implemented it was already too late.

It was of the very first importance that news of the probable arrival on the American coast of the French naval force under D'Estaing be sent immediately to the commanders, naval and military, on that station. It was further important that these commanders should know that, to meet this urgent threat, a British naval force of roughly equal strength was under orders for American service. Germain had stipulated this in presenting his opinion on 29 April. However, when the request went to the Admiralty for a frigate to carry these most important dispatches, Sandwich refused on the grounds of the scarcity of frigates. He asked Germain to send a packet.[73] The result was that news of the French force and of the intended British reinforcement did not reach Lord Howe until 29 June, when, after having assisted in the evacuation of Philadelphia, he spoke the packet off New York harbor. This was nine days before D'Estaing himself arrived off the American coast.[74] The slowness in the dispatch of intelligence to America was, however, overmatched by the slowness in the dispatch of the actual forces intended for service in that theater.

On 3 May, Germain drew up Byron's orders.[75] These orders were substantially the same as those contained in the instructions to the Admiralty of 29 April.[76] They were based on the supposition that Byron would put to sea immediately in hot pursuit of the French squadron.

The House of Commons was now aroused over ministerial ineptitude in the face of the threatening naval situation. Mr. William Pulteney, M.P. for Shrewsbury, alleged that, in view of the vast sums which Parliament had appropriated, if the ministers could not dispatch a fleet on twenty-four hours notice, they ought to answer with their heads.[77] North wrote plaintively to the King, who was at Portsmouth trying to hasten the naval preparations, that he hoped the fleet would soon sail because he was meeting violent opposition in the House.[78] The King replied that it was absurd that members of the House of Commons should pretend a knowledge of naval affairs, unacquainted as they were with its immense detail. High winds had made it extremely difficult to load the men-of-war with the necessary supplies. However, the fleet would sail in a day or so.[79] On the next day North wrote the King at great length, and it appears with true sincerity, on the subject of his own deficiencies, and the danger to the government inherent in his holding office. North reported that the government had been attacked with great severity and he was of the opinion that the only way to avert disaster was to initiate "a material change in the Ministry." "If your Majesty does not allow me to retire, you and the country are ruined." [80]

In fact the government on the two preceding days had been under heavy fire from the Opposition.[81] Both Fox and Burke had spoken, as well as Pulteney. Their main criticism had been that the government had allowed D'Estaing to sail unmolested. Fox asked "how it was possible to estimate the guilt of Ministers who could tamely suffer an hostile squadron to carry unmolested destruction to the British Army in America." [82] Germain spoke twice during the debate and both times briefly and with obvious embarrassment. He was forced to defend a policy against which he himself had rebelled. He admitted that "appearances were against the ministry but appearances were not to justify condemnation." [83] He then went on to argue that it would have been imprudent to have separated a squadron from the Home Fleet to go after D'Estaing until it was established what destination the French admiral had in mind. Such a course of action would have endangered the safety of the kingdom itself. Germain was using the language of Sandwich and obviously without conviction. Ordinarily, he was an astute debater and used clear and forceful language in the House. This was a pallid performance and for a good reason: he was now using the arguments and almost the words of his opponents within the cabinet. His best efforts during the past month had been devoted to confuting what he now advanced, and he had not changed his views. However, the disciplined majority in the House upheld the ministers and North's fears were, for the moment, dissipated.

In spite of this debate and the cabinet decision of 29 April, Keppel was still opposed to any detachment from the Home Fleet. In letters to Sandwich he developed the consequences which, it appeared clear to him, would follow from any policy of dispersal.[84] Sandwich shared his fears and needed no conversion. On 7 May, Sandwich wrote North that he still believed that there was a strong possibility that D'Estaing's destination was Cadiz and a junction with the Spanish fleet. In such a case the House of Bourbon would have a combined naval force of some 71 sail. Consequently, he wanted to know certainly of D'Estaing's destination before Byron was detached for the American service. He asked Lord North to give his views "the mature consideration that so momentous an affair demands." [85] On that same day North had written to the King:

But I am culpable, I am afraid, in a very great degree, in not having done what my own knowledge of my defects made it my duty to do. At present my disgrace, is, in a manner certain, whether I continue in office or leave it. But it is of the utmost importance to prevent the ruin and disgrace of the country, which must be the consequence of my remaining in the Cabinet, where I never could, nor can decide between different opinions.[86]

It is impossible not to feel some sympathy for North caught as he was between two such decided characters as Germain and Sandwich. North wrote to Sandwich that he would show his letter to the rest of the cabinet and take their opinion on the matter.[87] He added, as his own opinion, that there was more evidence to indicate that D'Estaing was bound for North America than for anywhere else. That day he wrote again to Sandwich to report that he had placed his (Sandwich's) position before Germain, Weymouth, Dartmouth, and Gower and that they had all agreed that nothing new had arisen which would justify any change in the intended destination of Byron's squadron.[88] Indeed, Sandwich was only bringing forth again the arguments he had used during April—arguments which had already been set aside by the cabinet.[89] They now were set aside again by North and the most important members of the cabinet. Yet within five days Sandwich gained his point and Germain wrote to Byron to remain at Plymouth until further orders. How did this startling change happen?

From the evidence which is available to us, it appears that Sandwich gained his point through arguments presented to the King. The King during the first week of May had visited Portsmouth navy yard in order to encourage the naval preparations under way there.

He had been attended by Sandwich. There can be no doubt that Sandwich had improved upon every opportunity, discreetly, to present his opinions. However, these opinions had had little effect during the King's stay at Portsmouth for, on the day before he left, he wrote North that he was "convinced of the propriety" of sending Byron to North America, and that he ought to sail without any delay.[90] The King arrived back in London late in the afternoon of 9 May, a Saturday. On that day Keppel wrote his gloomiest letter to Sandwich. He painted a truly alarming picture of the dire consequences which might result from the detachment of Byron: British sea power worsted in a major channel engagement. What would this mean to the safety of the kingdom? It was not a far-off threat either; it might occur within a week.[91] Obviously, it is not a small thing for the first lord of the Admiralty, nor for the sovereign, to disregard, upon naval matters, the strongly put advice of the admiral of the Home Fleet. In such a case a heavy responsibility is incurred. There was a further consideration which must have had its weight at this critical moment. The frigate "Proserpine" had been dispatched from England on 20 April to watch for D'Estaing's passage of the Straits of Gibraltar and, upon ascertaining the course he had set, the frigate was to race for home. Since D'Estaing had sailed from Toulon on 13 April, it seemed fair to assume that some certain word must soon reach England which would dispel ministerial hesitations. Under these circumstances, it was all too natural and too disastrous to decide upon delay. In any event, on 13 May Sandwich wrote to Weymouth with clarity: "I received His Majesty's commands today to send an express to Plymouth to stop the sailing of Admiral Byron's fleet till further orders...."[92] And on that same day Germain wrote Byron his delaying orders.[93] The next day these orders were formally approved by a cabinet meeting.[94] The intent was to hold Byron in home waters until some sure information as to the purposes of D'Estaing's squadron could be obtained. This was the final, the critical delay.

However, Byron's squadron was still regarded as *intended* for the American station upon the first positive intelligence of D'Estaing, and further instructions were issued to him on 18 May.[95] These instructions directed him to go directly to Sandy Hook rather than to Halifax [96] and must be considered as supplementary to his original orders to proceed to North America. In effect Byron was now ordered to delay sailing but, when he did sail, he was to set his course for New York rather than for Halifax.

The remainder of May was a period of great uncertainty and vacillation. Accounts reached England, which, though garbled and of uncertain reliability, seemed to indicate that D'Estaing had not passed the Straits of Gibraltar and that he had, in fact, put back to Toulon.[97] Rumors of this kind, introduced into a situation already highly complex, made clear and decisive action a remote possibility. The King, the ministers, the admirals were now trying to provide a naval policy for three contradictory possibilities: D'Estaing was bound for a junction with D'Orvilliers at Brest; D'Estaing was bound for North America; D'Estaing had put back to Toulon. The current confusion and indecision were well illustrated by a memorandum from the King:

I am very clearly of the opinion that the moment we hear d'Estaing has passed the Gulf of Gibraltar and gone forward to North America, that Byron must follow him. Should he be returned to Toulon, then Keppel must instantly sail off Brest with such ships as he has in condition, and be joined by Byron and his squadron; and as soon as Keppel can have a reinforcement to render him equal to the Brest fleet, then Byron must be detached with a sufficient force to the Gulf of Gibraltar.[98]

In other words, Byron might be dispatched on three possible missions. In the meantime, the conclusion was clear that he had best remain where he was—in home waters.

An effort was made on 25 May, in further instructions to Keppel, to formulate some kind of a policy to meet these distressing dilemmas.[99] The admiral was directed to proceed off Brest taking Byron's squadron with him. If it should appear through "good intelligence" that D'Estaing had gone to North America or the West Indies, he was to detach Byron in pursuit. If D'Estaing had not left the Mediterranean, Byron was to be dispatched in quest of him, with orders to pursue him if he had passed the Straits, bound out of Europe. In the latter eventuality Byron's original instructions were to become operative. By these instructions the cabinet had in fact passed the responsibility for decision to the admiral on the station. It was the negation of a policy. Certainly it so appeared to Keppel who wrote gloomily to Sandwich:

I cannot say that your instructions are such as I feel much satisfaction upon when I consider them over. It is impossible to avoid seeing that, both in the case of detaching Vice-Admiral Byron's squadron or detaining him a time that may be too long in the event, the blame must fall upon myself. Indeed there does appear *a positive period* for my sending him away where *the intelligence is certain*, and at which time my instructions decide positively: but suppose I have information at the time that the Brest fleet is ready to come out to sea, nearly three ships to two in force compared with the King's that will remain under my command, is it meant that I should with seventeen or eighteen of the line leave it to the choice of the French to come out or not, to give battle to the fleet under my command after it is reduced by detaching Vice-Admiral Byron's squadron.[100]

Further to add to the distraction of the ministers, there was a move set on foot in the Commons on 26 May to begin an enquiry into the conduct of Burgoyne's expedition.[101] This occupied almost all of Germain's energy and led to an altercation with Mr. Temple Luttrell, during which Germain said in the House that "old as he was, he would meet that fighting gentleman, and be revenged." [102] It was a time of frustration, indecision, and divided councils. A naval policy waited upon certain information of D'Estaing and that information, it appeared, must come by the frigate "Proserpine" expected daily at a British port.[103]

The "Proserpine," Captain Sutton, arrived at Falmouth on 2 June. Captain Sutton brought the certain intelligence so eagerly sought. He had sighted D'Estaing inside the Straits on 16 May and had followed him to sea, parting company on 18 May.[104] It now seemed certain beyond reasonable doubt that D'Estaing was bound out of European waters [105] and that, in all probability, his ultimate destination was North America.[106]

Byron was now ordered to put to sea "without one moment's" loss of time and to carry out his previous instructions.[107] Because of contrary winds, he did not sail until 9 June.[108] The voyage was stormy and his squadron was scattered and damaged. On 8 August—sixty-seven days out of Plymouth—the flagship, without a single ship in company, sighted, ninety miles off the south coast of Long Island, the French fleet of twelve sail of the line. Byron shaped his course for Halifax arriving there on 24 August.[109]

In the meantime, Howe by sea and Clinton by land, had evacuated Philadelphia. Howe reached New York on 29 June and Clinton, after a hazardous march through New Jersey, reached New York on 5 July. D'Estaing anchored off the Delaware on 8 July. He had, perhaps, missed by ten days doing in 1778 what De Grasse was to accomplish so decisively in 1781. As Washington wrote:

Had a passage of even ordinary length taken place, Lord Howe with the British Ships of war and all the transports in the river Delaware must inevitably have fallen; and Sir Henry Clinton must have had better luck than is commonly dispensed to men of his profession under such circumstances, if he and his troops had not shared at least the fate of Burgoyne.[110]

The naval operations on the American coast for the remainder of 1778 may be briefly summarized. D'Estaing sailed from the Delaware to New York, arriving off Sandy Hook on 11 July. Lord Howe had made a very skillful disposition of his inferior naval armament. Partly because of this and partly because D'Estaing, on the advice of his pilots, came to the conclusion that his ships drew too much water to cross the bar, no attempt was made to force the entrance to New York harbor.[111] On 22 July, D'Estaing sailed for Narragansett Bay to make an attempt on Rhode Island in concert with an American land force. Admiral Howe, tenacious of purpose and indefatigable in effort, gathered the effective units of his force together and, reinforced by the return of three further ships of his own squadron and one—the first—of Byron's squadron, sailed after D'Estaing. He arrived off Narragansett Bay on 9 August. The next day D'Estaing, cutting his cables in his hurry to take advantage of a favorable wind, put out of the bay. There followed three days of exciting naval maneuver. Neither D'Estaing nor Lord Howe wished to accept battle except under favorable conditions. They never did engage. A severe storm developed and separated the two fleets, doing considerable damage to both. Lord Howe returned to New York and, effecting some minor repairs, again put to sea on 22 August in search of the enemy. D'Estaing, after the storm, made some temporary repairs and returned to Rhode Island. He had, however, determined to give up the project of taking Rhode Island and communicated his decision to General Sullivan, the American commander, on 20 August. He further told Sullivan that he was going to Boston for repairs. He arrived at Boston on 28 August. On 4 November, D'Estaing sailed from Boston for service in the West Indies and thus ended the naval operations of the year 1778.[112]

We have seen what Lord Howe accomplished in the way of defensive naval action with the slender resources at his command. It is only fair to inquire what might not have been accomplished had Byron been dispatched, as Germain urged, at the beginning of May. D'Estaing did not pass the Straits of Gibraltar until 16 May and Byron would have had the opportunity to join with Howe before D'Estaing arrived off the American coast. In that case there would have existed all the elements which might reasonably be supposed necessary for a decisive British naval victory. The British weakness in 1778 was on the side of strategy, not of tactics, and strategy was determined in London. There Germain had urged in the first place that a sufficient force be sent against D'Estaing to engage him on fair terms before he passed the Straits of Gibraltar. When this policy was set aside by the cabinet he urged, as a second choice, that a force equal in strength to D'Estaing's be sent immediately to America. This policy was accepted, but due in part to stubborn obstructionism, in part to honest fears, in part to misguided judgment, the policy was not implemented until it was too late to be effective. Division of opinion among the political and service officials of the Crown in Great Britain had made impossible a bold and decisive action at the opening of the great naval war with France.

At almost the same time that D'Estaing and Lord Howe were maneuvering off Rhode Island, there occurred, in European waters, the first encounter between the main naval forces of France and Britain—the Battle of Ushant 23–28 July.[113] This encounter was indecisive in character, as the operations in North American waters had been, but these two actions combined mark the end of the transitional phase of the war. The American phase of the war had been concluded and the international phase had begun. With the departure of D'Estaing from the American coast for the West Indies in November 1778, a triangular naval pattern, emphasizing the relationship of Europe, the West Indies, and America had been established. For three years this pattern was combined with land operations on the continent of North America and in the West Indies. With the arrival of De Grasse, out of Europe via the West Indies, off the Capes of the Chesapeake in August 1781, the operations of the latter phase of the war had reached their climax. American independence resulted.

In the career of Germain, 1778 was a natural dividing point. Up to this point, as secretary of state for the American Department, he had been considered, and was often called, a colonial minister. He had a colonial policy and in the pursuit of it he had attempted to quell a rebellion. He had dealt with the American question, as well before Lexington and Concord as after, in terms of a domestic issue within the empire. From 1778 on, he was charged with the responsibility, not alone of subduing rebellion, but of prosecuting a patriotic war against an ancient enemy. Although in legal form he still continued to be secretary of state for the American Department—a colonial minister—his status during the latter years of the struggle more nearly approached that of war minister in the British government.

CONCLUSION

Certain over-all conclusions may be drawn from this study regarding the constitutional position of Germain, his abilities as an administrator, his part as a maker of strategy, military and naval, and the degree to which he understood the force of the Revolution as an idea.

Germain occupied a logical position on the constitutional issue of legislative supremacy. He took the simple and the legally tenable view that the authority of the British Parliament was complete and absolute. He rejected utterly the idea of a federal empire. For him it was necessary either to assert the right of Parliament to legislate for the colonies "in all cases whatsoever," or completely to give up the right to legislate. His intellect and temper were not so constituted as to lead him toward compromise and adjustment, and his knowledge and understanding of the historical development of the empire were not ample enough to show him that a federal relationship had, in fact, evolved. His position was, and today remains, respectable, though liberals in his own day found that position unsympathetic and history has denied it utterly. His view of the constitutional relationship between the colonies and the mother country was conservative, in an historical sense anachronistic, but, for his type of mind, intellectually satisfying.

And yet these concepts of conservatism and innovation work oddly in the Anglo-American world, where, except upon unusual occasions the American and English temperament have an innate predisposition toward conservatism and away from innovation. Thus, Englishmen of the generation of the 1760's had the image of themselves as the conservators of the Old Empire and of Americans as the innovators and radicals. Americans for their part, with a stronger sense of historical development, saw themselves as the true conservators, and Englishmen of that age as exhibiting tendencies toward innovation and radicalism, which contradicted the direction of a century of historical development. Something less than a century later Americans would divide among themselves upon the nature of their government whether in the tradition of loose federalism, which Southerners would espouse against the North and which Americans had espoused against England in the 1760's, or in the tradition of a strengthened centralism, which Northerners would support, and which in the 1760's in the imperial structure Englishmen had supported. Further, in this mid-nineteenth century crisis of the Union, Northerners would conceive of themselves as the true conservators of the Constitution, which now the South sought to overthrow, and Southerners would think of themselves as the conservators of the Old Constitution, and of Northerners as radical centralist innovators. This is the pragmatic temper of England and America which subscribes so readily to Burke's dictum: "One sure symptom of an ill society is the propensity of the people to resort to theories." Germain, though oppositional to Burke in the politics of the day, would have subscribed fully to this philosophic principle.

Yet in another direction Germain's constitutional position anticipated the future. In his belief in the divisibility of the secretariat, and above all because he fought for that principle as a custom of the constitution, he contributed substantially to the development of the modern cabinet system. If he was conservative on the item of legislative supremacy, he looked toward the future in his concept of a flexible secretariat.

By eighteenth-century standards, Germain was judged a good administrator. He infused new vigor into the office of the American secretaryship, did away with many of the superfluous forms and delays, and conducted business himself in a forthright manner. He took charge of American affairs when their aspect was dark and confused. His first year in office saw the raising, the equipping, and the sending beyond the Atlantic of the largest expeditionary force Great Britain had ever put in the field. From this point of view, 1776 was a triumph for Germain, and 1776, on the side of operations, was the most successful year for the British of all the years of the American struggle. The deficiency in 1776 lay not in the administration of the office of the American secretary but in the use in America of the men and materials supplied by that office.

Subsequently, because of the lack of support in Parliament and in the cabinet, because the war appeared to present afresh each year seemingly limitless demands, and because Germain himself came to rely more and more upon the chimera of Loyalist support, the flow of men and materials across the Atlantic began to dry up. Germain had not the energy nor the vision of that architect of victory, the elder Pitt, with whom he was sometimes rather absurdly compared, but he could, nevertheless, take hold of affairs, and it was in the field of administration that he was most successful.

It may be confidently asserted that the British did not lose the War of Independence because of the shortcomings of Germain as a strategist. It is much closer to the truth to say that on the side of land operations he was up to the standards of the soldiers who served under him and that, on the side of naval strategy, he displayed a vigorous insight which put him well above his cabinet colleague at the Admiralty, Sandwich, and the senior service chief in that department, Keppel.

It has become conventional to charge Germain with an impressive number of military sins, whether of commission or omission: he tied down his commanders in the field by minute directions; he failed to provide adequate reinforcements; he was ignorant of American geography and of the character of American rebels; he ordered one army (Burgoyne) to undertake a mission dependent for its success upon the cooperation of another army (Howe), and then failed to order the latter to initiate the necessary direct supporting action; and, finally, because he had been found guilty of the disobedience of orders in the face of the enemy, it was impossible for brave and honorable soldiers to serve under him.

It is my conclusion that none of these charges can be sustained, either in their entirety, or in any substantial degree. Germain gave, perhaps, too wide a discretion to his field commanders. By eighteenth-century British standards he put unexampled numbers of troops into the field. He was no more ignorant of American geography and American rebels than the officers of the regular army, many of whom had served in America, who advised and counseled him. He did not order Howe to march to Albany and rescue Burgoyne, because it was never conceived that Burgoyne would stand in need of a rescue party. There were important political implications in the conviction of Germain on the charge of disobedience of orders and, for long years after his court-martial, he retained the respect and support of so stout a soldier as General Murray and so doughty a sailor as Admiral Rodney. The general belief in the military incompetence and pusillanimity of Germain is a myth upon which too many historians have agreed.

Naval strategy did not become important in the War of Independence until the virtual entry of France into the struggle in the spring of 1778. Germain was the only member of the British cabinet to urge an imaginative and sound strategy to meet the initial threat of French sea power. This aspect of his career has been almost wholly neglected. When it is considered that, in the military sphere, he acquitted himself in a respectable manner, and that in the naval sphere, though his advice was not taken, he had seized upon the right principles of maritime warfare and had strenuously urged their adoption, it may be concluded that, as a strategist, Germain was not so calamitous a failure as he has been represented.

Germain never appreciated the force of the Revolution as an idea. He failed entirely to grasp that aspect of the revolutionary movement to which John Adams referred when he spoke of it as occurring "in the hearts and minds of the people." Germain conceived of the discontents in America as resulting from the agitation of a few radical leaders who were stirring up and misleading a fundamentally loyal, docile, and British people. He believed that such grievances as the colonists labored under could be redressed, upon loyal petition, by the magnanimous but authoritarian Parliament of Great Britain. The struggle between the mother country and the colonies had been precipitated, in Germain's view, by a small group of unmoral and discontented men who were exploiting the insubstantial grievances of a whole people for their own selfish profit. Consequently, throughout, Germain emphasized the need to go over the heads of the leaders to the people—the misguided people. Germain's attitude toward the part which conciliation might play in bringing the struggle to a conclusion is a case in point. He believed that the first essential was to get the British proposals, however limited and unimaginative they might be, broadcast to the general public. A meager concession, coupled with a vigorous use of force, would, when understood in America, lead the great bulk of the population to repudiate a radical leadership which, in any case, was only precariously maintained. Germain continually asserted that he was not fighting a people in arms.

In large measure Germain was right in believing that, at the beginning, only a minority in America were revolutionists. But success in revolution, and more often the feat of merely maintaining revolutionary resistance, attracted the more timid souls toward a commitment to the cause. As the years went on, the force of the revolutionary idea became more pervasive. Tempered by hard struggles and refined by the intellectual efforts of one of the most distinguished among all generations of Americans, the revolutionary ideal came to have a high validity and a wide appeal. Germain grasped nothing, or very little, of this and here was his major shortcoming. He held fast to the belief that his task was to check a civil broil within the empire, when in fact he was attempting to check the historic developments of more than a century.

NOTES

[1] "Warrant to Authorize Lord George Sackville Germaine to Countersign Commissions, 10 November 1775." The warrant is given in full in the Germain Papers, William L. Clements Library, Ann Arbor, Michigan. Subsequently, these papers will be cited as G.P. It was signed by Lord Suffolk, secretary of state for the Northern Department, 1771–79. It is calendared in the Historical Manuscripts Commission's *Report on the Manuscripts of Mrs. Stopford-Sackville of Drayton House, Northamptonshire* (London, 1904–10), II, 18. Subsequently, this work will be cited as *S.S.Mss.* A part of the material presented in this chapter has already appeared in the *William and Mary Quarterly*, Third Series, IX (1952), 317–37. It is reproduced here by the kind permission of the *Quarterly*.

[2] The official verbatim account of the proceedings at the court-martial is contained in *The Proceedings of a General Court Martial ... Trial of Lord George Sackville* (London, 1760). A study from a military point of view of the battle and incidentally of Sackville's part in it is contained in an article by Major Charles Winslow Elliott, "The Men Who Fought at Minden," *The Journal of the American Military Institute*, III (1939), 80–103.

[3] W. B. Willcox, "The British Road to Yorktown: A Study in Divided Command," *American Historical Review*, LII (1946), 1–35. Subsequently this journal is cited as *A.H.R.* For a lively, anecdotal, and highly flattering account of Germain's life down to Minden, see Louis Marlow, *Sackville of Drayton* (London, 1948). This account is not based on the G.P. Subsequently cited as Marlow, *Sackville*.

[4] The great bulk of the Germain Papers in the William L. Clements Library, University of Michigan, Ann Arbor, Michigan, relate to the American Revolution. There are, however, some earlier papers, but there is a gap from 10 August 1759 to 14 July 1760, the period of the court-martial. The *S.S.Mss.*, I, 312–22, has a section entitled "Minden Papers." George Coventry in his book, *A Critical Enquiry Regarding the Real Author of the Letters of Junius, Proving Them to Have Been Written by Lord Viscount Sackville* (London, 1825), related that he wrote to the then Duke of Dorset—Germain's son—asking him, in the aid of literary inquiry, to permit the examination of Germain's letters with re-

spect to Culloden and Minden. Subsequently, Coventry called upon the Duke, and described the visit as follows: "He received me in the most polite manner, but told me it was out of his power to render me assistance, not having any of his father's letters in his possession. Upon the whole he considered, that as the affair in question was now at rest it would be as well not to revive it, lest animadversions should be made that would tend to recall past events. His Grace more than once observed during the interview, that his father was an injured man; but he believed there never existed one who naturally possessed a better or more susceptible heart." P. xviii. Subsequently cited as Coventry, *Critical Enquiry.*

⁵ The military problem presented by Sackville's conduct at Minden centers largely upon the question of whether or not there was a confusion in orders, and the amount of time lost in bringing up the British cavalry. The time lost by Sackville's indecision came down to a very few minutes—perhaps eight minutes. Horace Walpole, Earl of Orford, *Memoirs of the Last Ten Years of George II* (London, 1822), II, 365. Subsequently, this work will be cited as Walpole, *Memoirs.*

⁶ "During the eighteenth century every Prince of Wales quarreled with the reigning monarch and went into opposition. As heir apparent George II co-operated in opposition with Walpole, Frederick with Pulteney, George III with the elder Pitt, and George IV with the younger Fox." Romney Sedgewick, ed., *Letters from George III to Lord Bute 1756–1766* (London, 1939), p. xi. This work will be cited as *Letters to Bute.*

⁷ "Lord George shows himself the man of honor you have often cited him to be." Prince to Bute, 10 June 1757, *Letters to Bute,* pp. 6–7.

⁸ Same to same, 2 July 1758, *ibid.,* pp. 10–11.

⁹ Pitt to Sackville, 15 October 1757, S.S.Mss., I, 51–52.

¹⁰ Hon. J. W. Fortescue, *A History of the British Army* (London, 1910), II, 345–52. Subsequently cited as Fortescue, *British Army.*

¹¹ Bute had agreed reluctantly in June to the dispatch of 9,000 troops to reinforce Prince Ferdinand, but upon the express condition that "a small body should not lead to a great one." *Letters to Bute,* p. 11.

¹² On 14 December 1757, Pitt had said that he would not "send a drop of our blood to the Elbe to be lost in that ocean of gore." But a year later, he advocated not only the spending of large sums in support of the German war, but also the sending of British troops. *Ibid.,* pp. 19–20.

¹³ *Letters to Bute,* pp. 347–48; Walpole, *Memoirs,* II, 306, 361–62. The King was against Sackville's posting to Germany. He left England without an audience.

¹⁴ Albert Von Ruville, *William Pitt, Earl of Chatham* (London, 1907), II, 243–48. Von Ruville, some fifty years ago, called attention to the political implications of Minden. Subsequently cited as Von Ruville, *Pitt.*

¹⁵ Two letters of November 1758 from the Prince to Bute report that

Sackville was getting on badly with the German officers. *Letters to Bute*, pp. 16–17.

[16] Prince to Bute, December 1758, *ibid.*, p. 19.

[17] Duke of Newcastle to Sackville, 31 October 1758, *S.S.Mss.*, I, 53.

[18] Ligonier to Sackville, 31 October 1758, *ibid.*, I, 53.

[19] Lord George Sackville to Mr. Pitt, 11 November 1758, in *Correspondence of William Pitt, Earl of Chatham*, edited by the executors of his son John, Earl of Chatham (London, 1838), I, 367–69. Subsequently cited as *Chatham Correspondence*. After his return from the expedition against the French coast in summer of 1758, Sackville had also written to Pitt about withdrawing "from the active part of my profession." Same to same, 3 July 1758, *ibid.*, I, 326–27.

[20] Bute to Sackville, 17 November 1758, *S.S.Mss.*, I, 54.

[21] Walpole, *Memoirs*, II, 417.

[22] Von Ruville, *Pitt*, II, 245, looks at this possibility and concludes that Bute was referring to Ferdinand.

[23] Walpole, *Memoirs*, II, 362–63; Sackville to Pitt, 11 November 1758, *Chatham Correspondence*, I, 368–69.

[24] Walpole, *Memoirs*, II, 359.

[25] Prince to Bute, December 1758, *Letters to Bute*, p. 19.

[26] Lord Fitzmaurice, *Life of William, Earl of Shelburne* (London, 1912), I, 239. Subsequently cited as Fitzmaurice, *Shelburne*.

[27] Holdernesse to Sackville, 5 June 1759; Duke of Newcastle to Sackville, 5 July 1759, *S.S.Mss.*, I, 56–57.

[28] Prince to King, 20 July 1759, *Letters to Bute*, p. 25. Von Ruville, *Pitt*, II, 245, makes a good deal of the Prince's request. He suggests that if the Prince had been given the command of the British land forces, Sackville's command in Germany would have had the character of "an independent auxiliary army." In this way, Sackville would have had much greater freedom of action.

[29] King to Prince, 27 July 1759, *Letters to Bute*, p. 26.

[30] Prince to Bute, 28 July 1759, *ibid.*, pp. 26–27.

[31] Prince to Bute, 30 July 1759, *ibid.*, p. 27.

[32] Sackville to Bute, 18 July 1759, *S.S.Mss.*, I, 310–11. Sackville had been in regular correspondence with Bute since taking the command in the previous October. Bute said his accounts of operations were the best reaching England. Bute to Sackville, 17 November 1758, *ibid.*, I, 54. Same to same, 26 April 1759, *ibid.*, I, 54.

[33] Sackville to Holdernesse, 18 July 1759, *ibid.*, I, 309.

[34] Fortescue, *British Army*, II, 494–506. This is a good standard account of the battle. See also Charles W. Elliott, "The Men Who Fought at Minden," *The Journal of the American Military Institute*, III (1939), 80–103.

[35] Walpole, *Memoirs*, II, 365; see also *Proceedings of a General Court Martial . . . Trial of Lord George Sackville*. Sackville's own defense in a

speech to the court appears on pp. 172–98. For a summary of the conflicting evidence at the court-martial, see Marlow, *Sackville*, pp. 114–24. Marlow concludes that what Sackville tried to prove "in his letters to Ferdinand, in his published *Apology*, and in his defence at the court-martial was justification of his uncertainty about orders and the necessity of preserving the alignment by halting and by avoiding such haste in marching as would have destroyed it." *Ibid.*, p. 121.

36 Sackville to Prince Ferdinand, 2 August 1759, *S.S.Mss.*, I, 312.

37 Prince Ferdinand to Sackville, 3 August 1759, *ibid.*, I, 313.

38 Von Ruville, *Pitt*, II, 246.

39 See p. 5.

40 Pitt to Bute, 6 August 1759, *Letters to Bute*, p. 28.

41 Bute to Pitt, 7 August 1759, *Chatham Correspondence*, I, 416–17.

42 Sackville to Holdernesse, 2 August 1759, *S.S.Mss.*, I, 313; *Letters to Bute*, p. 29.

43 *Ibid.*, p. 29.

44 Prince to Bute, 11 August 1759, *ibid.*, p. 29.

45 Holdernesse to Sackville, 14 August 1759, *S.S.Mss.*, I, 313.

46 Pitt to Bute, 15 August 1759, *Chatham Correspondence*, I, 417–18.

47 Sackville to Bute, 9 September 1759, *S.S.Mss.*, I, 315–16.

48 Bute to Sackville, before 7 September 1759, *ibid.*, I, 314.

49 Sackville to Holdernesse, 7 September 1759, *ibid.*, I, 314–15.

50 Holdernesse to Sackville, 8 September 1759, *ibid.*, I, 315.

51 Pitt to Sackville, 9 September 1759, *Chatham Correspondence*, I, 423–24.

52 Sackville to Bute, 9 September 1759, *S.S.Mss.*, I, 315–16.

53 Holdernesse to Sackville, 10 September 1759, *ibid.*, I, 316; Walpole, *Memoirs*, II, 379, says that Ligonier, commander in chief, and Barrington, secretary at war, told Sackville that if he wanted a court-martial, he might seek it himself in Germany.

54 Barrington to Sackville, 10 September 1759, *S.S.Mss.*, I, 316.

55 Sackville to Holdernesse, 1 December 1759, *ibid.*, I, 316.

56 Holdernesse to Sackville, 3 December 1759, *ibid.*, I, 317.

57 Holdernesse to Sackville, 15 January 1760, *ibid.*, I, 317.

58 Sackville to Holdernesse, 17 January 1760, *ibid.*, I, 317.

59 Walpole, *Memoirs*, II, 416.

60 H. B. Wheatley, ed., *The Historical and Posthumous Memoirs of Sir Nathaniel W. Wraxall*, 1772–1784 (London, 1884), I, 395; subsequently cited as Wraxall, *Memoirs*. See also Walpole, *Memoirs*, II, 414.

61 Holdernesse to Sackville, 22 January 1760, *S.S.Mss.*, I, 317.

62 Charles Gould, judge-advocate, to Sackville, 27 January 1760, *ibid.*, I, 317.

63 Sackville to Charles Gould, 27 January 1760, *ibid.*, I, 318.

64 Walpole, *Memoirs*, II, 424–25. For this aspect of the trial it is necessary to depend on Walpole. T. C. Hansard, publisher, *Parliamentary*

History of England to 1803 (London, 1813), XV, does not carry this debate. However, this volume covers the whole period 1753–65 and is even more defective than the volumes covering the American Revolution. Subsequently cited as *Parl. Hist.* We are on fairly safe ground in accepting the substance of Walpole's account, though his habit of introducing the actual words of the speakers may be more open to critical inquiry.

[65] Walpole, *Memoirs*, II, 430. For a general impression see *The Proceedings of a General Court Martial . . . , passim.*

[66] Sackville's able defense and summing up of his case may be found in *ibid.*, pp. 172–98.

[67] Walpole, *Memoirs*, II, 224.

[68] *Ibid.*, II, 431.

[69] *Ibid.*, II, 431. Major Elliot writing in the *Journal of the American Military Institute*, III (1939), 101–2, summarizes some of the interpretations of Germain's conduct as follows:

> "Historians have not yet been able to formulate a convincing and satisfactory explanation of Sackville's defection at Minden. The contemporary theory, popularly accepted, of personal cowardice, is incredible. The man had displayed marked courage at Fontenoy, where he had been wounded far within the enemy lines. The savage old Duke of Cumberland not only testified to his bravery but found in him 'a disposition to his trade which I do not always find in those of higher rank.' He fought duels without flinching and had been under fire many times. Professor Leadam dismisses the mystery with the remark that Lord George was a man 'whose courage fluctuated and on this occasion failed him altogether.' Smollett, a contemporary but not an unprejudiced observer, ardently defends him. Lord Mahon, whose historical writings are undoubtedly colored by his political views, inclines to the opinion that Sackville was swayed 'by one of those panics to which men of quick genius are sometimes prone.' Yet the same author remarks rather sapiently that for Lord George to appear on the night of the battle, at the Duke's supper table 'required full as much courage as to have led his cavalry to the charge.' Colonel Whitton, in an exhaustive study of the trial, carefully analyzes the evidence and arrives at the conclusion that the defendant has been misjudged by history. The theory of the German biographer of Pitt, Herr von Ruville, seems to be the most plausible—that Sackville was hoping to secure the supreme command and displace Brunswick, and was therefore unwilling to lend his German chief any but the most perfunctory cooperation."

Von Ruville's position was not so simple as this. He dismissed cowardice, a belief on Germain's part that the movement of the British cavalry was inadvisable, and "personal enmity" on Germain's part toward Ferdinand as explanations of Germain's conduct at Minden. Von Ruville's conclusion was "these different motives may have combined to influence him, but there was without doubt some more important factor, which can only be explained by a consideration of other facts, and the key as usual is to be found in English party spirit and controversy." Von Ruville, *Pitt*, II, 243.

70 *Letters to Bute*, p. 42.

71 *Ibid.*, p. 43.

72 Walpole, *Memoirs*, II, 431.

73 Prince to Bute, circa 23 April 1760, *Letters to Bute*, p. 43.

74 Same to same, circa 23 April 1760, *ibid.*, p. 43. This is another letter of the same day.

75 *Ibid.*, pp. 42–43.

76 *Parl. Hist.*, XXII, 999–1023; Coventry, *Critical Enquiry*, p. 330.

77 H. Flanders, ed., *Memoirs of Richard Cumberland* (Philadelphia, 1856), pp. 325–26. Subsequently cited as Cumberland, *Memoirs*.

78 Mrs. Paget Toynbee, ed., *The Letters of Horace Walpole, Fourth Earl of Orford* (London, 1904), IX, 285. Subsequently, this work will be cited as Walpole, *Letters*.

79 Wraxall, *Memoirs*, I, 393–94.

80 W. M. James, *The British Navy in Adversity* (London, 1926), pp. 139–42.

81 *Parl. Hist.*, XVI, 1284.

82 James Murray to Sackville, 14 July 1760, G.P.

83 Sir George Rodney to Germain, 12 November 1775, *ibid.*, calendared in *S.S.Mss.*, II, 19.

84 Sackville to Bute, end of October 1760, *ibid.*, I, 57.

85 W. J. Smith, ed., *The Grenville Papers. Being the Correspondence of Richard Grenville Earl Temple and the Right Honourable George Grenville, Their Friends and Contemporaries* (London, 1853), I, 359; III, xlv. Subsequently cited as *Grenville Papers*. See also William Hunt, *Political History of England 1760–1801* (London, 1905), p. 15. Subsequently cited as Hunt, *Political History*.

86 *Letters to Bute*, p. 179. See also King to Bute, 11 December 1761, *ibid.*, p. 73; same to same, 10 December 1762, *ibid.*, p. 173. It is clear that Sackville was being watched by the King during these years, as he singled him out for comment in his letters to Bute.

87 King to Bute, end of December 1762, *Letters to Bute*, p. 179.

88 The evidence here consists of two letters: Bute to Erskine, 8 April 1763, *S.S.Mss.*, I, 58–59; and Sackville to Erskine, 10 April 1763, *ibid.*, I, 59–60. The references to this third party with whom Lord George might ally himself are very vague. He is simply identified as "the greatest enemy man ever had, who aimed at no less than his blood." Bute to Erskine, 8 April 1763, *ibid.*, I, 58.

89 Bute to Erskine, 8 April 1763, *ibid.*, I, 58.

[90] Sackville to Erskine, 10 April 1763, *ibid.*, I, 59. Sackville says in this letter that the reference to what he might be reduced to do, in Erskine's letter to Bute, must have come from Erskine's own ideas. He did not remember having asked him to mention anything with respect to his possible future conduct.

[91] King to Bute, 21 April 1763, *Letters to Bute*, pp. 228–29.

[92] George Thomas, Earl of Albemarle, ed., *Memoirs of the Marquis of Rockingham and His Contemporaries* (London, 1852), I, 218 et seq.

[93] Charles Townshend to Sackville, 9 July 1765, *S.S.Mss.*, I, 62–63. A series of letters were exchanged between Townshend and Sackville in the summer of 1765 upon the subject of the latter's taking office. See Sackville to Townshend, between April and August 1765, *ibid.*, I, 61–62; same to same, 9 July 1765; Townshend to Sackville, 12 July 1765; Sackville to Townshend, 13 July 1765, *ibid.*, I, 63–66.

[94] Sackville to Irwin, 23 December 1765, *ibid.*, I, 103. In the *Grenville Papers*, II, 487, under date of 22 January 1764, Grenville tells a similar story with considerable circumstantial detail with respect to the friendship between Lady George Sackville and the Hereditary Princess.

[95] Sackville to Irwin, 23 December 1765, *S.S.Mss.*, I, 103. See also *London Chronicle*, Thursday, 24 January 1766, for an argument against Sackville's having any office in government so long as anybody who was at all capable was available.

CHAPTER 2

[1] "If you understand the difference between representative and legislative capacity, it is more than I do, but I assure you, it was very fine when I heard it." Sackville to Irwin, 17 January 1766, *S.S.Mss.*, I, 103–5. If this distinction was not clear to Sackville it was clear to colonial Americans, and lay strongly at the base of the "search of Americans for principle." Americans believed that Parliament could legislate but not tax because taxation touched property and to eighteenth-century Americans property and liberty were almost synonymous, since property in the form of land was so widely held. Americans made no distinction between external and internal taxes; they denied the authority of Parliament to tax them at all. Edmund S. Morgan, *The Birth of the Republic, 1763–1789* (Chicago, 1956), Ch. II, pp. 14–27, *passim*, and in more detail Edmund S. and Helen M. Morgan, *The Stamp Act Crisis: Prologue to Revolution* (Chapel Hill, 1953), *passim*. See also Oliver M. Dickerson, *The Navigation Acts and the American Revolution* (Philadelphia, 1951), pp. 290–300, where it is argued with great force that the Navigation Acts were not among the important causes of the American Revolution. Americans, in general, did not dispute the right of the imperial government to regulate trade, and indeed the great trade system established for over a century by the Navigation Acts was a mutually advantageous system. What

Americans objected to was that the legislation after 1763 was not trade legislation but was anti-trade legislation and was designed to raise a revenue, to tax. This Americans were adamantly opposed to, and the activities of the customs racketeers established under the Townshend Act of 1767 as a Board of Customs Commissioners made the new policy seem naked tyranny.

[2] Sackville to Irwin, 17 January 1766, *S.S.Mss.*, I, 104.

[3] Same to same, 2 September 1762 and 5 September 1764, *ibid.*, I, 93–94, 95–96.

[4] *Parl. Hist.*, XVI, 161.

[5] Sackville to Irwin, 31 January 1766, *S.S.Mss.*, I, 105–6.

[6] *Ibid.*, I, 105. A recent writer, though recognizing the Stamp Act crisis as important in bringing on the separation of England and America, states: "My conclusion and thesis are that, while the British Stamp Act of 1765 greatly contributed to and touched off the colonial uprising of 1765–1766, the colonists had been brought to the brink of rebellion by a number of other provocative British measures from 1759 to 1764, most of which persisted after the Stamp Act was repealed in 1766 and contributed to the mounting discontent culminating in the American Revolution 1775–1783." Bernhard Knollenberg, *Origin of the American Revolution, 1759–1766* (New York, 1960), p. 1. See especially "Introduction," pp. 1–11.

[7] *Annual Register* (2d ed.; London, 1779), XIX, 93.

[8] Sackville to Irwin, 31 January 1766, *S.S.Mss.*, I, 106.

[9] Same to same, 10 February 1766, 11 March 1766, 25 April 1766, *ibid.*, I, 106–8, 108–9, 110–11.

[10] *Parl. Hist.*, XVII, 1194–96.

[11] *Ibid.*, XVI, 228–35.

[12] *Ibid.*, XVI, 228–34. The footnotes in the *Parl. Hist.* give a full account of this negotiation. These footnotes, because of the detailed account of the fine shades of political allegiance and family connection, elusive and difficult of access elsewhere, constitute an invaluable source.

[13] Conway to Sackville, 30 July 1766, G.P. In the Germain Papers, Conway's formal letter of dismissal is enclosed under the same cover with a personal note from Conway in which he expressed concern at his unpleasant duty. Sackville replied (31? July 1766) in a gracious manner. *S.S.Mss.*, I, 66. Conway became secretary of state for the Northern Department in Chatham's administration; Sackville's correspondent Townshend, forsaking the Grenville connection, became chancellor of the Exchequer, with fatal consequences for the British Empire. See Townshend to Sackville, 1 August 1766, *S.S.Mss.*, I, 66–67, and Sackville to Townshend, 3 August 1766, *ibid.*, I, 67.

[14] Whately to Grenville, 19 July 1766, *Grenville Papers*, III, 271.

[15] Sackville to Irwin, 9 December 1766, *S.S.Mss.*, I, 117.

[16] Same to same, 13 February 1767, *ibid.*, I, 118–19.

17 Same to same, 2 March 1767, *ibid.*, I, 119–20. The *Parl. Hist.*, apparently in error, has placed this defeat under the date of 2 June 1767. *Parl. Hist.*, XVI, 364.

18 *Parl. Hist.*, XVI, 375–76.

19 Sackville to Irwin, 13 February 1767, *S.S.Mss.*, I, 119.

20 Whately to Sackville, 21 July 1767, *Grenville Papers*, IV, 71–79.

21 Sackville to Whately, 23 July 1767, *ibid.*, IV, 76.

22 Whately to Sackville, 21 July 1767, *ibid.*, IV, 76.

23 Sackville to Grenville, 30 July 1767, *ibid.*, IV, 124.

24 Sackville to Irwin, 10 August 1768, *S.S.Mss.*, I, 127.

25 Sir Henry Cavendish, *Debates of the House of Commons During the Thirteenth Parliament of Great Britain, Commonly Called the Unreported Parliament*, edited by J. Wright (London, 1841), I, 84. This valuable work breaks off in the middle of a sentence in reporting the debates of 27 March 1771. No more of the work was published, and the copy available to this writer was certified as an exact copy of the one in the possession of the British Museum. Subsequently cited as Cavendish, *Debates.*

26 The most complete account of the parliamentary debates for the years 1768–71, is Cavendish, *Debates.* During this period Sackville spoke only once on affairs relating to America, i.e., in December 1768. In this period, however, he spoke fifteen times on other questions. *Ibid.*, I and II, *passim.* The *Parl. Hist.*, covering the whole period (1769–74), is equally silent. His correspondence is no more rewarding.

27 Germain to Irwin, 23 October 1770, *S.S.Mss.*, I, 132.

28 Hunt, *Political History*, p. 115. See also M. M. Spector, *The American Department of the British Government 1768–1782* (New York, 1940), p. 16. Subsequently cited as Spector, *American Department.*

29 *Annual Register*, XIX, 93.

30 Germain to Irwin, 30 October 1771, *S.S.Mss.*, I, 133.

31 Cavendish, *Debates*, II, 143.

32 Lord Vere to Earl Temple, 19 December 1769, *Grenville Papers*, IV, 490–92. This letter gives a full account of Lady Betty Germain's will. She also left Lady Vere £20,000. Lord Vere remarked of the bequest to Sackville: "Great part of the world we hear, are extremely angry at her leaving Drayton to Lord George Sackville, and, I conclude, will not believe neither Lady Vere nor I are the least disappointed, though we can, with the greatest truth, affirm we never one hour in our lives ever expected it, not only from the ascendent we daily saw the Duke of Dorset [Sackville's father] had with her, but from its' being the wish and desire of Sir John [Lady Betty's husband]." *Grenville Papers*, IV, 491.

33 Cumberland, *Memoirs*, pp. 322–23.

34 *Parl. Hist.*, XVII, 1162.

35 *Ibid.*, XVII, 1194–96.

36 *Ibid.*, XVII, 1195.

37 *Ibid.*, XVII, 1196.

38 *Ibid.*, XVII, 1196. See R. E. Brown, *Middle Class Democracy and the Revolution in Massachusetts* (Cornell University Press, 1955), *passim*, where it is argued that essentially by the 1760's Massachusetts was a political democracy, and the belief expressed that this was generally true of the other colonies. See especially Brown's conclusions, pp. 401–8. This thesis is strongly challenged in Merrill Jensen, "Democracy and the American Revolution," *Huntington Library Quarterly*, XX (1956–57), 321–41.

39 *Parl. Hist.*, XVII, 1196.

40 *Ibid.*, XVII, 1196–97.

41 Shelburne to Chatham, 4 April 1774, *Chatham Correspondence*, IV, 340.

42 *Parl. Hist.*, XVII, 1312.

43 *Ibid.*, XVII, 1313.

44 *Ibid.*, XVII, 1408.

45 *Ibid.*, XVIII, 192.

46 *Ibid.*, XVIII, 192.

47 As an instance of the government majority, it may be noted that the petition of the London merchants praying for an opportunity to be heard on the American question was lost, 250 to 89. It was on this petition that Germain spoke on 29 January. *Ibid.*, XVIII, 193.

48 Germain to Irwin, 30 May 1775, *S.S.Mss.*, I, 134–35. The news arrived "yesterday," that is, 29 May.

49 Germain to Irwin, 13 June 1775, *ibid.*, I, 315.

50 *Ibid.*, I, 135.

51 Wedderburn to Germain, 7(?) March 1776, *S.S.Mss.*, II, 24. This letter was written sometime after Germain had taken office, but it reflects clearly his position. In it Wedderburn remarked that Germain's presence in the government was absolutely necessary to the "plan of coercion." His withdrawal from government would be fatal to that "plan."

52 Suffolk to Germain, 15 June 1775, *ibid.*, II, 1.

53 Germain to Suffolk, 16 or 17 June 1775, *ibid.*, II, 2–3.

54 *Ibid.*, II, 2. John R. Alden in his *General Gage in America* (Baton Rouge, 1948) covers the American career of Gage from the Seven Years' War down to his recall as commander in chief in 1775. He pictures the dilemma of Gage as emerging from his position between "the views of stubborn men in power in London" and "the attitude of the equally stubborn patriot leaders. He stood between antagonistic forces, whose clash he could not avert. The hurricane which resulted he could not stay, although he could and did postpone it for many months. In the wreckage left behind by the hurricane was his own career." P. 298.

55 It is interesting to note that General Howe's brother, Lord Howe, wrote to Germain (7 August 1775) stating that he understood from a letter which he had received from Germain that his brother was to re-

place Gage, who had been recalled. *S.S.Mss.*, II, 6. This is significant as indicating the influence Germain had with government three months before he took office. See Chapter 3.

[56] Germain to Suffolk, 16 or 17 June 1775, *S.S.Mss.*, II, 3. This, of course, must be read as French Canadians.

[57] Germain to Irwin, 29 June 1775, *ibid.*, I, 135.

[58] Same to same, 26 July 1775, *ibid.*, I, 136.

[59] Same to same, 13 September 1775, *ibid.*, I, 137.

[60] Eden to Germain, 15, 18, 27 September 1775, *ibid.*, II, 8, 8–9, 9–10.

[61] Same to same, 3 October 1775, *ibid.*, II, 10–11.

[62] *Ibid.*, II, 10.

[63] *Ibid.*, II, 11. Howe, of course, was to replace Gage as the commanding general in America, exclusive of Canada.

[64] Germain to Eden, 1775, G.P. The letter has never been published. The letter is undated, but Eden's reference, in his letter to Germain of 21(?) October 1775, to the latter's refusal of the vice-regal position dates it as between 3 October and 21 October 1775.

[65] Eden to Germain, 1775 (probably 21 October), *S.S.Mss.*, II, 12.

[66] *Parl. Hist.*, XVIII, 697.

[67] *Ibid.*, XVIII, 761.

[68] Germain to Irwin, 27 October 1775, *S.S.Mss.*, I, 137–38.

[69] *Annual Register*, XIX, 192. See also W. E. H. Lecky, *History of England in the Eighteenth Century* (London, 1906–7), IV, 331. Subsequently cited as Lecky, *Eighteenth Century*. Lecky stated that Germain was an efficient administrator, an excellent debater in the House, and infused new life into the administration.

[70] "News of tomorrow—Lord George Germain, Secretary of State." Walpole to Countess of Upper Ossory, 9 November 1775, Walpole, *Letters*, IX, 280.

[71] *S.S.Mss.*, II, 18.

[72] Germain to Irwin, 4 November 1775, *ibid.*, I, 138. A sharp, ironic, and almost undoubtedly apocryphal story was told of Germain in office, which turns upon his change of name from Sackville to Germain. It is related that a country curate of timid nature became alarmed by the location of a gunpowder magazine close by his home. He proceeded to London to protest to Lord George Germain, the secretary of state, and in graphically describing his alarm he declared to the secretary that he was as afraid of gunpowder as Lord George Sackville. (The story I have read, but after diligent search I must confess I cannot give the reference.)

CHAPTER 3

[1] V. Sackville West, *Knole and the Sackvilles* (London, 1931), p. 157. Subsequently cited as Sackville West, *The Sackvilles*.

² There is a truly formidable body of recent sophisticated historical interpretation of the nature of parties in English politics of the 1760's. One suspects that Sackville was innocent of any true comprehension of these intricacies, save that he lived in the midst of them and had the feel of "connection," "faction," and "interest." The late Sir Lewis Namier was the founder, inspirer, and indefatigable researcher and expositor of one school. He and his followers saw the political complexion of the House of Commons in the 1760's as exhibiting the characteristics of a spectrum. At one end of the spectrum was the court-administration group, which would support the King's government as a matter of course. At the other end of the spectrum were the country gentlemen of independent mind and election who regarded themselves as Tories, but whose chief characteristic was a kind of high-minded but unpredictable independency. In the middle of the spectrum were the politicians with their eye on "party," "faction," and "connection." Out of these untractable materials, majorities and ministries were formed. In this analysis ideas are important only when connected with political weight and votes. Sir Lewis was also an irrationalist in the classic tradition, in that he placed little faith upon purposive declaration, when such declaration was made questionable by virtue of contrary action and personality. See Lewis B. Namier, *The Structure of Politics at the Accession of George III* (London, 1929; 2d ed., 1957); Richard Pares, *George III and the Politicians* (Oxford, 1953); John Brooke, *The Chatham Administration, 1766–1768* (New York, 1956); Ian R. Christie, *The End of North's Ministry, 1780–1782* (London, 1958).

Professor Herbert Butterfield in his *George III and the Historians* (London, 1957) is critical of the whole Namier school as being merely structural or static analysis, and unaware of the "higher political considerations" and that the play of ideas in debate was the play of the rational faculty of man and of his higher nature. Thus, Butterfield would credit the Rockingham party with a "higher purpose," while the Namierites, at least in Butterfield's view, reduced "the programme of this party to a mere device of eighteenth-century faction." See the insightful article of Jacob Price on Namier and his critics in *Journal of British Studies*, I (November 1961), 71–93. For a generalized over-all review of the various schools of historical interpretation relating to the causal factors of the American Revolution, see Edmund S. Morgan, "The American Revolution: Revisions in Need of Revising," *William and Mary Quarterly*, Third Series, XIV (1957), 3–15.

³ "Memoranda: Secretaries of State, November 1775," Historical Manuscripts Commission's *Report on Manuscripts in Various Collections* (Dublin, 1909), VI, 256. Subsequently, this work will be cited as *Various Collections*, VI.

⁴ King to North, 6 November 1775: North to King, 7 November 1775. Sir John Fortescue, *The Correspondence of King George III* (London,

1928), III, Nos. 1740, 1741. Subsequently cited as Fortescue, *Correspondence*.

[5] King to North, 7 November 1775, *ibid.*, III, No. 1742.

[6] North to King, 7 November 1775, *ibid.*, III, No. 1743.

[7] King to North, 8 November 1775, *ibid.*, III, No. 1745.

[8] North to King, 8 November 1775, *ibid.*, III, No. 1746.

[9] King to North, 9 November 1775, *ibid.*, III, No. 1748.

[10] *Various Collections*, VI, 256.

[11] See Chapter 3.

[12] North to King, 9 November 1775, Fortescue, *Correspondence*, III, No. 1749.

[13] *Various Collections*, VI, 256.

[14] There is an interesting item by Benjamin Franklin defending the new office of secretary of state for the American Department. It was in answer to a letter signed "Old England" in the *Gazeteer* for 12 January 1768. "Old England" attacked the new office on the following grounds: (1) It would create new lucrative offices with dependents. (2) It would provide a secret channel for conventions between the government and the colonies destructive of the freedom and the trade of England. (3) It would tend to range America, "child of Prerogative," on the side of the crown in some future imagined contest between Crown and Parliament. Franklin answered each of these charges with good humor but acute insight. Verner W. Crane, *Benjamin Franklin's Letters to the Press, 1758–1775* (Chapel Hill, 1950), pp. 108–10.

[15] A. H. Basye, "The Secretary of State for Colonies," *A.H.R.*, XXVIII (1922), 14.

[16] Act of 6th of Queen Anne. Section 25, "... no person who shall have in his own name ... any new office or place of profit whatsoever under the crown, which at any time since the 25th Oct. 1705, has been created or elected ... shall be capable of being elected or voting as a member of the House of Commons...." *Parl. Hist.*, XX, 255.

[17] *Various Collections*, VI, 256.

[18] *Parl. Hist.*, XX, 255. There had been at least two cases before 1707 when three secretaries of state had held office: one case in 1553 and the other in 1616–17. See Spector, *American Department*, p. 12. Sir Joseph Mawbey in his speech in the Commons on this subject (1779) took notice of the precedent in 1553 (Sir John Cheke was a third secretary), but dismissed it as a bad precedent because of the irregular character of the times. No account was taken, if indeed there was knowledge, of the precedent of 1616–17, when Sir John Herbert, Sir Ralph Wynood, and Sir Thomas Lake were all secretaries of state under James I. *Parl. Hist.*, XX, 250 *et seq.*

[19] In 1716 there were three secretaries; in 1723, four. Spector, *American Department*, p. 13.

[20] A document in Wedderburn's hand purporting to be a summary of

a debate in the House of Lords on the American secretaryship. Reprinted in Mark Thomson's, *Secretaries of State 1681–1782* (Oxford, 1932), pp. 171–73. Subsequently cited as Thomson, *Secretaries of State*.

[21] *Various Collections*, VI, 256–57.

[22] Wedderburn to Eden, 17 December 1775, in B. F. Stevens, ed., *Facsimilies of Manuscripts in European Archives Relating to America* (London, 1889–95), No. 859. Subsequently cited as Stevens, *Facsimilies*.

[23] "Minutes for a Royal Order Touching the Appointment of Lord Geo. Germain as Secretary of State for the Colonies. About December 1775," *ibid.*, No. 857. Benjamin Stevens dated it December 1775. Eden in a letter to Wedderburn of 16 December 1775, referred to it as "a paper which I proposed to you this morning." Eden to Wedderburn, 16 December 1775, *ibid.*, No. 858. Thomson (*Secretaries of State*, p. 60) gives the impression that the negotiation with respect to the "barrier treaty" took place before Germain was sworn into office. This gives a different and, it would appear, an incorrect interpretation of the whole proceeding. Thomson reprints the document as Appendix VI, pp. 173–74, of his book. A. H. Basye had already given some attention to this matter in his article, "The Secretary of State for the Colonies," *A.H.R.*, XXVIII (1922), 13–23.

[24] Eden to Wedderburn, 16 December 1775, Stevens *Facsimilies*, No. 858.

[25] Wedderburn to Eden, 17 December 1775, *ibid.*, No. 859.

[26] Eden to Wedderburn, 17 December 1775, *ibid.*, No. 460. "I am willing to hope you will hear no more on the subject." However, he still defended the idea of the "treaty," pointing out that there must always be delimitations between different offices.

[27] *Parl. Hist.*, XX, 266. Germain missed only seventeen out of 179 meetings of the Board of Trade between November 1775 and November 1779. Shortly after Germain made the above statement, the Board of Trade passed a minute to the effect that since the presence of the secretary of state at Board meetings was made necessary by the commissions, the privileges of the first lord of trade should properly belong to the secretary of state. A. H. Basye, the authority on the Board of Trade, in his book, *The Lords Commissioners of Trade and Plantations 1748–1782* (Yale University Press, 1925), sums up Germain's relations to the Board in the following way: "Lord George was ready, in other words, to claim either that he was not a regular and organic member of the board by virtue of the terms of the board's commission and was therefore on the same footing as the other great officers or that he was a 'bona fide' successor of the first lord and entitled to all the perquisites of that position." P. 180. Germain is reported to have said that "he is no more a lord of trade than the Archbishop of Canterbury who 'nominally' (says the noble lord) stands in the commission as well as myself." *Parl. Hist.*, XX, 263. Apparently, Germain made a mistake here as the bishop of

London, not the archbishop of Canterbury, was named in the commission.

28 *Ibid.*, XXI, 194.

29 Sackville West, *The Sackvilles*, p. 156.

30 Germain to Irwin, 18 November 1775, *S.S.Mss.*, II, 138.

31 *Parl. Hist.*, XVIII, 989, 991. See p. 45.

32 Germain to Irwin, 18 November 1775, *S.S.Mss.*, II, 138.

33 Walpole to Countess of Upper Ossory, 23 November 1775, Walpole, *Letters*, IX, 285.

34 Wraxall, *Memoirs*, I, 389.

35 Fitzmaurice, *Shelburne*, I, 238. One of Germain's elder brothers— Lord John—"went off his head" and the other elder brother—Lord Middlesex—is described as "that proud, disgusted, melancholy, solitary man whose conduct savoured so strongly of madness." When Lord John heard of Germain's court-martial he is reported to have said, "I always told you that George was no better than myself." Sackville West, *The Sackvilles*, p. 55. To say that Lord John "went off his head," is almost certainly too gross a diagnosis to stand. He was subject to agonizingly painful fits of depressive melancholia, which makes him a truly pathetic figure.

36 Other adjectives applied to him were "hot, haughty, ambitious, and obstinate." *Ibid.*, p. 157.

37 Wraxall, *Memoirs*, I, 384.

38 Cumberland, *Memoirs*, p. 201. Both Wraxall and Cumberland were friends of Germain.

39 Wraxall, *Memoirs*, I, 385.

40 Sackville West, *The Sackvilles*, p. 156.

41 Cumberland, *Memoirs*, p. 210.

42 Spector, *American Department*, Ch. VIII, *passim*. Mrs. Spector has made a detailed and thoroughly admirable study of the administrative aspects of the office. This chapter is one of her best.

43 Germain to Knox, 19 October 1776, *Various Collections*, VI, 126.

44 Same to same, 19 September 1777, *ibid.*, VI, 138.

45 Pownall to Knox, 13 November 1776, *ibid.*, VI, 127.

46 Lecky, *Eighteenth Century*, IV, 330.

47 Fitzmaurice, *Shelburne*, I, 238–39. Prominent among these, according to Shelburne, were the following: Mr. Murray, later Lord Mansfield; the two Stones, one of whom became secretary to the Duke of Newcastle and virtually ruled him, and the other became primate of Ireland; and Mr. Markham, later archbishop of York. "... his Westminster connections never failed to advise and support him underhand, even when he was most pressed." *Ibid.*, I, 250.

48 Cumberland, *Memoirs*, pp. 326–28. It has been put forward as a possible explanation of this oddly disturbing scene that Germain was attempting to disabuse Lord Mansfield of any idea that he had been the author of the Junius papers. Coventry, who was convinced that Germain

was Junius, pointed out a speech of Germain's made 6 December 1770 regarding a proposed inquiry into the conduct of criminal justice and involving the investigation of charges against Mansfield. The speech, Coventry argues, though nominally that of one friendly toward Mansfield, was full of satire and invective. Coventry, *Critical Enquiry*, pp. 185–90.

[49] Fitzmaurice, *Shelburne*, I, 250.

[50] Wraxall, *Memoirs*, I, 387. One unfriendly critic described the only good feature of Germain's speaking as "his arrogance and his presumption." James Hare to Carlisle, 1 January 1782, in Historical Manuscripts Commission's *Report on the Manuscripts of the Earl of Carlisle, Preserved at Castle Howard*. Fifteenth Report, Appendix, Part VI (London, 1897), 561. Subsequently cited as *Carlisle Mss.*

[51] Wraxall, *Memoirs*, I, 388.

[52] Coventry, *Critical Enquiry*, pp. 298–302; *Parl. Hist.*, XVI, 1328, 1330.

[53] *Ibid.*, XIX, 1199–1203; Coventry, *Critical Enquiry*, pp. 54–60.

[54] *Parl. Hist.*, XXII, 999–1203.

[55] Cumberland, *Memoirs*, p. 292.

CHAPTER 4

[1] Sir George Savile made merry by comparing the gentlemen on the Treasury Bench to the gentlemen in the Congress. He compared Wedderburn to Franklin, Germain to General Putnam, and Lord North to John Adams. Germain sat between Wedderburn and North. *Parl. Hist.*, XVIII, 982–83. See Germain's speech, *ibid.*, XVIII, 989–91.

[2] Walpole, *Letters*, IX, 133.

[3] *Parl. Hist.*, XVIII, 997.

[4] Indeed, he was referred to in the House as "the Pitt of the day." Col. Barré threw ridicule upon this idea by saying that it only conveyed to him that "there had been a Mr. Pitt, a great man, but he did not see how the noble lord was like him." *Parl. Hist.*, XVIII, 1154–55.

[5] Knox tells an amusing story of Germain's last days in office (1782). "The King told him (Lord George) Lord North had spoken of the necessity for his going out because of his avowed principle of resisting treaty with America upon any footing but the preservation of sovereignty. 'If you mean by his going out,' said the King, 'to relinquish that principle you must make other removes.' 'No,' replied Lord North, 'for no one else has declared that principle.' 'Yes,' says the King, 'you must go further; you must remove me.'" "Account of What Passed in Consequence of Lord Cornwallis's Surrender," *Various Collections*, VI, 272–76.

[6] Germain to Howe, 18 November 1775, in *The Parliamentary Register or History of the Proceedings and Debates of the House of Commons* (London, 1802), X, 306. Subsequently referred to as *Parl. Reg.* He was

probably heartened to begin his correspondence with military and naval men by the compliment Rodney paid him upon hearing of his appointment. After extending congratulations, Rodney went on to say that the appointment would in part compensate for the "gross, cruel, base, unjustifiable persecution you underwent in the late reign." Rodney to Germain, Paris, 12 November 1775, G.P.

[7] See Chapter 2, p. 27 *et seq.*, for a brief notice of this letter. Germain to Suffolk, 16 or 17 June 1775, S.S.Mss., II, 2–3.

[8] Allen French, *First Year of the American Revolution* (Boston, 1934), p. 566, relates that at the time Lord Howe—the general's brother—took the sea command in 1776, he had not spoken to Germain for seventeen years. Yet on 22 July 1775, Lord Howe wrote to Germain thanking him for his goodness to General Howe in his late appointment: he was sent out as a major general to reinforce Gage in March 1775. Lord Howe remarked that it laid him under an equally deep debt of gratitude. Lord Howe to Germain, 22 July 1775, G.P. This letter is only calendared in S.S.Mss., II, 5. On 29 July there is another letter from Lord Howe to Germain, *ibid.*, II, 5–6, enclosing one of his brother's letters with his own comments. On 25 September 1775, Lord Howe in a letter to Germain spoke of "seeing your Lordship in town . . ." G.P. This part of the letter is not included in the summary given in S.S.Mss., II, 9. The context makes it clear that "seeing" Germain meant seeing and speaking to him. See note 17 following.

[9] King to North, 28 July 1775, Fortescue, *Correspondence*, III, No. 1685.

[10] Dartmouth to Gage, 2 August 1775; Dartmouth to Howe, 2 August 1775; Dartmouth to Carleton, 2 August 1775, in Historical Manuscripts Commission's *Report on the Manuscripts of the Earl of Dartmouth.* Fourteenth Report, Appendix, Part X (London, 1898), 344–45. Subsequently, this work will be cited as *Dartmouth Mss.*

[11] Walpole with heavy irony (and some truth) remarked: "Well, General Gage is recalled, and is to be hanged. We had conquered America by this time they say if he had not betrayed us and desired the provincials to block him up; so 'en attendant' Hancock and Adams and Putnam and Washington, you may divert yourselves with executing your own general. Voltaire will abuse you, as he did about poor Byng; but really a government must condemn somebody . . ." Walpole, *Letters*, IX, 229.

[12] King to North, 28 July 1775, Fortescue, *Correspondence*, III, No. 1685.

[13] Dartmouth to Gage, 2 August 1775, *Parl. Reg.*, X, 253–55. This letter is only calendared in *Dartmouth Mss.*, 345.

[14] Germain was later to inquire into some of the results of this policy. See Germain to Howe, 5 January 1776, and Howe to Germain, 7 May 1776, *Parl. Reg.*, X, 309–10. See p. 76.

[15] Gage to Dartmouth, 1 October 1775, in C. E. Carter, ed., *The*

Correspondence of General Thomas Gage with Secretaries of State 1763–1775 (New Haven, 1931), I, 418. Gage handed over his command to Howe on 10 October and arrived in England 14 November.

[16] Howe to Dartmouth, 9 October 1775, *Parl. Reg.*, X, 259–62.

[17] Mention has already been made in note 8 of Lord Howe's letters to Germain of 22 and 29 July and 25 September 1775. The first two are hardly more than calendared in the *S.S.Mss.*, and the one of 25 September has, for our purposes, essential omissions. This correspondence is, of course, complete in the G.P. However, Germain's letters to Lord Howe, to which the latter constantly refers, are not in the G.P.

[18] Lord Howe to Germain, 25 September 1775, G.P.

[19] Same to same, 29 July 1775, *ibid.*

[20] Same to same, 7 August 1775, *ibid.*

[21] Same to same, 25 September 1775, *ibid.* As noted, Chapter 2, Germain was at this very time being considered by North for a mission to America which was vice-regal in character. The primary thought in North's mind, however, was that such a personage would be chiefly devoted to making peace, not war.

[22] Lord Howe's letter to Germain of 25 September was based on a letter from his brother of 20 August. Troyer Anderson in his study, *The Command of the Howe Brothers During the American Revolution* (New York, 1936), p. 115, in comparing Howe's earlier and later plans, speaks of a few weeks intervening between the two. In fact more than seven weeks intervened. Is there some confusion between the date of Lord Howe's letter to Germain (25 September) and General Howe's letter to Admiral Howe (20 August)? Anderson, in his admirable study, fails, except for a passing reference (p. 115), to note the probable interplay of ideas between Germain and Sir William Howe via the latter's brother, Viscount Howe. Of course Anderson's focus of attention was not on this aspect of the situation. Subsequently cited as Anderson, *Command of the Howe Brothers.*

[23] Anderson, *Command of the Howe Brothers*, p. 117, remarks in this connection: "The earliest of his formal requests (9 October) probably represented the largest force he hoped to get under existing conditions. Thus a divergence appears between the numbers he felt free to demand and those he really felt necessary. He recognized that the apparent circumstances of his situation did not warrant as extensive an effort by the government as he felt inwardly to be needed. This feeling that the problem was more formidable than appearances indicated or than the government was willing to recognize grew on Howe and, as we shall see, played a very important part in shaping his later actions and attitude." The comment naturally arises that if "he felt free" to suggest 24,000 to Germain out of office, would he not have felt equally free to do so had he known his request would be read by Germain in office in the stead of the hesitant Dartmouth?

[24] Dartmouth to Howe, 5 September 1775, *Parl. Reg.*, X, 262–64.

[25] Howe to Dartmouth, 26 November 1775, *ibid.*, X, 264–68.

[26] Dartmouth to Howe, 22 October 1775, *ibid.*, X, 287–90.

[27] Howe to Dartmouth, 16 January 1775, *ibid.*, X, 291–94.

[28] Howe to Dartmouth, 22 January 1775, *ibid.*, X, 295–96.

[29] Germain to Howe, 18 November 1775, *ibid.*, X, 306.

[30] Germain was perhaps more sanguine than Dartmouth about this, because Dartmouth two days before leaving office referred to the southern expedition in a letter to Howe in the following terms: "I say of the possible advantage (of this expedition) because the effect of it is very precarious." Dartmouth to Howe, 8 November 1775, *ibid.*, X, 304–5.

[31] Anthony Storer to Lord Carlisle, 14 December 1775, *Carlisle Mss.*, p. 311.

[32] The so-called "Olive Branch Petition," the work of Dickinson and Jay, passed the Congress in July 1775. There is a copy in the G.P. entitled "Petition of Congress to King." It is misdated September 1775. It was an effort to conciliate the issues at stake. Richard Penn presented it to Lord Dartmouth in August. He was given to understand that no answer would be forthcoming. On 23 August, a royal proclamation declared the Americans to be rebels and warned against giving them any aid and comfort. The American Prohibitory Bill was the next step in coercion. See Edward Channing, *A History of the United States* (New York, 1912), III, 186–88. Subsequently cited as Channing, *History*.

[33] *Parl. Hist.*, XVIII, 1060. The full debate appears *ibid.*, XVIII, 992–1000, 1028–38, 1056–65, 1103–6.

[34] *Parl. Hist.*, XVIII, 1058–59.

[35] Channing, *History*, III, 188. John Adams wrote on hearing of the Act: "I know not whether you have seen the Act of Parliament called a Restraining Act or Prohibitory Act or Piratical Act or Act of Independency—for by all these titles it is called. I think that the most apposite is the Act of Independency; the King, Lords, and Commons have united in sundering this country from that, I think, forever." Adams to Gates, 23 March 1776, in C. F. Adams, ed., *The Works of John Adams* (Boston, 1850–56), I, 206–8.

[36] Howe to Germain, 26 November 1775, *Parl. Reg.*, X, 264–69. Burgoyne arrived in London from America on 27 December 1775. He was a member of Parliament and it was not uncommon for members to return home during the period the army was in winter quarters. Burgoyne was also in England during the winter 1776–77.

[37] Dartmouth to Howe, 5 September 1775, *ibid.*, X, 262–64.

[38] Germain to Howe, 5 January 1776, G.P. (Military Dispatches Secret). Subsequently cited as M.D.S. Germain's dispatch of 18 November was little more than an acknowledgment of Howe's letters of 5 and 9 October. See p. 53.

[39] Howe's forces at Boston on 21 November 1775 amounted to 7,605

men, made up of 1,315 commissioned officers, 4,865 rank and file fit for duty and 1,425 sick. "Abstract of the Latest Returns of His Majesty's Forces at Boston. Dated 21st November 1775." G.P.

[40] Howe had asked for 6,100 British recruits to fill out his battalions. Germain was able to offer him only 4,400. This latter number is the one used to reach the total of approximately 22,000.

[41] It seems clear that Germain was thinking of a force of 7,000 foreign troops and 3,000 British, since the total of foreign troops provided for by the treaties with the German states was 17,000, and of these 10,000 were to be sent to Howe. The negotiations with the Russians had failed.

[42] See p. 51.

[43] There is a long document (15 pages) in the G.P. (Supplementary Mss. Vol. I) entitled "The Importance of Canada. Humbly Inscribed to the Right Hon. Lord George Germain." This document emphasizes the absolutely critical position of Canada in the whole British empire in America. "The ridiculous present situation of Canada is a matter of amusement to all who have the least conception of its importance. It's worth twenty Bostons.... The whole can be retaken in the spring by an army and fleet up the River St. Lawrence, the only way to conquer this country with ease." The author of this memorandum then went on to advocate the invasion of the territory of the rebellious provinces, after Canada had been taken, one column entering New York by way of Oswego, another by way of Lake Champlain, and a third should penetrate to the Connecticut River and so on to New England. "If this is done, which it may easily and ought, what would be the situation of the enemy, but begging peace. England then has the whole northern government from New York at her mercy." What more effective support could be offered for Howe's campaign against New York?

[44] Germain to Howe, 1 February 1776, M.D.S.

[45] This was the fact. Clinton had sailed for the rendezvous off Cape Fear on 20 January. Howe to Germain, 22 January 1776, *Parl. Reg.*, X, 295–96.

[46] Shortly after this (Germain to Clinton, 25 April 1776, M.D.S.), Germain issued a dormant commission to Clinton to succeed Howe, in the case of the latter's death or incapacity. It was, of course, not to be made public until the eventuality it looked toward should have occurred.

[47] Germain to Suffolk, 16 or 17 June 1775, S.S.Mss., II, 2–3.

[48] *Parl. Hist.*, XVIII, 1180.

[49] *Ibid.*, XVIII, 1180. Germain in an earlier debate had referred, rather ironically, to the greater supposed propriety in sending native rather than foreign troops to fight in America, *ibid.*, XVIII, 1139.

[50] *Parl. Hist.*, XVIII, 1188, 1227.

[51] *Ibid.*, XVIII, 1156–85. Copies of the treaties are given 1156–67.

[52] Germain to Carleton, 17 February 1776, in *Report on Canadian Archives for 1885* (Ottawa, 1886), p. 234. In a calendar of the Haldi-

mand Collection, partly covered in this volume, the section devoted to the correspondence of the ministers with Generals Amherst, Gage, and Carleton, 1760–88, notices only two previous letters to Carleton, i.e., of 10 November and 23 December 1775. The former announced Germain's appointment as secretary of state and the latter merely enclosed a copy of a parliamentary act—the Prohibitory Act.

[53] Germain to Howe, 28 March 1776, G.P.

[54] Germain's original commitment (5 January) was for a reinforcement of 14,400. See p. 55.

[55] Germain's original commitment (5 January) had been for 10,000 foreign troops for Carleton. See p. 56. Actual figures for forces in Canada at the beginning of the campaign were: British 8,147; foreign 2,964; total 11,111. To these during the campaign were added 2,298 foreign troops, making a total of 13,409. "State of the Army in Canada at the Beginning and End of the Campaign of 1776." G.P. (Supplementary Mss., Vol. I).

Germain's dispatch of 3 May to Howe (*Parl. Reg.*, X, 332–35) gives details of sailing dates of both Howe's reinforcement and Carleton's. The former would sail during the first week in May (partly); the latter had sailed on 7 and 8 April. The former arrived during July and early August (*Parl. Reg.*, X, 335–39); the latter on 6 May.

[56] Germain to Howe, 28 March 1776, G.P. Even Dartmouth had consented to the use of Indians. In a letter to Gage, 2 August 1775 (Dartmouth Mss., p. 345), he wrote: "The steps which you say the rebels have taken for calling in the assistance of the Indians leave no room to hesitate upon the propriety of your pursuing the same measures."

[57] Germain to Tonyn, 23 December 1775, G.P.

[58] He later congratulated Tonyn on his handling of the Indians during a recent conference, when the Creeks had been persuaded to help in any operations proposed against the rebels in neighboring provinces. Germain to Tonyn, 14 June 1776, G.P.

[59] Germain to Burgoyne, 28 March 1776, G.P.

[60] See J. A. James, ed., *George Rogers Clark's Papers 1771–1781* (Springfield, 1912), pp. viii, xxxv et seq. Also for the use of Indians under Haldimand after Spain's entry into war, *ibid.*, pp. viii, cxxv et seq.

[61] John D. Barnhart, "A New Evaluation of Henry Hamilton and George Rogers Clark," *Mississippi Valley Historical Review*, XXXVII (1950–51), 650. See also John C. Barnhart (ed.), *Henry Hamilton and George Rogers Clark in the American Revolution with the Unpublished Journal of Lieut. Gov. Henry Hamilton* (Crawfordsville, Ind., 1951), *passim*.

[62] Hamilton to Dartmouth, 2 September 1776, G.P.

[63] Carleton to Hamilton, 19 July 1776. Calendared in *Report on Canadian Archives for 1885*, p. 282, and summarized in Hamilton's letter to Dartmouth.

[64] Germain to Carleton, 26 March 1777, in *Report of the Pioneer Society of the State of Michigan, Together with Reports of the County Pioneer Societies* (2d ed.; Lansing, 1908), IX, 346–48. The letter is also in the G.P.

[65] Germain to Carleton, 26 March 1777, G.P. There are two letters from Germain to Carleton of 26 March. The one cited here on the use of Indians and another (see note 88, Ch. 6) in which Germain criticized Carleton for withdrawing from Crown Point in November 1776. Carleton answered both letters on 20 May 1777 (Carleton to Germain 20 May 1777, C.O. 42, Vol. 36, No. 19). This is a long and bitterly ironic letter defending his conduct of military operations in 1776 (see note 40, Ch. 7). In a single paragraph he refers to Germain's letter on the use of Indians as follows: "Your Lordship's letter No. 14 contains orders for Captain Hamilton, Lt. Gov. of Detroit, in consequence of his correspondence directly with your office. These likewise have been forwarded." There is not a word of criticism of the orders to Hamilton in a letter which was one long wail of complaint.

A few months before Hamilton's expedition against Vincennes, which culminated in his capture by George Rogers Clark and subsequent imprisonment, Hamilton had met Daniel Boone at Detroit. Boone was at that time the captive of the Shawnees. Hamilton offered the Shawnees the enormous sum of £100 for the release of Boone but was refused. See Howard Peckham, *Captured by Indians* (New Brunswick, N.J., 1954), 108–9. For Hamilton's own account, see "Report by Lieutenant Governor Henry Hamilton on his Proceedings from November 1776, to June 1781," *S.S.Mss.*, II, 223–48.

[66] *Parl. Hist.*, XIX, 700–701.

[67] *Ibid.*, XIX, 699.

CHAPTER 5

[1] Germain to Howe, 28 March 1776, G.P. In subsequent references Howe will be used to indicate General Sir William Howe and Lord Howe will indicate his brother, the Admiral.

[2] Anderson, *The Command of the Howe Brothers*, Ch. IX (*passim*), has an admirable account of the work of the Howes as commissioners. The conflict preceding the drawing up of the instructions to the Howes, however, is given only brief treatment.

[3] This aspect of the commission has been treated in Chapter 2 of this work.

[4] *Parl. Hist.*, XVIII, 695–97.

[5] Eden to Germain, 1775. Probably 21 October, *S.S.Mss.*, II, 11.

[6] *Parl. Hist.*, XVIII, 990–91.

[7] *Ibid.*, XVIII, 993.

[8] *Ibid.*, XVIII, 1029–30.

⁹ There is a memorandum in Knox's hand in the Knox Papers in the W. L. Clements Library entitled: "Account of the First Peace Commission of 1776 (2 March 1776)." A précis with a few quotations from this memorandum is reprinted in *Various Collections*, VI, 258–60. The précis leaves some points obscure and does not reflect as emphatically as the original does the contest of views and wills which came to the fore during the drawing up of the commission.

¹⁰ Germain to Eden, 18 February 1776, Stevens, *Facsimilies*, No. 465. Knox was suggested as a secretary for the commission, but he turned this post down.

¹¹ Knox Papers, "Memorandum on the Peace Commission of 1776."

¹² Knox Papers. A document in Knox's hand entitled "Ideas of What Might Facilitate an Accommodation under the Intended Commission." The document contains this statement of principle: "The difficulty to be apprehended in the outset of a treaty with the colonies is the jealousy they entertain that nothing more is intended than to divide them and as their division ought to be one great object of the treaty, it is necessary to open it by a step which will remove all ground of such jealousy, but at the same time hold forth inducements for their entering into separate treaties." This document is calendared in *S.S.Mss.*, II, 221, and in *Various Collections*, VI, 260.

¹³ Knox Papers, "Memorandum on Peace Commission."

¹⁴ Suffolk to Germain, 7 March 1776, *S.S.Mss.*, II, 23–24.

¹⁵ Wedderburn to Germain, 7 (?) March 1776, *ibid.*, II, 24–25.

¹⁶ Knox Papers, "Memorandum on Peace Commission."

¹⁷ Lord Howe to Germain, 26 March 1776, *S.S.Mss.*, II, 25–26.

¹⁸ Lord Howe to Germain, 1 April 1776, *ibid.*, II, 26–27. The explanations were made before 1 April, but are referred to in this letter.

¹⁹ Lord Howe to Germain, 1 April 1776, *ibid.*, II, 25–26.

²⁰ Wedderburn to Germain, 2 April 1776, G.P.

²¹ Germain to Lord Howe, 2 April 1776, *S.S.Mss.*, II, 28.

²² A common enough usage in the eighteenth century and not charged with the unpleasant connotation it would bear today. But it was then a cold and formal usage.

²³ Lord Howe to Germain, 3 April 1776, *S.S.Mss.*, II, 28. He referred to having received Germain's letter of 2 April "last night."

²⁴ Wedderburn to Germain, 24 April 1776, *ibid.*, II, 28–30. This is the only source from which we can collect the opinions of the taciturn Lord Howe. It is a long letter and Wedderburn canvasses the whole position of Lord Howe and the problem which he presented to the government.

²⁵ Wedderburn to Germain, 24 April 1776, *ibid.*, II, 28–30.

²⁶ Same to same, 24 April 1776, *ibid.*, II, 28–30.

²⁷ Germain to Howe, 27 April 1776, M.D.S.

²⁸ There are copies of both in the Knox Papers. There is an excellent

précis of the commission in a volume of photostats in the W. L. Clements Library, entitled Library of Congress Photostats, "Précis of Correspondence with General Howe."

[29] Lord Howe to Germain, 11 August 1776, G.P.

[30] Howe to Germain, 25 April 1776, *Parl. Reg.*, X, 311.

[31] Same to same, 7 July 1776, *ibid.*, X, 329.

[32] Howe to Dartmouth, 21 March 1776, *ibid.*, X, 298–302. It is interesting to note that Howe had had no word from the Home Government since 22 October 1775.

[33] Howe to Germain, 25 April 1776, *Parl. Reg.*, X, 310–13. He had received his first letters from England since 22 October in Nantucket Road on 26 March. This was the first news he had had of the appointment of Germain as American secretary.

[34] Howe to Germain, 26 April 1776, *S.S.Mss.*, II, 30–31.

[35] Germain to Howe, 3 May 1776, *Parl. Reg.*, X, 332–35.

[36] Same to same, 5 January 1776, *ibid.*, X, 307–10. This dispatch has already been considered in a different connection. See above, p. 59 *et seq.*

[37] Howe to Germain, 7 May 1776, *ibid.*, X, 313–17.

[38] Germain to Howe, 11 June 1776, *ibid.*, X, 337–38.

[39] Possibly in compliance with the suggestions of Dartmouth in his letter to Gage of 2 August, *ibid.*, X, 253–55. This has been noted above, pp. 48 *et seq.*

[40] Howe to Germain, 7 June 1776, *S.S.Mss.*, II, 33–36.

[41] Same to same, 12 May 1776, *ibid.*, II, 31–32.

[42] "...we have seen so much of a defensive situation that we must avoid another of the same nature, and hope by the offensive to see the northern and southern armies united upon the Hudson's River this campaign, if the Canadians are hearty." Howe to Germain, 12 May 1776, *ibid.*, II, 31–32.

[43] Howe to Germain, 7 June 1776, *ibid.*, II, 33–36.

[44] Germain to Carleton, 22 August 1776, G.P. This letter, noticed later, did not reach Canada. The ship carrying it was forced back to England.

[45] Germain to Howe, 22 August 1776, *Parl. Reg.*, X, 352.

[46] Howe to Germain, 8 June 1776, *ibid.*, X, 328–29.

[47] Same to same, 8 June 1776, *ibid.*, X, 328–29.

[48] Burgoyne to Germain, 1 June 1776, *S.S.Mss.*, II, 33.

[49] A. L. Burt, "The Quarrel Between Germain and Carleton—An Inverted Story," *Canadian Historical Review*, XI (1930), 221. This article, for the first time, directs attention to Carleton's conduct at the beginning of the campaign of 1776 rather than his conduct at the end of the campaign—the refusal to attack Ticonderoga—as being the determining factor in the failure of the northern army to achieve any large objectives in 1776. Subsequently the *Canadian Historical Review* is cited as *C.H.R.*

[50] A. T. Mahan, *The Major Operations of the Navies in the War of American Independence* (Boston, 1913), p. 25. Mahan also remarked: "The little American navy was wiped out; but never had any force, big or small, lived to better purpose or died more gloriously, for it saved the Lake for that year."

[51] A. L. Burt in *C.H.R.*, XI, 212.

CHAPTER 6

[1] "Even of those great conflicts in which hundreds of thousands have been engaged, and tens of thousands have fallen, none has been more fruitful of results than this surrender of 3,500 fighting men at Saratoga. It has not merely changed the relation of England and the feelings of Europe toward those insurgent colonies, but it has modified for all time to come, the connection between every colony and every parent state." Lord Mahon, *History of England, 1713–1783* (Boston, 1853), VI, 190.

[2] *Parl. Hist.*, XX, 818.

[3] Indispensable to a study of the campaign of 1777 is the contemporary material. The chief sources, exclusive of the documents subsequently published or those now available in manuscript form, are the following: *Parl. Reg.*, X, 253–480. This volume contains the papers upon which the Howe Inquiry was based. It includes the greater part of the official correspondence of Dartmouth, Gage, Germain, Howe, and Burgoyne relating to the war in America from August 1775 to October 1777. *Ibid.*, XII, *passim*. The whole of this volume is given over to a record of the debates in committee on "the several papers which were presented to the House by Mr. De Grey," that is to say the Howe Inquiry. It also includes the cross-examination of witnesses. *Parl. Hist.*, XX, 678–818. This source has the debates, but not the cross-examination. It is not as satisfactory as the *Parl. Reg. The Narrative of Sir William Howe . . . Relative to His Conduct During His Late Command of the King's Troops in North America to Which Are Added Some Observations upon a Pamphlet Entitled Letters to a Nobleman* (2d ed.; London, 1781). This is Howe's own defense. Subsequently cited as Howe, *Narrative. A State of the Expedition from Canada as Laid before the House of Commons by Lt. Gen. Burgoyne with a Collection of Authentic Documents* (2d ed.; London, 1780). Subsequently cited as Burgoyne, *State of the Expedition.* This, beside being the official Burgoyne version of the campaign, reproduces some valuable documents not easily available elsewhere. There is a good deal of pamphlet material, signed and anonymous. Joseph Galloway and Israel Mauduit stand out by virtue of the virulence of their attack upon the Howes. See Robert J. Taylor, "Israel Mauduit," *New England Quarterly*, XXIV (June, 1951), 208–30. W. C. Ford, "Parliament and the Howes," *Proceedings of the Massachusetts Historical Society*, XLIV, 120–43, is the best guide to the mass of controversial material

relating to the Howe Inquiry. C. F. Adams, "Contemporary Opinion of the Howes," *ibid.*, XLIV, 94–120, is made up largely from the collection of pamphlets preserved by Israel Mauduit. The most recent and the best study of the Howes is Troyer Anderson's *The Command of the Howe Brothers.*

⁴ Claude Van Tyne, *The War of Independence: American Phase* (Boston and New York, 1929), p. 383.

⁵ Carleton to Gage, 15 February 1767, in A. Shortt and A. G. Doughty, eds., *Documents Relating to the Constitutional History of Canada, 1759–1791* (Ottawa, 1918), I, 280.

⁶ Dartmouth to Gage, 15 April 1775, Gage Papers, English Series, Vol. XXVIII, in W. L. Clements Library, Ann Arbor, Michigan.

⁷ Canadian Archives, Q Series, XI, 263–64.

⁸ "Précis of Measures and Orders Respecting Quebec." Letter of 28 March 1776 to Carleton. G.P.

⁹ See Ch. 5.

¹⁰ Germain to Carleton, 22 August 1776, G.P.

¹¹ "Précis of Orders Respecting Quebec." G.P. Supplementary Mss., Vol. I.

¹² Pownall to Knox, 2 December 1776, *Various Collections*, VI, 127.

¹³ King to North, 2 July 1777, Fortescue, *Correspondence*, III, No. 2024.

¹⁴ See A. L. Burt, "The Quarrel Between Carleton and Germain," *C.H.R.*, XI (1930), 204–8. This aspect of the problem relating to the administration of Quebec under Carleton is fully treated in this article. See also A. L. Burt, *The Old Province of Quebec* (Minneapolis, 1933), *passim.*

¹⁵ See A. L. Burt in *C.H.R.*, XI (1930), 203–4.

¹⁶ Germain to Burgoyne, 23 August 1776, *S.S.Mss.*, II, 39–40. Later on (Germain to Howe, 18 October 1776, *ibid.*, II, 42–43), Germain told Howe that he had opposed giving Carleton the Red Ribbon before he had any claim to it by his operations in Canada. He felt especially strongly in this matter, he asserted, because the King had also given Howe the same mark of distinction for services (1776) far more valuable than those of Carleton. He had only agreed to this arrangement when the King pointed out that Howe's honor was greater because he had been granted the order "unasked." The King also undertook that this would not stand in the way of further honors for Howe. Howe replied (Howe to Germain, 31 December 1776, *ibid.*, II, 53–55) that he wished that he had been able to refuse the Red Ribbon "without ostentation." Burgoyne also objected to the Red Ribbon (Derby to Germain, 31 August 1777, *ibid.*, II, 75). All this objection occurred after the granting of the Ribbon to Carleton, as though there were something in the circumstances surrounding that grant which made it of little value.

¹⁷ Germain to Howe, 22 August 1776, *Parl. Reg.*, X, 352.

[18] Much controversy has centered around this point: should Carleton have made an attempt on Ticonderoga in the fall of 1776? For a severe criticism of Carleton by a biased contemporary see Christie to Germain, 26 October 1776, *S.S.Mss.*, II, 44–46. For the view of a fair-minded soldier who was with Carleton and who believed that the failure to make an attempt on Ticonderoga was justified only on the condition that Crown Point was to be held, see Major General Phillips to Burgoyne, 23 October 1776, in E. B. De Fonblanque, *Political and Military Episodes Derived from the Life and Correspondence of the Rt. Hon. John Burgoyne* (London, 1876), pp. 218–21.

[19] Howe to Germain, 30 November 1776, *S.S.Mss.*, II, 49–51.

[20] "Memorandum of General Carleton relative to the next campaign communicated to Lieut. General Burgoyne, to be laid before government." *Ibid.*, II, 222.

[21] Howe to Germain, 30 November 1776, *ibid.*, II, 49–51; Howe, *Narrative*, p. 10.

[22] Dundas, speaking later in the Commons, made this distinction. He said "the plan was a wise one; that it was attended to in the execution with assiduity and ability; that it was a plan of cooperation, not a junction of the bodies of the armies...," *Parl. Reg.*, VIII, 166.

[23] W. B. Donne, *The Correspondence of King George III with Lord North, 1768–1783* (London, 1867), II, 45. Subsequently cited as Donne, *Correspondence.*

[24] Burgoyne to Clinton, 7 November 1776, Clinton Papers.

[25] Underlining is in the original, as if to raise an ironic query.

[26] He said Carleton ought to have ignored "the drawings and technical reasonings of dull, formal, methodical, fat engineers." Burgoyne to Clinton, 7 November 1776, Clinton Papers.

[27] Burgoyne to Clinton, 7 November 1776, *ibid.* Later Burgoyne spoke of Carleton as treating him like a brother. See Burgoyne, *State of the Expedition*, p. 10.

[28] Burgoyne to Germain, 3 March 1776, *S.S.Mss.*, II, 23. Burgoyne had asked for a few days' postponement of his embarkation due to the ill health of his wife. Germain to Burgoyne, 23 August 1776, *ibid.*, II, 39–40. Germain conveyed his sympathies on the death of Lady Charlotte.

[29] Burgoyne to Clinton, 7 November 1776, Clinton Papers. Burgoyne said he expected he would see Clinton in England shortly, as he knew the latter did not intend to spend successive winters in America. He cautioned Clinton to keep his criticisms of Carleton "in your own breast."

[30] "Carleton's Evidence before the House." An undated document in the G.P. It is included at the end of the volume for 1778; Carleton's evidence was in May, 1779, *Parl. Reg.*, XII, 145–54.

[31] Shelburne Papers, LXVI, 149, in W. L. Clements Library, Ann Arbor, Michigan.

[32] Carleton's "Evidence before the House," G.P.

[33] Germain to King, 10 December 1776, Fortescue, *Correspondence*, III, No. 1936.

[34] Fonblanque, *Burgoyne*, p. 225.

[35] Donne, *Correspondence*, II, 45; Fonblanque, *Burgoyne*, p. 227.

[36] Germain to King, 10 December 1776, Fortescue, *Correspondence*, III, No. 1936.

[37] Fonblanque, *Burgoyne*, p. 227.

[38] "Memorandum of General Carleton Relative to the Next Campaign, Communicated to Lieut. General Burgoyne, to be Laid Before the Government." *S.S.Mss.*, II, 222.

[39] See p. 86 *et seq.*

[40] King to North, 13 December 1776, Fortescue, *Correspondence*, III, No. 1938.

[41] *Ibid.*

[42] See Jane Clark, "The Command of the Canadian Army in 1777," *C.H.R.*, X (1929), 130.

[43] *Ibid.*

[44] Donne, *Correspondence*, II, 76. "On his [Germain's] trial after the battle of Minden, Haldimand had been a witness for and Carleton against Lord George."

[45] See L. B. Namier, *The Structure of Politics at the Accession of George III* (2 vols., London, 1929), *passim*; and *England in the Age of the American Revolution* (London, 1930), *passim*. See also review of further literature on this matter. See Chapter 3, note 2.

[46] *C.H.R.*, XI (1930), 202.

[47] See p. 84 *et seq.*

[48] King to North, 13 December 1776, Fortescue, *Correspondence*, III, No. 1938. The King spoke of the "general's application for 4,000 men." Donne, *Correspondence*, II, 45, misread this passage. He attributed the "application" to Howe, who was asking for 15,000 rather than 4,000.

[49] "Memorandum and Observations relative to the Service in Canada submitted to Lord George Germain." Shelburne Papers, LXVI, 149. There are two columns in this document. One is headed "General Carleton's Requisition" and the other "Observations."

[50] Burgoyne, *State of the Expedition*, Appendix, pp. 1–3.

[51] Burgoyne to Germain, 1 January 1777, G.P.

[52] *Parl. Hist.*, XIX, 1187. Much later, May 1778, Burgoyne taxed Germain in the House with having included this private letter among papers submitted to the House. It tended, he said, to create the impression that he was trying to supplant his good friend Carleton in the Canadian command, when it had already been determined that Carleton should not have that command. Germain replied that it had accidentally been placed by clerks among the papers presented to the House and that he was sorry. *Ibid.*, 1195. Again in May 1779, during the Howe Inquiry, Burgoyne returned again to the effect that the letter had had upon public opinion.

He said that he accepted Germain's explanation, but that "it is a notorious fact . . . that it has been held a reflection upon my character (by the part of the public with whom the noble lord is unpopular) that I addressed him as a patron and a friend." *Ibid.*, XX, 781.

53 *Ibid.*, XX, 782. This comes from a speech of Burgoyne's, 20 May 1779. Carleton was rather vague on the extent of his authority in the military sphere. As commander in chief he believed his authority extended to Ticonderoga, but in consequence of the orders Burgoyne took out in the spring of 1777 he was confined to the province of Quebec. See Carleton's "Evidence Before the House." G.P.

54 *Parl. Hist.*, XX, 684.

55 Howe to Germain, 20 December 1776, S.S.Mss., II, 52–53.

56 Same to same, 30 November 1776, *ibid.*, II, 49–51.

57 Howe had stated this in Howe to Germain, 30 November 1776, *ibid.*, II, 49–51.

58 Howe to Germain, 20 December 1776, *ibid.*, II, 52–53.

59 "Germain's Own Account of Plans for Campaign of 1777" (1778). G.P. The letter before the House is in S.S.Mss., II, 66–67. This letter approved the move against Philadelphia, provided it was executed "in time for you to cooperate with the army ordered to proceed from Canada and put itself under your command." This letter is noted in a wider context in Chapter 7, pp. 112 *et seq.*

60 *Studies Military and Diplomatic, 1775–1865* (New York, 1911), p. 148.

61 Germain to Howe, 14 January 1777, S.S.Mss., II, 56–57.

62 *Parl. Hist.*, XX, 684; Howe, *Narrative*, p. 11.

63 *Parl. Hist.*, XX, 804.

64 Howe to Germain, 20 January 1777, *Parl. Reg.*, X, 377–78.

65 Germain to Howe, 3 March 1777, S.S.Mss., II, 58–59; Howe, *Narrative*, p. 12.

66 Howe to Germain, 31 December 1776, S.S.Mss., II, 53–55.

67 Germain to King, 24 February 1777, Fortescue, *Correspondence*, III, No. 1963.

68 King to North, 24 February 1777, *ibid.*, No. 1964.

69 This document may be found in printed form in a variety of places. It may be conveniently consulted in H. Nickerson, *The Turning Point of the Revolution* (New York, 1928), pp. 89 *et seq.* Fonblanque, *Burgoyne*, p. 483, contains only extracts. There is a copy of Burgoyne's "Thoughts" in G.P.

70 Fonblanque, *Burgoyne*, p. 229; Germain to King, 18 March 1777, and Sandwich to King, 18 March 1777, Fortescue, *Correspondence*, III, Nos. 1970, 1971.

71 This must mean in Burgoyne's addition to the original Carleton memorandum, for that document did not mention artillery.

72 Fortescue, *Correspondence*, III, Nos. 1996, 1997. Both of these are

dated 5 March 1777. The second document here is really "remarks" upon Burgoyne's earlier "Memorandum and Observations."

[73] For instance, the first document mentioned above begins: "In general, I conceive, that the outlines are founded on a proper foundation." The King's "Remarks" begin: "The outlines of the plan seem to be on a proper foundation." The King then went on to give precisely the same allocation of forces by regiment and by number. Other details correspond.

[74] G. H. Guttridge, "Germain in Office 1775–1782," A.H.R., XXXIII, 29, states: "... in the hands of the King and his ministers significant alterations in Burgoyne's 'Thoughts' were made, and the probability is that these alterations were due originally to the King."

Jane Clark, "Responsibility for the Failure of the Burgoyne Campaign," A.H.R., XXXV, 543, is of the opinion that Germain "possibly" made the suggestion with respect to one item, implying that he was the author of the document, i.e., "Remarks on the Conduct of the War—from Canada." No detailed analysis was made by either Guttridge or Clark because the focus of their attention was elsewhere.

[75] On 26 March 1777, the date on which the final plan for 1777 in Canada took form, Germain wrote separate letters to both Carleton and Burgoyne on the subject of Indians which would "put them out of doubt" on the propriety of using Indians. G.P. See pp. 61, 104, and below note 97.

[76] *The War of Independence*, pp. 381–382.

[77] "Observations on the War in America. To Lord George Germain. 1776." G.P. (Supplementary Mss., Vol. I). There is an even earlier document in G.P., Jonathan Boucher to Germain (?), 27 November 1775, in which the suggestion is plainly made that the colonies ought to be cut in two by a campaign up the Hudson to Canada.

[78] "Germain's Own Account of Plans for Campaign of 1777" (1778). G.P.

[79] King to North, 24 February 1777, Fortescue, *Correspondence*, III, No. 1964.

[80] Howe to Germain, 2 December 1776; same to same, 31 December 1776, S.S.Mss., II, 51, 53–55.

[81] Germain to Knox, 31 December 1776, *Various Collections*, VI, 128.

[82] Germain to Howe, 1 February 1776, M.D.S.

[83] Jane Clark, "The Command of the Canadian Army in 1777," C.H.R., X, 133.

[84] Thomas Jones, *History of New York During the Revolutionary War* (New York, 1879), I, 131–32. Jones was a justice of the Supreme Court of the Province of New York. He removed to England in 1781 and died there in 1792. The book was written between 1783 and 1788. The manuscript was not published until 1879. It is a Loyalist history and is bitter about the conduct of many of the British leaders in the Revolution. W. B. Willcox has edited with an introduction Sir Henry Clinton's own nar-

rative of his campaigns, 1775–82, under the title *The American Rebellion* (New Haven, 1954). Toward the end of his introduction, Willcox introduces the theme that Clinton's failures "come from a cause that he would have died rather than admit. His nemesis was himself." P. li. In collaboration with a psychotherapist Frederick Wyatt, Willcox developed this theme further in: "Sir Henry Clinton: A Psychological Exploration in History," *William and Mary Quarterly*, Third Series, XVI (January 1959), 3–26. In a paper read at a session of the American Historical Association meeting in New York (29 December 1960), dealing with the subject "Sir Henry Clinton and the Problem of Unconscious Motivation," Willcox showed that after Yorktown, in an effort to justify his own inactivity, he fabricated an order from Germain forbidding him to detach troops from Virginia, inserted the order in a dispatch from Germain, and in his memoirs maintained that the supposed Germain order had brought on the catastrophe.

[85] Jane Clark, in *C.H.R.*, X, 134. Clinton refused this post out of respect for Carleton. It must be kept in mind that what Clinton refused was not the command of the northern army, which had gone to Burgoyne, but Carleton's virtual "garrison duty" command at Quebec, which was all that was left to him after Germain's orders of 22 August 1776. These orders, however, did not reach Carleton until 6 May 1777.

My colleague Professor Willcox, who is engaged in writing a biography of Clinton, has discovered a letter (Clinton to Drummond, 23 December 1777, filed under date of 26 January 1778), in which Clinton, speaking of the offer made him of Carleton's post, declared that it was not "the government of Canada but the command in chief there." The statement is clear, but I must believe that Clinton misunderstood. If Clinton's statement is to be credited, it means that Carleton's original command of 1776 had now been divided into three: Burgoyne's, Clinton's, and Carleton's. Even if, following an old prejudice, it might be contended that Germain was capable of this lunacy and malice (and I do not for a moment so contend), it is, I think, beyond the bounds of sound historical judgment to conclude that the King and North would have concurred in such a decision.

[86] Clinton-Germain conversation 7 April 1777; undated memorandum and journal of events, both filed at end of 1777. Clinton Papers. Further reference is made to this conversation in the next chapter.

[87] Germain to Howe, 19 April 1777, M.D.S.

[88] Fonblanque, *Burgoyne*, p. 496.

[89] Shelburne gave currency to many of these stories. One of the least pleasant of these related to Germain's youth and Shelburne told it in this manner. "This shrewd old man Mr. Carter observed Lord George Sackville's [Germain's] countenance and manner dining at a side-table in his own house with some persons of his own age—Mr. Carter's table being full—when a slight dispute occured; and saw enough into his character

to make him advise the Duke of Dorset when he returned to Ireland, whatever he did with his son, never to put him in the army." Fitzmaurice, *Shelburne*, I, 239. Another Shelburne story: "He commanded a regiment in Flanders and in Scotland. I have heard the officers of the regiment affirm that he was frequently found in Scotland listening at the officers' tents to hear what was said of him." *Ibid.*, I, 239.

[90] Germain to Carleton, 26 March 1777, S.S.Mss., II, 61–63.

[91] Germain to Carleton, 22 August 1776, G.P. See p. 82.

[92] See Ch. 5.

[93] A. L. Burt in *C.H.R.*, XI, 212.

[94] Germain to King, 16 October 1779, G.P. The further details of the quarrel between Germain and Carleton are given in the following chapter.

[95] Knox Papers. This letter was not published by the Historical Manuscripts Commission.

[96] Fitzmaurice, *Shelburne*, I, 247–48. For substantiating evidence see next chapter, p. 116.

[97] These familiar categories in Germain's thought relating to the use of Indians and precise disposition of troops have been referred to (p. 99) in an attempt to establish Germain's authorship of "Remarks on the Conduct of the War" and "Remarks on the Requisitions." See also Germain to Carleton, 26 March 1777, and Germain to Burgoyne, 26 March 1777, G.P., for instructions on the use of Indians. See p. 64.

CHAPTER 7

[1] Burgoyne, *State of the Expedition*, p. 9. Germain complained of Burgoyne's tardiness in setting out for America in 1777: "I didn't know that two winds were necessary at Plymouth before they could put to sea." Germain to Knox, 2 April 1777, *Various Collections*, VI, 129.

[2] *Parl. Hist.*, XX, 787.

[3] *Ibid.*, XX, 694–96.

[4] Howe to Germain, 2 April 1777, S.S.Mss., II, 63–65.

[5] Howe to Carleton, 5 April 1777, *ibid.*, II, 65–66.

[6] There is an interesting comment in "Abstract of Précis 1777–1778," G.P. (Supplementary Mss., Vol. II), on Howe's letter of 2 April. "He proposed with a reinforcement of 15,000 men [30 November] to have had 12,000 at Rhode Island, 15,000 at New York—10,000 of which to go up the Hudson River and 8,000 to cover Jersey and alarm Philadelphia. He is told his reinforcement will be only 4,800 which is 10,200 less than his expectation. He then gives up 10,000 at Rhode Island, which leaves his force for other operations exactly what it would have been had he received the whole 15,000."

[7] Howe to Carleton, 5 April 1777, S.S.Mss., II, 65–66.

[8] Howe to Germain, 2 April 1777, *ibid.*, II, 65.

[9] Howe to Germain, 22 October 1777, *ibid.*, II, 79–81.

[10] "Carleton's Evidence Before the House," G.P. Dated 1778.

[11] See p. 113.

[12] Germain to Carleton, 26 March 1777, S.S.Mss., II, 60–63. See Ch. 6, p. 104 *et seq.*

[13] Fonblanque, *Burgoyne*, pp. 232–33. If Fonblanque, an employee at the War Office, had ever seen this document, it is a pity he did not publish it; the document is unknown today.

[14] *Parl. Hist.*, XX, 796.

[15] Fitzmaurice, *Shelburne*, I, 247–48.

[16] G. O. Trevelyan, *The American Revolution* (New York, 1917–20), IV, 216. Trevelyan further remarked: "...Lord Shelburne, when jotting down reminiscences in the seclusion of his study was no safe authority for anecdotes reflecting upon the public men of his own time."

[17] *Various Collections*, VI, 277. George Bernard Shaw utilized this story about Germain in his play, *The Devil's Disciple* (1897); Ayot St. *Lawrence Edition of the Collected Works of Bernard Shaw* (New York, 1930), IX, 3–86. Shaw discusses in his notes to this play (p. 86) Fonblanque and Shelburne as sources for the story. He indulges in dramatic license by contriving to have Burgoyne discover the facts of the "pigeon-holed dispatch" before the battle of Saratoga. F. J. Huddleston, in a flippant book, *Gentleman Johnny Burgoyne*, published as late as the 1920's (New York, 1927), plays the story very broadly: "...so my Lord George Germain, who ruined the chances of a magnificent British victory at Minden by *not* being in a hurry to advance against the enemy, also ruined any prospect Burgoyne might have had of being successful, by *being* in a hurry to spend a week-end in Sussex." P. 118. Huddleston, like Fonblanque, was an employee at the War Office.

[18] There is a short sketch of D'Oyley in Spector, *American Department*, pp. 105–6.

[19] Israel Mauduit was the pamphleteer. See W. C. Ford, "Parliament and the Howes," *Proceedings of the Mass. Historical Society*, XLIV, 122–23. See also Taylor's article on Mauduit in *New England Quarterly*, XXIV, 208–30.

[20] Germain to Carleton, 26 March 1777, G.P.

[21] Howe to Germain, 3 June 1777, *Parl. Reg.*, X, 399.

[22] Same to same, 5 June 1777, G.P. This letter is summarized in S.S.Mss., II, 68, but this important section is omitted. The letter was received in England on 10 July. There was also a public letter from Howe to Germain of 5 June. *Parl. Reg.*, X, 400.

[23] Same to same, 5 July 1777, *ibid.*, X, 407.

[24] See W. B. Willcox, "Too Many Cooks: British Planning Before Saratoga," *The Journal of British Studies*, II (November, 1962), 65–67. Willcox says that "strong hints" were thrown out to Clinton that the northern command would be his for the asking, but that he would not ask. *Ibid.*, II, 58–59.

[25] *Ibid.*, II, 66–67.

[26] Germain to Howe, 18 May 1777, *S.S.Mss.*, II, 66–67.

[27] Willcox, *Journal of British Studies*, II, 67–76.

[28] *Ibid.*, II, 69.

[29] *Ibid.*, II, 74.

[30] Germain to Howe, 18 May 1777, *S.S.Mss.*, 66–67.

[31] Same to same, 3 March 1777, *ibid.*, II, 58–59.

[32] Howe to Germain, 3 June 1777, *ibid.*, II, 68. Germain immediately approved of Howe's decision: "When I say what I wished and what I imagined, I am persuaded that you upon the spot must be a better judge of what is right and practicable." Germain to Howe, 4 August 1777, G.P. But later Germain voiced some criticism on directions from the King. Same to same, 6 August 1777, *ibid.*

[33] Germain to Knox, 11 June 1777, *Various Collections*, VI, 30.

[34] Germain to Knox, 24 June 1777, *ibid.*, VI, 131.

[35] *Parl. Hist.*, XX, 743–44.

[36] Germain to Knox, 22 August 1777, *Various Collections*, VI, 136–37. In this letter Germain coupled a complaint against Howe's slowness with a mild protest against the slowness of the messengers in his office: "I wish the messengers for the future would take places in the stage coach when they are too fat to ride above five miles an hour."

[37] See Ch. 6, pp. 103 *et seq.*

[38] One of the letters of 22 August 1776 related to the reshuffling of civil offices in Quebec. The other related to Carleton's supersession in command of the northern army. For the problems of internal government in the province of Quebec, to which the first letter above refers, see *C.H.R.*, XI, 208 *et seq.*

[39] Germain to Knox, 1 July 1777, *Various Collections*, VI, 132. Germain clearly considered that Carleton's resentment of his letter of 26 March would arise from the particularity of the orders contained in that dispatch. He felt that Carleton would perceive that the plain implication of these orders was a censure upon his inactivity in 1776. The paragraph in the dispatch of 26 March which Germain had ordered deleted, traced a categorical connection between Carleton's withdrawal from Crown Point in November and the success of Washington at Trenton in December. Censure on the point of inactivity would indubitably have been collected from the "Trenton paragraph" rather than from the particular character of the orders. This passage appears further to substantiate the interpretation, earlier advanced, that Germain intended that the "Trenton paragraph" should have been omitted. See Chapter 6, pp. 103–4.

[40] North to King, 2 July 1777, Fortescue, *Correspondence*, III, No. 2023.

[41] King to North, 2 July 1777, *ibid.*, III, No. 2024.

[42] Carleton to Germain, 20 May 1777, C.O. 42, Vol. 36, No. 19.

[43] Same to same, 22 May 1777, quoted by Burt in *C.H.R.*, XI, 218.

[44] Same to same, 23 May 1777, summarized in *ibid.*, XI, 208.

[45] Germain to Knox, 24 June 1777, *Various Collections*, VI, 131.

[46] Carleton to Germain, 20 May 1777, *Canadian Archives Report for 1885*, pp. cxxxii–cxxxv.

[47] Lt. Col. Christie observed Carleton's conduct during the time when arrangements were being made to bring a naval force together and pursue the enemy across Lake Champlain. He said that everything was in complete chaos due to poor administration. Necessary supplies were scattered from Montreal to St. Johns, with no central control. No person knew where anything was. "Confusion and embarrassment appeared everywhere under a commander absorbed within himself, giving orders to few and saying little who follows a scheme or plan absolutely incomprehensible." Christie to Germain, 26 October 1776, *S.S.Mss.*, II, 44–46. Christie was prejudiced against Carleton, but this was the picture given to Germain.

[48] Quoted in Burt, *C.H.R.*, XI, 218.

[49] *Ibid.*, XI, 218.

[50] A third letter (Carleton to Germain, 23 May 1777) charged Germain with upsetting the civil government of Canada by interfering in the internal affairs of the province. This letter was very bitter in tone. Carleton declared that Germain's interference would "occasion no small exultation among the King's enemies." *C.H.R.*, XI, 208.

[51] Germain to King, G.P. Undated, but written at the time when Carleton was being considered as commander in chief in America (1782). It is possible that this letter might have been written in 1779 when Carleton was first considered for that post, and there is a letter of Germain's on that subject in 1779 (Germain to King, 16 October 1779, G.P.). But a reference in the former letter to "the most calamitous situation of your distracted and divided Empire" would seem to indicate 1782 as the date of this letter.

[52] The rough draft is undated. The letter, in fair copy in the Knox Papers, is endorsed "This was shewed to the King and approved by H.M." *Various Collections*, VI, 132–33. It is dated 10 July 1777. The copy in the Colonial Office Records is dated 25 July 1777. *Canadian Archives Report for 1885*, pp. cxxxvi–cxxxvii. Germain's answer to Carleton's charges with respect to the interference of Germain in the civil affairs of Quebec was a separate letter of 25 July. See *C.H.R.*, XI, 208 *et seq.* Germain recapitulated his side of the case in this affair in a letter to the King of 3 August (Germain to King, 3 August 1777, Fortescue, *Correspondence*, III, No. 2038).

[53] *Parl. Hist.* XIX, 1374–75.

[54] Germain to King, undated, probably 1782, G.P.

[55] Germain to King, 3 August 1777, Fortescue, *Correspondence*, III, No. 2038.

[56] Germain to Knox, 4 August 1777, Knox Papers.

[57] Burgoyne to Germain, 14 May 1777, *Parl. Reg.*, X, 470–72.

[58] *Parl. Hist.*, XX, 787.

[59] Germain's own "Account of Plans for Campaign of 1777," G.P.

[60] Germain to Knox, 2 August 1777, Knox Papers.

[61] Same to same, 8 August 1777, *Various Collections*, VI, 134–35.

[62] Same to same, 12 August 1777, *ibid.*, VI, 135. "I thank you for your invitation to the turtle, but as I do not care to be robb'd in returning hither at night I hope you will excuse my being of the party."

[63] Germain to Knox, 22 August 1777, *ibid.*, VI, 136–37. Howe's letter of 15 July, enclosing Burgoyne's of 2 July, arrived in London 22 August. *S.S.Mss.*, II, 72.

[64] Howe to Germain, 7 July 1777, *ibid.*, II, 70–71.

[65] "Abstract of Précis," G.P.

[66] Burgoyne to Howe, 2 July 1777, *S.S.Mss.*, II, 72.

[67] Howe to Burgoyne, 17 July 1777, Burgoyne, *State of Expedition, App.*, IX.

[68] Howe to Germain, 16 July 1777, *S.S.Mss.*, II, 72–73.

[69] See Jane Clark in *A.H.R.*, XXXV, 550 *et seq.* Miss Clark has based her account upon the reports of conversations between Clinton and Howe at New York, committed to writing by Clinton shortly after they took place. The originals are in the Clinton Papers. See also Willcox in *Journal of British Studies*, II, 67–76. I have already dealt with these conversations between Clinton and Howe, pp. 114 *et seq.*

[70] "Distribution of Troops Under the Command of Lt. Gen. Sir H. Clinton at N.Y. and Posts Depending"; "Abstract of Précis," G.P. A document in the G.P., "State of Sir William Howe's Army Campaign 1777," gives 15,942 as the number of troops Howe took with him. This must include those troops which Howe later ordered to join him from New York.

[71] Quoted in Jane Clark in *A.H.R.*, XXXV, 554.

[72] Howe to Germain, 2 April 1777, *S.S.Mss.*, II, 65.

[73] "Abstract of Précis," G.P.

[74] *Ibid.*

[75] *S.S.Mss.*, II, 67.

[76] Howe to Germain, 30 August 1777, *S.S.Mss.*, II, 74–75.

[77] Germain to Howe, 3 September 1777, M.D.S.

[78] Burgoyne to Germain, 14, 19 May, 11 July, 1777, *Parl. Reg.*, X, 470–75.

[79] Burgoyne to Germain, 11 July 1777, *ibid.*, X, 473–75.

[80] *Parl. Hist.*, XX, 786–87.

[81] Burgoyne to Germain, 20 August 1777, *Parl. Reg.*, X, 475–79.

[82] Burgoyne summarized Howe's letter of 17 July in his dispatch to Germain of 20 August, *ibid.*, X, 477.

[83] Burgoyne to Germain, 20 October 1777, *ibid.*, X, 479–80.

84 "Abstract of Précis 1777–1778," G.P.; Jane Clark in *A.H.R.*, XXXV, 556.

85 Clinton to Burgoyne, 8 October 1777, G.P.

86 "Copy of Sir Henry Clinton's Message by Capt. Campbell to Lt. Gen. Burgoyne in answer to a letter from the Lt. Gen.," G.P.

87 Burgoyne to Germain, 20 October 1777, *Parl. Reg.*, X, 479–80.

88 Burgoyne to Col. Phillipson, 20 October 1777, quoted in Fonblanque, *Burgoyne*, pp. 313–16.

89 Germain to King, 15 December 1777, Fortescue, *Correspondence*, III, No. 514.

90 Germain to Carleton, 26 March 1777, S.S.Mss., II, 60–63.

91 Burgoyne, *State of the Expedition*, p. 4; *Parl. Hist.*, XIX, 1189–90; *ibid.*, XX, 783.

92 "Germain's Own Account of Plans for Campaign of 1777 (1778)," G.P.

93 *Ibid.*

94 *Parl. Hist.*, XIX, 523–24. Lord North remarked to Fox after one of these strident attacks upon Germain: "Charles, I am glad you did not fall on me today for you was in full feather." Reginald Lucas, *Lord North* (London, 1913), II, 201–2.

95 *Parl. Hist.*, XIX, 525–29.

96 *Ibid.*, XIX, 531.

97 *Ibid.*, XIX, 533.

98 *Ibid.*, XIX, 533–34.

99 *Ibid.*, XIX, 537.

100 *Ibid.*, XIX, 540.

101 *The Eighteenth Century*, IV, 439. Lecky added: "More than any other man he gave the Whig party that cosmopolitan and un-national character which was one of the chief sources of its weakness, and which it only lost at the Reform Bill of 1832." G.M. Trevelyan in his *Earl Grey of the Reform Bill* (London, 1920) has a very effective Whiggish eulogy of Fox: "He had loved life too well to be a perfect statesman, but he brought human life and love with him into the political world and since he passed out of it, though it has been dignified by equal genius and higher virtue it has never again been made Shakespearian by such a kind, grand, human creature." P. 148.

102 *Parl. Hist.*, XIX, 534–35.

103 *Ibid.*, XIX, 538.

104 *Ibid.*, XIX, 539.

105 *Ibid.*, XIX, 540–41.

106 *Ibid.*, XIX, 541.

107 The relationship of the two was reported by Walpole: "Charles Fox on Wednesday told Lord George he hoped to see him brought to a second trial." Walpole to Countess of Upper Ossory, 5 December 1777, Walpole, *Letters*, X, 164.

[108] *Parl. Hist.*, XIX, 538.

[109] *The Diary and Letters of His Excellency, Thomas Hutchinson* (Boston, 1884–86), II, 210. Fonblanque, *Burgoyne*, says that there was a story current that Fox went down to meet Burgoyne on his arrival in England and intercepted him at Hounslow. In an interview Fox persuaded Burgoyne to join his party. Fonblanque does not contradict this, but points out that Burgoyne "had anticipated the course Lord G. Germain adopted and had determined not to allow himself to be made the victim of ministerial blunders. He continued, however, for some time after his return to avoid joining the opposition." P. 351, note 2. Fonblanque was the official biographer of Burgoyne. His work is very favorable to that general.

[110] *Parl. Hist.*, XX, 818. One of the puzzles surrounding the pamphlet warfare which preceded, accompanied, and outlasted the "Inquiry" was the lack of a pamphlet from Sir William Howe's brother, Lord Howe. This pamphlet, in manuscript, turned up among the Howe Mss. recently acquired by the W. L. Clements Library. It was edited with a critical introduction by myself, and published as *Reflections on a Pamphlet intitled "a Letter to the Right Honble Lord Vic^t H—E."* (Ann Arbor: University of Michigan Press, 1959).

"A Letter to Right Honble, etc.," was a pamphlet attacking Lord Howe written by Joseph Galloway. See Ch. 6, note 3.

[111] The renewed interest in Burke by our own generation, and yet the failure really to place him in terms of his times and the issues which inspired them is the subject of W. T. Laprade, "Edmund Burke: An Adventure in Reputation" in the *Journal of Modern History*, XXXII (December 1960), 321–32, but especially 327–32, where Laprade reviews chronologically the biographies of Burke from McCormick (1797) to Cone (1957).

[112] For a good example of this type of treatment see Alan Valentine, *Lord George Germain* (Oxford University Press, 1962), *passim*.

[113] Jane Clark in A.H.R., XXXV, 545.

CHAPTER 8

[1] Charles Francis Adams, *Works of John Adams* (1850–56), I, 271.

[2] In two letters of 22 October 1777; one is in *S.S.Mss.*, II, 79–80; the other in G.P.

[3] North to King, 2 July 1777, Fortescue, *Correspondence*, III, No. 2023.

[4] Donne, *Correspondence*, II, 76.

[5] Two days earlier Germain had written of his wife's dangerous condition which might prevent him from attending to any business. Germain to King, 13 January 1778, Fortescue, *Correspondence*, IV, No. 2162.

[6] Germain to Knox, 16 January 1778, *Various Collections*, VI, 141–42.

[7] Suffolk to Germain, 15 January 1778, *S.S.Mss.*, II, 90.

[8] Suffolk to Germain, 20 January 1778, *ibid.*, II, 91.

[9] Cumberland to Knox, 22 January 1778, G.P.

[10] Lord Milton to Germain, 17 January 1778, G.P.

[11] Germain to Knox, 25 January 1778, *Various Collections*, VI, 142.

[12] Germain to Howe, 11 December 1777, *S.S.Mss.*, II, 83–84.

[13] King to North, 9 January 1778; North to King, 10 January 1778, Fortescue, *Correspondence*, IV, Nos. 2152, 2154. Germain had given the King the impression that D'Oyley had said it would be unsafe and imprudent to keep Sir William and Lord Howe in their commands. D'Oyley, however, repudiated this and said he had meant only that it would be difficult to persuade the general and the admiral to retain their commands.

[14] North to King, 12 January 1778; King to North, 13 January, 1778, *ibid.*, IV, Nos. 2156, 2162.

[15] Germain to King, 13 January 1778, *ibid.*, IV, No. 2162.

[16] "Minute of a Cabinet," 17 January 1778, *ibid.*, IV, No. 2170.

[17] North to King, 18 January 1778, *ibid.*, IV, No. 2171.

[18] King to North, 13 January 1778, *ibid.*, IV, No. 2161.

[19] Same to same, 2 February 1778, *ibid.*, IV, No. 2184.

[20] Germain to Howe, 4 February 1778, *S.S.Mss.*, II, 92–93.

[21] King to North, 17 February 1778, Fortescue, *Correspondence*, IV, No. 2194.

[22] Bathurst to Germain, 16 February 1778, *S.S.Mss.*, II, 93.

[23] King to North, 17 February 1778, Fortescue, *Correspondence*, IV, No. 2194.

[24] *Parl. Hist.*, XIX, 355.

[25] *Ibid.*, XIX, 591–92. For a useful but brief account of the Carlisle commission, which grew out of North's policy of conciliation, see Alan S. Brown, "The British Peace Offer of 1778: A Study in Ministerial Confusion," *Michigan Academy of Science, Arts, and Letters, Papers*, XL (1955), 249–60. This volume covers the *Papers* given at the 1954 meetings of the Academy.

[26] Germain to Eden, 31 July 1778, G.P.

[27] King to North, undated, Fortescue, *Correspondence*, IV, No. 2188.

[28] Germain to Irwin, 3 February 1778, *S.S.Mss.*, I, 139.

[29] *Parl. Hist.*, XIX, 762 et seq.

[30] *Ibid.*, XIX, 762–815.

[31] *Ibid.*, XIX, 834–67.

[32] Germain to Knox, 18 February 1778, *Various Collections*, VI, 143.

[33] "Draft of a Circular Letter to Commissioners for Restoring Peace Sir Wm. Howe, Gov. Tryon, Sir H. Clinton, Commanding Officer at R. I. Governor Tryon," G.P.

[34] Germain to Howe, 18 February 1778, *S.S.Mss.*, II, 93–94.

[35] King to North, 17 February 1778, Fortescue, *Correspondence*, IV, No. 2194.

[36] Mahon, *History of England*, VI, 219. See also Jane Clark, C.H.R., X, 130.

[37] Germain to Irwin, 3 February 1778, S.S.Mss., I, 139.

[38] King to North, 3 March 1778, Fortescue, *Correspondence*, IV, No. 2202.

[39] The common interpretation of this incident has been largely drawn from this letter of George III. There has been no effort to evaluate the whole of Germain's position at the time.

[40] Mr. Jackson was later replaced by Governor Johnstone. Carlisle had only consented to the appointment of Jackson because of his familiarity with America. Carlisle felt this would "outbalance the insignificance of his situation and the obscurity of his name." *Carlisle Mss.*, 377.

[41] W. A. Brown, *Empire or Independence, A Study in the Failure of Reconciliation 1774–1783* (Louisiana State University Press, 1941), p. 245.

[42] See the sketch in *Various Collections*, VI, 265–67. See also A. S. Brown's "William Eden and the American Revolution," an unpublished Ph.D. dissertation, University of Michigan (1953).

[43] Eden to Germain, 5 March 1778, S.S.Mss., II, 94.

[44] *Carlisle Mss.*, 377.

[45] On 15 March, Lord North, feeling that Chatham's support would be valuable at this time of crisis, suggested an organization of the cabinet which would include him. In this reorganization he had suggested a peerage for Germain. The King was opposed to Chatham and declared he would rather lose his Crown than be in shackles to Chatham or any other branch of the Opposition. Nothing came of North's suggestion and nothing further was heard of Germain's resignation. Fortescue, *Correspondence*, IV, Nos. 2219, 2220, 2221.

[46] The subsequent progress and the ultimate failure of the Carlisle Peace Commission belongs in the general histories of the American Revolution. (For a specialized treatment see W. A. Brown, *Empire or Independence*, Ch. X, pp. 244–92.) Germain played no significant part in the later developments. As secretary of state for the American Department, he carried on a desultory and formal correspondence with the commissioners. Eden wrote complaining of the accommodation aboard the "Trident" which was to carry him, his wife and children, and four female attendants to America. Eden to Germain, 11 April 1778, G.P. He also wrote to Germain suggesting that Clinton ought to be made a commissioner if Howe had left for England. Same to same, 12 April 1778, S.S.Mss., II, 106. After the commissioners arrived in America and discovered that Philadelphia was in the process of being evacuated by the British, they were very angry. They had not been informed of this move, though it had been determined upon before they left England. Eden reproached Germain for his lack of candor. Eden to Germain, 19 June

1778, *ibid.*, II, 115–16. Germain replied that he had not been at liberty to reveal to anybody the government's most secret policies at so critical a juncture in the national life. Germain to Eden, 31 July 1778, G.P. In July, Germain pointed out the necessity for the commissioners sticking precisely to their instructions, Germain to Commissioners, July 1778, G.P.; in November he gave the commissioners permission to return home. Draft to Commissioners, 4 November 1778, G.P.

CHAPTER 9

[1] A. T. Mahan, *Major Operations of the Navies in the War of American Independence* (Boston, 1913), Ch. IV, pp. 58–81. This is the best available account of naval operations in 1778. Quite naturally it does not touch upon the problem of the formulation of naval policy by the British cabinet. Mahan's account was originally prepared for the cooperative work W. L. Clewes *et al.*, *The Royal Navy: A History from the Earliest Times to the Present* (7 vols., London, 1897–1903), III, Ch. XXXII, 394–412. Subsequently cited as Mahan, *Major Operations*. A briefer and less critical treatment is provided by G. W. Allen, *A Naval History of the American Revolution* (2 vols., Boston and New York, 1913), I, 327–36. W. M. James, a British naval officer, in his *British Navy in Adversity* (London, 1926), Ch. VII, pp. 87–111, has four short paragraphs at the beginning of his account with respect to an Admiralty "War Plan." He goes little further, however, than to say "there was no plan, nor, indeed, was there very much to plan with." P. 87. His account of naval tactics is brisk and clear and his maps, bold in outline and free of superfluous detail, are especially commendable. Sydney Fisher, *The Struggle for American Independence* (2 vols., Philadelphia and London, 1908), II, Ch. LXXIII, 206–16, is an older, standard account. The best French treatment is Georges La Cour Gayet, *La Marine militaire de la France sous le règne de Louis XVI* (2 vols., Paris, 1905), II, Chs. VII and VIII, 138–77. La Cour Gayet is primarily interested in tactics, though he does (pp. 144–45) discuss what, up to that time, had been the normal character of French naval strategy. Other French accounts may be mentioned although they add little to the clarification of the larger problems of naval strategy: Louis Edouard Chevalier, *Historie de la marine française pendant la guerre de l'independence americaine* (Paris, 1877), Ch. III, pp. 107–23; Vicomte de Noailles, *Marins et soldats français en Amérique 1778–1783* (Paris, 1903), pp. 31–49; and E. Augier, *Traité d'historie maritime de la France* (Brest, 1902), pp. 291–97, 306–10. Some of the material contained in this chapter, in a different and abbreviated form, appeared in my article, "The Anglo-French Naval Crisis, 1778: A Study of Conflict in the North Cabinet," in the *William and Mary Quarterly*, Third Series, XIII (January 1956), 3–25. It is reprinted here by permission of the *Quarterly*.

[2] The French Ambassador announced the treaty of amity and commerce between France and the United States to the British government on 13 March 1778. The British immediately recalled their ambassador. Mahan, *Major Operations*, p. 58. The French Ambassador was also recalled in March. Allen, *Naval History*, p. 327. The formal French declaration of war did not come until 10 July 1778 and took the form of a letter from the King to the admiral of France. La Cour Gayet, *La Marine militaire de la France*, II, 118–20. The British orders "to seize or destroy all ships or vessels belonging to France" without restriction were given to Admiral Keppel on 19 July, to Admirals Montague and Barrington on 27 July. G.P. However, after 13 March 1778, both the French and British governments conducted themselves as though a state of war existed between the two countries.

[3] Mahan, *Major Operations*, p. 79, states precisely the "fault" of the ministry as seen from the point of view of naval operations: "When war with France threatened, the Ministry, having long warning, committed an unpardonable fault in allowing such a force, i.e. Howe's to be confronted by one so superior as that which sailed from Toulon in April 1778. This should have been stopped on its way, or, failing that, its arrival in America should have been preceded by a British reinforcement." James, *British Navy in Adversity*, p. 87, says that "the obvious course" was that "of forbidding freedom of movement to the enemy fleet," by a squadron based on Gibraltar or by concentrating off Brest and thus preventing the French fleet from getting to sea.

W. B. Willcox in his article "Why Did the British Lose the American Revolution," *Michigan Alumnus Quarterly Review*, LXII (August, 1956), 317–24, stated the problem whose solution I attempt in the following pages, as follows: "The entrance of France converted the struggle into a world war, in which North America became a subordinate theater. But this need not have happened. If the British had employed the naval strategy which had served them so well in their previous duel with France —and which served them as well in their next—they would have precluded French operations overseas by a blockade in home waters. In that case their own American squadron, while decreased in size might still have patrolled the coast unchallenged; and their prospects in the colonies would have been little impaired. Instead the Cabinet decided that the Royal Navy was too weak for a blockade of France. *The reasons for this decision, the most important and disastrous made in London during the war, are obscure to this day*; it seems to have been reached without awareness of its strategic meanings. Its ill effects were felt wherever British squadrons were exposed to French attack, from the Indian Ocean to the Caribbean, and nowhere more forcefully than in North America." P. 321. It is argued below that not only was Germain aware of the strategic meaning of the decision but that he argued vigorously for adoption of the classic and proper strategy. (The italics are mine.)

⁴ Germain to Sir H. Clinton, Whitehall, 8 March 1778, G.P. There is also a copy of this letter in M.D.S.; it is printed in *S.S.Mss.*, II, 94–99, and in Stevens, *Facsimilies*, No. 1062. Germain's letter to Clinton of 8 March 1778 was received by Clinton at Philadelphia on 9 May 1778. Clinton Letter Books No. 2. The latter part of the Clinton Papers consists of bound volumes (8) of fair copies of the Germain-Clinton correspondence. In each case the date of the receipt of the letter is noted.

⁵ A reference to the Carlisle Peace Commission which still, before the announcement of the Franco-American Alliance, appeared to have some chance of success.

⁶ Germain wrote: "I am not without hopes we shall be able to send out, in the course of the summer, ten or twelve thousand British soldiers to which I expect will be added a regiment or two of Germans." Germain to Sir H. Clinton, 8 March 1778, G.P.

⁷ Lord Howe remained in the naval command until the autumn of 1778. He returned to England at that time and was not employed afloat again until 1782. Mahan, *Major Operations*, pp. 80–81.

⁸ These instructions to Clinton have a special interest in view of the charge laid against Germain that, in the campaign of 1777, he issued peremptory, detailed, and precise orders to Burgoyne which gave that general no discretionary power. With respect to the proposed campaign in the south, Germain now wrote to Clinton: "But your own knowledge of those provinces and the information you can collect from the naval and military officers that have been on service there, will enable you to give the officer to whom you entrust the command, better instructions than I can pretend to point out to you at this distance." At the end of the dispatch with respect to the military operations as a whole, he wrote, "I have thus stated the King's wishes and intentions, but he does not mean you to look upon them as orders, desiring, on the contrary that you use your own discretion in planning as well as executing all operations which shall appear the most likely means of crushing the rebellion." It is perhaps not going too far to suggest that these sentences reflect Germain's desire to protect himself against further charges, whether grounded or not in the original case (1777), of attempting narrowly and categorically to direct a commander three thousand miles distant.

⁹ Lord North to King, 6 January 1778, Fortescue, *Correspondence*, IV, No. 2149.

¹⁰ *Ibid.*, Nos. 2147, 2148, 2150. In the latter reference (King to North, 7 January 1778), the King wrote: "However insidious the conduct of France may appear, it is pleasant to feel we are taking all the steps that would be necessary if it should end in a war, and my mind is perfectly prepared to meet what I should certainly think a very unhappy event from the consciousness that I have scrupulously attempted to avoid and that without one single grievance, France chooses to be the Aggressor ..." For a detailed account of the conclusion of the Franco-American treaty,

see E. S. Corwin, *French Policy and the American Alliance* (Princeton, 1916), particularly Chapter VII. The most elaborate treatment of the whole subject is Henri Doniol's *Histoire de la participation de la France à l'établissement des Etats-Unis d'Amérique* (5 vols., Paris, 1886–92). Vols. I and II give a detailed account of the negotiation of the alliance and the last chapter of Vol. II tells of the final rupture with Great Britain.

[11] Germain's agent in Paris, James Hutton, was the leader of the Moravian sect in England. Hutton was an acquaintance of Franklin, though by no means a confidant. It is not clear whether or not he was in the pay of Germain, who received £3,000 a year for the secret service work of his department. It has been commonly believed that he considered this sum part of the perquisites of office and pocketed the greater part of it himself. See Spector, *American Department*, p. 128. There is little evidence in the G.P. to indicate that the American Department had organized an espionage system in any regular or methodical manner. It would appear rather that spying activities were on an *ad hoc*, day to day, basis. This is further borne out by a statement of Germain to Knox: "I do not wonder that Sir Stanier has no accounts from Paris even if your friend's intelligence be true, I do not find that any minister except Lord North has any regular information from France . . ." Knox Papers. No date, probably 1778.

For a general account of the British secret service in this connection see S. F. Bemis, "British Secret Service and the French-American Alliance," A.H.R., XXIX, 474–95. See also F. P. Renaut, "Le secret service de l'amirauté britannique" in *L'Espionage naval au XVIII siècle* (Paris, 1936).

[12] Hutton to Germain, Paris, 20 January 1778, G.P. Hutton was in touch with Lord Stormont, but he did not like to visit his home, as he felt sure he was being followed. Hutton was modest with respect to the amount and the character of the information he was able to collect: "I have sent the Light I could get at. Not much. When a man gives his all, he can do no more." Hutton to Germain (?), Paris, 14 January 1778, G.P.

[13] Hutton to Germain, one-half past six at night, Queen's Row, Pimlico, 25 January 1778, *ibid*.

[14] Hutton to Germain, 26 January 1778, *ibid*. Hutton reported in this letter that the American delegate who approached him was "Alderman Lee"—that is William Lee. The section of the letter identifying the delegate as "Alderman Lee" is omitted in *S.S.Mss.*, II, 92.

[15] The time limit of 10 days is interesting. This time limit was set on 25 January, and would have expired on 4 February. The final drafts of the treaty were signed 6 February.

[16] Stormont to Weymouth, 20 February 1778, in *The Private Papers of John, Earl of Sandwich, First Lord of the Admiralty 1771–1782*, edited

by G. R. Barnes and J. H. Owen (4 vols., London, 1932–38). Publications of the Navy Records Society, I, 343–44. Subsequently cited as the *Sandwich Papers*. See also King to North, 3 March 1778, Fortescue, *Correspondence*, IV, No. 2204. There is an interesting letter from Sir George Rodney, probably to Lord Stormont, in the G.P. under date of 13 March, relative to the first official recognition by the French armed forces of the independence of the United States. Rodney relates that Commodore Jones, senior sea officer "belonging to the States of America now in Europe," secured on 25 February 1778, a salute from the French naval commander M. La Motte Picque. The Frenchman however would grant to the American naval forces only a reply of nine guns to the American thirteen. This was in line, M. La Motte Picque explained, with what the French customarily accorded to republics and instanced the Dutch. Commodore Jones boasted: "I am the first person who have occasioned France openly to avow the independence of America, who by returning the salute of her ships has acknowledged them as free States." Rodney asked his correspondent to show this letter to Germain.

17 As indicated above, the instructions were general in character, setting only long-range objectives and leaving more discretionary powers in the hands of the military and naval officers in America than was at all customary.

18 "Minute of a Cabinet at Lord Weymouth's house, 14 March 1778. Present—Lord President, Lord Privy Seal, Lord Suffolk, Lord Sandwich, Lord G. Germain, Lord North, Lord Weymouth." *Sandwich Papers*, I, 361. See also an unsigned and undated memorandum in Sandwich's hand entitled "Advice Given About the Change of War in America," *ibid.*, I, 359–60. This was probably prepared for the consideration of the cabinet meeting of 14 March 1778, as the main proposals advanced in it were embodied in the cabinet minute of 14 March. See Dora M. Clark, "British Opinion of Franco-American Relations," *William and Mary Quarterly*, Third Series, IV (July 1947), 305–16. The bulk of this article deals with the later period, but see especially pp. 305–8.

19 Since the detailed disposition of the military and naval forces set forth in the minute and slightly modified by the cabinet minute of 18 March are fully explained below in connection with the secret instructions of 21 March, it has been thought unnecessary to go further into detail at this point.

20 Lord Amherst attended the cabinet of 18 March, and there is a document entitled "Lord Amherst's Idea about Change of War in America," *Sandwich Papers*, I, 365. This document indicates that Lord Amherst approved fully of the expedition against St. Lucia.

21 M.D.S.; Clinton's Letter Book No. 7; Stevens, *Facsimilies*, No. 1069. These "secret instructions" together with Germain to Clinton, 21 March 1778, and Germain to Clinton, 8 March 1778, were all received by Clinton at the same time, that is, on 9 May. He acknowledged their

receipt in a letter to Germain 10 May 1778. See Clinton's Letter Book No. 2 under this date. It is fortunate that he received all three together, since the operations ordered on 21 March were quite incompatible with those ordered on 8 March.

[22] M.D.S.; Clinton's Letter Book No. 8; Stevens, *Facsimilies*, No. 1068. As secretary of state for the American Department, Germain had special and individual responsibility for North America and the West Indies; as a secretary of state, on a footing of equality with the two "ancient secretaries," he had, of course, a general and real responsibility for all advice submitted to the King.

[23] Germain wrote to Sandwich, 21 March 1778, *Sandwich Papers*, I, 366, and to the Admiralty (*ibid.*, I, 368) on the same day, giving the necessary information so that orders might be sent to the naval commander.

[24] See Chapter 8, note 46.

[25] See above note 22.

[26] Sandwich to North, 6 March 1778, *Sandwich Papers*, I, 349. At this time the French fleet was reported as follows: Brest: 21 ships of the line and 35 frigates; Toulon: 12 ships of the line and 13 frigates. The Spanish fleet was reported as being 32 of the line and 8 frigates. Thus, "the House of Bourbon have in Europe an actual force of 65 of the line."

[27] Two months later and on the basis of much more extended and elaborate intelligence reports, the French force was reported as follows: Brest, 25 ships of the line; Toulon, 18. The Spanish naval strength is given as 28 ships of the line. Thus the naval force of "the House of Bourbon amounts to upward of 70 sail." Sandwich to North, 7 March 1778, *ibid.*, II, 49.

[28] *Ibid.*, II, 49. G. S. Graham, "Considerations on the War of American Independence," *Bulletin of the Institute of Historical Research*, XXII (1949), 22–34, writes with respect to the rejuvenation of French naval power after 1766: "Had the French fully comprehended the significance of real 'command of the sea,' the issue of the war might have been different. A scientifically wrought instrument lay in skilled hands, but the audacity was lacking. A century of almost constant numerical inferiority had left an indelible mark on the French naval mind. The dead-hand of *passive defence* still clutched the Ministry of Marine, and prevented it from securing the full benefit of its new strength." P. 30.

[29] Fortescue, *Correspondence*, IV, No. 2218. The greater part of the "Line of Battleships" abroad were on the American station under Lord Howe. "Advice Given About the Change of the War in America." In Lord Sandwich's hand. Probably March 1778, *Sandwich Papers*, I, 359. See also: "State of the Force in North America," 15 March 1778, *ibid.*, I, 362. This was written by Stephens, Sandwich's secretary. There is some disparity between these two accounts in actual numbers.

[30] "State of the Force at Home," March 1778, *ibid.*, II, 19–21. This

document also lists, in addition, 13 ships of the line in commission, several of which "may very soon be ready for sea." This would make a total of 53 ships of the line at home rather than the 55 ships noted above. Some light is thrown upon the rather complex problem of what precisely the British naval strength was in the spring of 1778, by papers prepared for a debate in the House of Lords on 23 April 1779 upon a motion made to remove Lord Sandwich from office. *Parl. Hist.*, XX, 426–67. These papers show that on 9 June 1778, there were 47 ships of the line, "actually at sea or nearly ready to proceed to sea." This indicates that six or eight ships listed in the documents we have been considering must, in March, have been still on the ways and far from completion. *Sandwich Papers*, II, 270–71.

31 *Ibid.*, II, 21–22. One ship, the "Ruby," had been added to the list, making in all 21 ships ready for foreign service.

32 *Ibid.*, II, 21, note 2.

33 This was actually done in May, when the King had taken a personal interest and instilled a sense of urgency. See Fortescue, *Correspondence*, IV, No. 2324.

34 See above p. 154.

35 D'Estaing was a soldier turned sailor. Born in 1729, he served in India under Lally Tollendal in 1758. After having been taken prisoner in 1759, he exchanged into the Navy. He was in command in American waters 1778–80 and was guillotined in 1794. Mahan, *Major Operations*, p. 59, note 1, and James, *British Navy in Adversity*, p. 90. He never displayed that confidence at sea which comes from having followed it from youth. Augier, *Traité d'histoire maritime*, p. 307, accounts in part for the slowness of D'Estaing's passage to America in 1778, by the fact that he tried out naval "evolutions" "de se familiariser avec la manoeuvre et la conduite d'un escadre avant d'arriver sur le theatre des operations. . . ." D'Estaing himself said it was due to the slowness of some of his vessels. Allen, *Naval History of the American Revolution*, I, 328.

36 When Admiral Darby went to the relief of Gibraltar in March, 1781, he left in home waters no vestige of naval protection, and this in the face of a considerable French naval force at Brest. Indeed, De Grasse was there with part of the French naval power destined to play so significant a part in the Yorktown campaign. *Sandwich Papers*, IV, 4–7.

37 "Lord Sandwich's Opinion 4 April 1778." Endorsed by him, "written at the Cabinet Council"; *ibid.*, II, 22–23.

38 Fortescue, *Correspondence*, IV, No. 2275.

39 Lord George Germain to Lord North, 27 April 1778, *ibid.*, IV, No. 2316.

40 See above p. 149. Mahan, *Major Operations*, p. 79.

41 Charles R. Ritcheson, *British Politics and the American Revolution* (Norman, Okla., 1954), pp. 252–57, accepts the Sandwich view and dismisses that of Germain on what seems to me meager evidence. His treat-

ment of Germain *passim* is the old caricature which grew out of the Minden court-martial (1760). He repeats (p. 213) the story that Germain was spiteful toward Carleton because the latter testified against him at the court-martial. This story was exploded a quarter century ago by A. L. Burt in *Canadian Historical Review*, XI (1930), 202. See also Chapter 1 of the present work.

[42] *Sandwich Papers*, II, 6–7. A further difficulty with respect to Keppel's appointment arose from the fact that his third in command was Sir Hugh Palliser, the senior professional member of the Board of Admiralty. Palliser belonged to the ministerial party and Keppel to the opposition. The court-martial arising out of the indecisive action between the French and British at Ushant, 23–27 July 1778 aroused great bitterness. It made the fleet "politics conscious."

[43] King to Lord North, 16 March 1778: "I have this day seen Admiral Keppel who will very properly accept the Command of the Fleet proposed for the defense of this Kingdom." Fortescue, *Correspondence*, IV, No. 2227. Four days earlier, the King had written: "By the list of Speakers yesterday in favor of Mr. Fox's motion, I see Admiral Keppel took a part that will disappoint Lord Sandwich, he having uniformly pretended that the Admiral, though very adverse on all political points, is much of his opinion in Marine affairs." King to North, 12 March 1778, *ibid.*, IV, No. 2213.

[44] Admiral Keppel to the King, April 1778: "I never allow myself to form plans in my imagination for exertion and enterprise upon the enemy, without continually meeting a complete check or stop, for the want of force, both of land and sea, that is employed in North America, but I will interfere as little as possible with that great question. It seems decided, yet I may be permitted to say that the great land force as well as sea force in that part, the number of transports, victuallers, of ordnance ships and other store ships employ the largest stock of seamen belonging to this country . . . ," *ibid.*, IV, No. 2312. See also "Memorandum by Keppel," *Sandwich Papers*, II, 29.

[45] Admiral Keppel to King, April 1778, Fortescue, *Correspondence*, IV, No. 2312.

[46] Keppel to Sandwich, 16 April 1778, *Sandwich Papers*, II, 30–31.

[47] See above pp. 156–57.

[48] Fortescue, *Correspondence*, IV, No. 2301. Lord North's opinion began to change as the result of intelligence reports he had received.

[49] *Ibid.*, IV, No. 2304.

[50] *Sandwich Papers*, II, 8. See also Mahan, *Major Operations*, pp. 58–59. D'Estaing took from 13 April to 16 May to get from Toulon to Gibraltar. Calms were the reason for this slow passage. La Cour Gayet, *Marine militaire*, II, 149. But see above note 35.

[51] North to Sandwich, 23 April 1778, *Sandwich Papers*, II, 33–34. North was right in the number of ships of the line—12—which made

up D'Estaing fleet. He was wrong on the date of sailing, as shown above. North also told Sandwich that D'Estaing was to be assisted by several American frigates and smaller ships.

[52] As noted p. 159, on the fifteenth he had believed the fleet might be headed for the East or West Indies.

[53] *Sandwich Papers*, II, 34–35.

[54] Germain to North, 27 April 1778, Fortescue, *Correspondence*, IV, No. 2316.

[55] *Ibid.*, IV, No. 2316.

[56] *Sandwich Papers*, II, 35–36. North had now in hand the information mentioned in his letter to Sandwich of 23 April (see above note 51), the information from Turin (see above p. 160), and information from Paris. The last intelligence was to the effect that "d'Estaing is not to come to Brest. He is going on a secret expedition, but nobody at Paris will venture to declare even what their conjectures are upon that subject." *Ibid.*, II, 36.

[57] See above p. 157.

[58] This last conjecture was either shrewd or fortuitous. As will become apparent, D'Estaing was just ten days too late in his arrival on the American coast to have achieved what Sandwich feared in his latter alternative.

[59] Sandwich to Keppel, 28 April 1778, *Sandwich Papers*, II, 37–38.

[60] See above note 44.

[61] Keppel to King, April 1778, Fortescue, *Correspondence*, IV, No. 2312.

[62] Silas Deane and Conrad Alexander Gerard, the first French Minister to the United States, left Paris on 31 March 1778 to go to Toulon on their way to America. See Carl Van Doren, *Secret History of the Revolution* (New York, 1941), p. 72.

[63] King to Sandwich, 29 April 1778, 5 m. past 9 A.M., *Sandwich Papers*, II, 38–39.

[64] Close to a third of the Germain Papers, now at the W. L. Clements Library, were not listed by the Historical Mss. Commission's *Report on the S.S.Mss.*

[65] G.P. There is a copy of this document in Germain's hand and a fair copy made by a clerk in the office. They exactly correspond. It is curious that this document, perhaps the most important among the G.P. on the question of naval strategy, was neither printed nor listed by the Historical Mss. Commission. It does not appear in any of the printed collections such as Stevens, *Facsimilies*; Fortescue, *Correspondence*; *Sandwich Papers*; S.S.Mss., etc., and understandably, since it was unknown, it is not considered by the standard writers on naval affairs.

[66] Cabinet Minute of 29 April 1778. M.D.S.

[67] Germain to King, 29 April, 50 m. past 7 P.M., Fortescue, *Correspondence*, IV, No. 2318.

[68] Germain to Lords of the Admiralty, 29 April 1778, M.D.S.

[69] At first Admiral Parker was the selection but, since he was junior to Admiral Gambier, and no great opinion was held of Gambier's prudence, Bryon was selected for the command. See North to King, 30 April 1778 (two letters), Fortescue, *Correspondence*, IV, Nos. 2320, 2321. King to Sandwich, 30 April 1778; North to Sandwich, 30 April 1778; *Sandwich Papers*, II, 39–40.

[70] Stephens to Sandwich, 30 April 1778, *ibid.*, II, 40–41.

[71] Sandwich to Stephens, 1 May 1778, *ibid.*, II, 41–43. Both Mulgrave and Palliser were on the Admiralty Board.

[72] Germain to Knox, 2 May 1778, *ibid.*, II, 42, note 1. It was common for Germain and Sandwich to put forth their views to each other through their secretaries Knox and Stephens.

[73] G.P. and *S.S. Mss.*, II, 110.

[74] Mahan, *Major Operations*, p. 63. The news reached Clinton 1 July 1778 at New York. Clinton replied to Germain's letter of 4 May, which had gone by packet, on 11 July 1778. Clinton's Letter Book, Nos. 6 and 15.

[75] To Vice Admiral Byron, 3 May 1778, G.P.

[76] See above p. 169.

[77] Robinson to Sandwich, 5 May 1778, *Sandwich Papers*, II, 45. This W. Pulteney later became Sir William Johnstone Pulteney. He was the brother of Governor George Johnstone. *S.S.Mss.*, II, 59. Late in 1777 he had carried on a correspondence with Germain relative to the possibility of beginning, through him, a negotiation with the Americans at Paris looking toward an accommodation. See G.P. and *S.S.Mss.*, II, 81–82, 82–83. Mr. Pulteney's language as reported in *Parl. Hist.*, XIX, 1132, was not so colorful as that attributed to him by Robinson. However *Parl. Hist.* was not a verbatim account at this period, and Robinson, writing on the same day, probably reported accurately.

[78] North to King, ?6 May 1778, Fortescue, *Correspondence*, IV, No. 2327.

[79] King to North, 6 May 1778, *ibid.*, IV, 2328.

[80] North to King, 7 May 1778, *ibid.*, IV, 2329.

[81] *Parl. Hist.*, XIX, 1131–37.

[82] *Ibid.*, XIX, 1135.

[83] *Ibid.*, XIX, 1135.

[84] Keppel to Sandwich, 5, 6 May 1778, *Sandwich Papers*, II, 46–47, 47–48.

[85] Sandwich to North, 7 May 1778, *ibid.*, II, 49–50.

[86] North to King, 7 May 1778, Fortescue, *Correspondence*, IV, No. 2329.

[87] North to Sandwich, 8 May 1778, *Sandwich Papers*, II, 51–52.

[88] North to Sandwich, 8 May 1778, *ibid.*, II, 53–54. Interestingly enough this letter found its way into the G.P. It decisively rejects

Sandwich's views, and for this reason Germain may have sought and obtained a copy. It is not in *S.S.Mss.*

⁸⁹ The presumed reason for Sandwich again raising the whole question was a dispatch from Admiral Duff, commander of the Mediterranean squadron. However, Duff's dispatch was dated 10 April, and the cabinet in making its decision had had fresher and what appeared to be more authentic information on which to rely.

⁹⁰ King to North, 8 May 1778, Fortescue, *Correspondence*, IV, No. 2330.

⁹¹ Keppel to Sandwich, 9 May 1778, *Sandwich Papers*, II, 54–56. Palliser was of the same opinion. Palliser to Sandwich, 12 May 1778, *ibid.*, II, 56–58.

⁹² Sandwich to Weymouth, 13 May 1778, *ibid.*, II, 58.

⁹³ To Vice Admiral Byron, 13 May 1778, G.P.

⁹⁴ *Sandwich Papers*, II, 58.

⁹⁵ To Vice Admiral Byron, 18 May 1778, G.P.; also *Sandwich Papers*, II, Appendix B, 375.

⁹⁶ This change came as the result of Commodore Hood's advice to the King. A fleet was more mobile at New York than at Halifax due to the prevailing southwest wind during the summer months. See Hood to King, 9 May 1778, Fortescue, *Correspondence*, IV, No. 2332. For more on this point, a matter of real significance in naval dispositions in the days of sailing ships, see also North to Sandwich, 12 May 1778, *Sandwich Papers*, II, 56; and Germain to King, 17 May 1778, Fortescue, *Correspondence*, IV, No. 2345.

⁹⁷ Keppel to Sandwich, 18 May 1778, *Sandwich Papers*, II, 66. Same to same, 24 May 1778, *ibid.*, II, 71–74.

⁹⁸ This is an undated memorandum but the contingencies looked at date it unmistakably as having been written during the last two weeks of May. *Ibid.*, II, 74–75.

⁹⁹ To Admiral Keppel, 25 May 1778, G.P.; and *Sandwich Papers*, II, Appendix A, 370.

¹⁰⁰ Keppel to Sandwich, 26 May 1778, *ibid.*, II, 77–78.

¹⁰¹ *Parl. Hist.*, XIX, 1176–99; Fortescue, *Correspondence*, IV, No. 2360.

¹⁰² *Parl. Hist.*, XIX, 1201.

¹⁰³ D'Estaing left Toulon 13 April; he passed the Straits of Gibraltar 16 May.

¹⁰⁴ *Sandwich Papers*, II, 8. Mahan, *Major Operations*, 59, says that D'Estaing had been followed 90 leagues into the Atlantic.

¹⁰⁵ Sutton reported: "From the regular courses the fleet steered and the great press of sail they carried, I cannot help supposing it is for the West Indies." *Sandwich Papers*, II, 89.

¹⁰⁶ For the reasons why North America rather than the West Indies

was thought the most likely destination, see King to Sandwich, 5 June 1775, *ibid.*, II, 89; and Palliser to Sandwich, 5 June 1778, *ibid.*, II, 91.

[107] To Vice Admiral Byron, 5 June 1778, G.P.; *Sandwich Papers*, II, Appendix B, 375.

[108] Mahan, *Major Operations*, 59.

[109] *Ibid.*, 62.

[110] Quoted in *ibid.*, 63.

[111] *Ibid.*, 64–68. The relative strengths of the two fleets were: Lord Howe, six 64's; three 50's and six frigates. D'Estaing, one 90-gun ship; one 80; six 74's, and one 50.

[112] *Ibid.*, 100.

[113] *Ibid.*, 82–97.

BIBLIOGRAPHY

I. Contemporary Writings

  A. Manuscripts

Clinton Papers (260 vols.). William L. Clements Library, Ann Arbor, Michigan.

    Clinton took over the command in America from Howe in the spring of 1778, and the Clinton Papers are most valuable for the later years of the revolutionary struggle. However, Clinton held important secondary commands from 1775 to 1778 and he was a voluminous letter writer.

    These Papers were used chiefly for the problem of command in 1776–77 as reflected in Burgoyne's correspondence with Clinton; for the latter part of the campaign of 1777 as reflected from Clinton's post in New York; and for the relations of Clinton and Germain in the first part of 1778. (Clinton's Letter Books, No. 1: Clinton to Germain 2 May to 26 December 1778. No. 1: Germain to Clinton 4 February 1778 to 2 June 1779).

    Clinton was very sensitive (see Harold Murdock, *Bunker Hill. Notes and Queries on a Famous Battle* [Boston, 1927], Ch. V, "The Sensitiveness of General Clinton," pp. 121–34), and in his later years he wrote, to explain his part therein, a history of the "American War: An Historical Detail of Seven Years Campaign in North America." This manuscript has been edited with an introduction by W. B. Willcox under the title *The American Rebellion* (New Haven, 1954). Willcox is presently engaged in writing a biography of Clinton.

    The Clinton Papers are discussed in H. H. Peckham, *Guide to the Manuscript Collections in the William L. Clements Library* (Ann Arbor, 1942), pp. 46–65, and in Randolph G. Adams, *The Headquarters Papers of the British Army in North America* (Ann Arbor, 1928).

Gage Papers (180 vols.). William L. Clements Library, Ann Arbor, Michigan.

    Gage was recalled in the fall of 1775, and Germain did not correspond with him at all. These Papers were useful chiefly for the purpose of following the British plans for 1776 as they had developed by the time Germain took office. A section of this collection was examined. Important Gage correspondence is available in printed form in the *Parliamentary Register* (London, 1902), X, and in Clarence E. Carter, *The Correspondence of General*

Thomas Gage with the Secretaries of State (2 vols., New Haven, 1931 and 1933). For a full description of the scope of this manuscript collection see Peckham, *Guide*, pp. 82–100.

Germain Papers (22 vols.). William L. Clements Library, Ann Arbor, Michigan.

This collection is made up of about 2,000 pieces covering the years 1683–1785. There is also a separate volume entitled Military Dispatches Secret. The documents have been described by Randolph G. Adams in Clements Library Bulletin No. 18, *The Papers of Lord George Germain* (Ann Arbor, 1928), and in Peckham, *Guide*, pp. 106–11. The Historical Manuscripts Commission reported on this collection in its *Ninth Report*, Part III, 1884, and again in a fuller manner in two volumes, *Report on the Manuscripts of Mrs. Stopford-Sackville of Drayton House, Northamptonshire* (London, 1904 and 1910). This *Report* included the Irish Papers and the Minden Papers which were not purchased by Mr. Clements. However, about one-third of the collection in the Clements Library was not catalogued by the Commission.

The great bulk of the Germain Papers relate to the period of the American Revolution (16 vols.). They were examined fully for this study and constitute its main documentary source. The Papers provide an excellent account of the main outlines of Germain's public policy, but they are disappointingly meager on the personal side. In the latter connection the Knox Papers (see below) are much fuller. The rough drafts of many dispatches in Germain's hand appear among his Papers as well as the fair copies. By a close examination of the portions of a dispatch which have been struck out, and the additions which have been made in the original, it is possible to follow the development of a line of policy from its rough formulation to its final statement.

The collection also contains a great many rather lengthy documents on various aspects of the American struggle, apparently submitted to Germain in an effort to influence the government one way or another. These are useful, when considered with due caution, to establish the genesis of a policy. There are also a number of summaries, précis of correspondence, etc., with marginal comments which are a most useful source to establish chronology. They also give many clues as to the grounds upon which a certain line of action was based.

Whenever a satisfactory printed source existed for the material in the Germain Papers, it has been cited in this study rather than the original. Only where a document was unavailable in printed form, or where, in its printed form, it was defective because of being cast as a précis, or because of essential omissions, was citation made to the original Papers.

Knox Papers (11 vols.). William L. Clements Library, Ann Arbor, Michigan.

These Papers contain about 650 pieces. Roughly 80 percent of this material was calendared by the Historical Manuscripts Commission in its *Report on Manuscripts in Various Collections*, VI (London, 1909), 81–296. Most of the material which appears in this *Report* is quite satisfactory from the point of view of fullness (see Peckham, *Guide*, pp. 148–50).

In a number of cases, however, the Knox Papers made possible a fuller interpretation (Peace Commission, 1776) and a different interpretation (Trenton Affair) in the relations of Germain and Carleton, from what would have been possible with the material in the *Report*.

The Knox Papers constitute perhaps the best single source from which to collect impressions of Germain as he conducted business from day to day. He lived on easy and friendly terms with Knox, and his few sallies of wit are found in these Papers. His letters to Knox are also a valuable guide to Germain's whereabouts on certain dates, and they also indicate the periods he spent away from London, whether at Stoneland or Drayton.

Shelburne Papers (179 vols.). William L. Clements Library, Ann Arbor, Michigan.

These Papers were helpful in throwing some light upon Carleton's ideas for the campaign of 1777, as included in a letter to Burgoyne, and as set down by Burgoyne in a memorandum presented to the Home Government. For the whole scope of the Shelburne Papers see Peckham, *Guide*, pp. 220–35.

B Printed
   1. Collections of Documents
      Adams, C. F., ed., *The Works of John Adams* (Boston, 1850–56, in 10 vols.).

      Barnes, G. R. and Owen, J. H., eds., *The Private Papers of John, Earl of Sandwich, First Lord of the Admiralty, 1771–1782* (Navy Records Society, London, 1932–38, in 4 vols.).

      Carter, C. E., ed., *The Correspondence of General Thomas Gage with the Secretaries of State* (New Haven, 1931 and 1933, in 2 vols.).

      Cavendish, Sir Henry, ed., *The Debates of the House of Commons During the Thirteenth Parliament of Great Britain, Commonly Called the Unreported Parliament* (London, 1841, in 2 vols.).

      Donne, W. B., ed., *The Correspondence of King George III with Lord North from 1768 to 1783* (London, 1867, in 2 vols.).

      Executors of John, Earl of Chatham, eds., *Correspondence of William Pitt, Earl of Chatham* (London, 1838–40, in 4 vols.).

Force, Peter, ed., *American Archives Fourth Series* (Washington, 1846).

Fortescue, Sir John, ed., *The Correspondence of King George III from 1760 to December 1783* (London, 1928, in 6 vols.).

Historical Manuscripts Commission:
Report on the Manuscripts of the Earl of Carlisle, Preserved at Castle Howard. Fifteenth Report, Appendix, Part VI (London, 1897).

Report on the Manuscripts of the Earl of Dartmouth. Fourteenth Report, Appendix, Part X (London, 1895).

Report on the Manuscripts of Mrs. Stopford-Sackville of Drayton House, Northamptonshire (London, 1904 and 1910, in 2 vols.).

Report on the Manuscripts in Various Collections, VI (London, 1909).

Hutchinson, P. O., ed., *The Diary and Letters of His Excellency, Thomas Hutchinson* (Boston, 1884–86, in 2 vols.).

James, J. A., ed., *George Rogers Clark Papers* (Springfield, 1912).

Parliamentary History of England from the Earliest Period to the Year 1803. Published under the superintendence of T. C. Hansard (London, 1813–14).

Parliamentary Register or History of the Proceedings and Debates of the House of Commons (London, 1802).

Proceedings of a General Court Martial ... Trial of Lord George Sackville (London, 1760).

Report on Canadian Archives for 1885 (Ottawa, 1886).

Report of the Pioneer Society of the State of Michigan, Together with Reports of County Pioneer Societies, IX (2d ed.; Lansing, 1908).

Sedgwick, Romney, ed., *Letters from George III to Lord Bute 1756–1766* (London, 1939).

Shortt, A., and Doughty, A. G., eds., *Documents Relating to the Constitutional History of Canada 1759–1791* (Ottawa, 1918, in 2 vols.).

Smith, W. J., ed., *The Grenville Papers: Being the Correspondence of Richard Grenville, Earl Temple, K.G., and the Right Honourable George Grenville, Their Friends and Contemporaries* (London, 1853, in 4 vols.).

Stevens, B. F., ed., *Facsimilies of Manuscripts in European Archives Relating to America* (London, 1889–95, in 25 vols.).

Toynbee, Mrs. Paget, ed., *The Letters of Horace Walpole* (Oxford, 1903–5, in 16 vols.).

2. Works by Contemporaries

Albemarle, George Thomas, Earl of, ed., *Memoirs of the Marquis of Rockingham and His Contemporaries* (London, 1852).

Annual Register (2d ed.; London, 1779).

[Anon.], *A Letter to Lt. Gen. Burgoyne Occasioned by a Second Edition of His State of the Expedition from Canada* (London, 1780).

————, *Reply to Lt. Gen. Burgoyne's Letter to His Constituents* (London, 1779).

————, *A Brief Examination of the Plan and Conduct of the Northern Expedition in America 1777* (London, 1780).

————, *A View of the Evidence Relative to the Conduct of the War Under Sir Wm. Howe, Lord Viscount Howe and General Burgoyne as Given Before a Committee of the House of Commons Last Session of Parliament. To Which Are Added a Collection of Celebrated Fugitive Pieces That Are Said to Have Given Rise to That Inquiry* (London, 1779).

————, *Essay on Modern Martyrs; with a Letter to Gen. Burgoyne* (London, 1780).

Burgoyne, Right Hon. John, *State of the Expedition from Canada* (London, 1780).

————, *The Substance of Gen. Burgoyne's Speeches ... with an Appendix Containing Gen. Washington's Letter to Gen. Burgoyne* (London, 1778).

————, *A Letter from Lt. Gen. Burgoyne to His Constituents* (London, 1779).

————, *A Supplement to the State of the Expedition from Canada, Containing Gen. Burgoyne's Orders Respecting the Principal Movements of the Army to the Raising of the Siege of Ticonderoga* (London, 1780).

Clinton, Sir Henry, *Observations on Mr. Stedman's History of the American War* (London, 1794).

Crane, Verner W., *Benjamin Franklin's Letters to the Press, 1758–1775* (Chapel Hill, 1950).

Flanders, H., ed., *Memoirs of Richard Cumberland* (Philadelphia, 1856).

Galloway, Joseph, *A Reply to the Observations of the Lt. Gen. Sir Wm. Howe on a Pamphlet Entitled Letters to a Nobleman, in Which His Misrepresentations Are Detected, and Those Letters Are Supported by New Matter and Argument* (London, 1780).

————, *Letters to a Nobleman on the Conduct of the War in the Middle Colonies* (London, 1779).

Howe, Admiral Lord, *Reflections on a Pamphlet Intitled "a Letter to the Right Honble Lord Vic^t H . . . E."* Edited with an Introduction by Gerald S. Brown (Ann Arbor: University of Michigan Press, 1959).

Howe, Sir William, *The Narrative of Lt. Gen. Sir William Howe in a Committee of the House of Commons on 29th April 1779, Relative to His Conduct During His Late Command of the King's Troops in North America, to Which Are Added Some Observations upon a Pamphlet Entitled Letters to a Nobleman* (London, 1780).

Jones, Thomas, *History of New York During the Revolution* (New York, 1879, in 2 vols.).

Mauduit, Israel, *Three Letters to Lt. Gen. Sir Wm. Howe* (London, 1781).

Stedman, Charles, *The History of the Origin, Progress and Termination of the American War* (London, 1794, in 2 vols.). For a general statement of the authenticity of the contemporary histories and especially Stedman, see R. Kent Newmayer, "Charles Stedman's History of the American War," *American Historical Review*, LXIII (July, 1958), 924–34. Newmayer shows that a large part of Vol. I of Stedman's work and much less of Vol. II was plagiarized from the *Annual Register*. Stedman was not unique in this for "Stedman's *History* is the tenth contemporary account to be derived entirely or in part from the *Annual Register*." Pp. 933–34.

Walpole, Horace, *Journal of the Reign of George III 1771–1783* (London, 1859, in 2 vols.).

———, *Last Journals* (London and New York, 1910, in 2 vols.).

———, *Memoirs of the Last Ten Years of George II* (London, 1822, in 2 vols.).

Wheatley, H. B., ed., *The Historical and Posthumous Memoirs of Sir Nathaniel W. Wraxall 1772–1784* (London, 1884, in 5 vols.).

II. Histories and Studies

Adams, Charles F., "Contemporary Opinion on the Howes," Massachusetts Historical Society, *Proceedings*, XLIV (October, 1910), 94–120.

———, "The Revolutionary Campaign of 1777," *ibid.*, XLIV, 13–65. This monograph was subsequently reprinted in *Studies Military and Diplomatic 1775–1865* (New York, 1911).

Alden, John R., *General Gage in America* (Baton Rouge, 1948).

Allen, Gardner W., *A Naval History of the American Revolution* (Boston and New York, 1913, in 2 vols.).

Anderson, Troyer, *The Command of the Howe Brothers During the American Revolution* (New York, 1936).

Augier, E., *Traité d'histoire maritime de la France* (Paris, 1903).

Barnhart, John D., "A New Evaluation of Henry Hamilton and George Rogers Clark," *Mississippi Valley Historical Review*, XXXVII (1950–51), 643–52.

————, *Henry Hamilton and George Rogers Clark in the American Revolution with the Unpublished Journal of Lieut. Gov. Henry Hamilton* (Crawfordsville, Ind., 1951).

Bayse, Arthur H., *The Lords Commissioners of Trade and Plantations 1748–1782* (Yale University Press, 1925).

————, "The Secretary of State for Colonies," *American Historical Review*, XXVIII (October, 1922), 12–23.

————, "The Earl of Carlisle and the Board of Trade," *American Historical Review*, XXII (January, 1917), 334–39.

Bemis, Samuel F., "British Secret Service and the French Alliance," *American Historical Review*, XXIX (April, 1924), 474–95.

Bird, Harrison, *March to Saratoga: General Burgoyne and the American Campaign* (New York, 1963).

Brooke, John, *The Chatham Administration, 1766–1768* (New York, 1956).

Brown, Alan S., "The British Peace Offer of 1778: A Study in Ministerial Confusion," Michigan Academy of Science, Arts, and Letters, *Papers*, XL (1955), 249–60.

Brown, Gerald S., "The Court Martial of Lord George Sackville, Whipping Boy of the Revolutionary War," *William and Mary Quarterly*, Third Series, IX (July, 1952), 317–37.

————, "The Anglo-French Naval Crisis, 1778: A Study of Conflict in the North Cabinet," *William and Mary Quarterly*, Third Series, XIII (January, 1956), 3–25.

Brown, Robert E., *Middle Class Democracy and the Revolution in Massachusetts* (Cornell University Press, 1955).

Brown, Sanborn, "Count Rumford: International Reformer," *New England Quarterly*, XXI (March, 1948), 34–49.

Brown, Weldon A., *Empire or Independence* (Louisiana State University Press, 1941).

Burt, Alfred L., *The Old Province of Quebec* (Minneapolis, 1933).

————, "The Quarrel Between Germain and Carleton: An Inverted Story," *Canadian Historical Review*, XI (September, 1930), 202–22.

Butterfield, Herbert, *George III and the Historian* (London, 1957).

Channing, Edward, *History of the United States* (New York, 1905–25, in 6 vols.).

Chevalier, Louis, *Histoire de la marine française* (Paris, 1886–1902, in 5 vols.).

Christie, Ian R., *The End of North's Ministry 1780–1782* (London, 1958).

Clark, Dora M., "British Opinion of Franco-American Relations," *William and Mary Quarterly*, Third Series, IV (July, 1947), 305–16.

Clark, Jane, "The Command of the Canadian Army in 1777," *Canadian Historical Review*, X (June, 1929), 129–35.

————, "The Responsibility for the Failure of the Burgoyne Campaign," *American Historical Review*, XXXV (April, 1930), 542–54.

————, "The Perfidy of Sir William Howe," *American Historical Review*, XXXVII (July, 1932), 721–22.

Corwin, E. S., *French Policy and the American Alliance of 1778* (Princeton, 1916).

Coventry, George, *A Critical Enquiry Regarding the Real Author of the Letters of Junius* (London, 1825).

Dickerson, Oliver M., *The Navigation Acts and the American Revolution* (Philadelphia, 1951).

Doniol, Henri, *Histoire de la participation de la France à l'établissement des Etats-Unis d'Amérique* (Paris, 1886–92, in 5 vols.).

Elliott, Major C. W., "The Men Who Fought at Minden," *Journal of the American Military Institute*, III (1939), 80–103.

Fisher, Sydney G., *The Struggle for American Independence* (Philadelphia and London, 1908, in 2 vols.).

Fitzmaurice, Edmond George Petty, 1st Baron, *Life of William, Earl of Shelburne* (2d and rev. ed.; London, 1912, in 2 vols.).

Fonblanque, Edward B. de, *Political and Military Episodes . . . Derived from the Life and Correspondence of the Right Hon. John Burgoyne* (London, 1876).

Ford, Worthington C., "Parliament and the Howes," Massachusetts Historical Society, *Proceedings*, XLIV (October, 1910), 120–43.

Fortescue, Hon. John W., *A History of the British Army* (London, 1910, 13 vols. in 14).

French, Allen, *First Year of the American Revolution* (Boston, 1934).

Graham, Gerald S., "Considerations on the War of American Independence," *Bulletin of the Institute of Historical Research*, XXII (1949), 22–34.

Guttridge, George H., "Lord George Germain in Office," *American Historical Review*, XXXIII (October, 1927), 23–43.

Hudleston, F. J., *Gentleman Johnny Burgoyne* (New York, 1927).

Hunt, William, *History of England 1760–1801* (London, 1905).

James, W. M., *The British Navy in Adversity* (London, 1926).

Jensen, Merrill, "Democracy and the American Revolution," *Huntington Library Quarterly*, XX (1956–57), 321–41.

Knollenberg, Bernhard, *Origin of the American Revolution* (New York, 1960).

La Cour Gayet, Georges, *La Marine militaire de la France* (Paris, 1905, in 2 vols.).

Laprade, W. T., "Edmund Burke: An Adventure in Reputation," *Journal of Modern History*, XXXII (December, 1960), 321–32.

Lecky, W. E. H., *History of England in the Eighteenth Century* (London, 1906–7, in 7 vols.).

Lucas, Reginald, *Lord North* (London, 1913, in 2 vols.).

Mahan, Alfred T., *The Major Operations of the Navies in the War of American Independence* (Boston, 1913).

Mahon, Lord, *History of England 1713–1783* (Boston, 1853, in 7 vols.).

Morgan, Edmund S., *The Birth of the Republic* (Chicago, 1956).

———, "The American Revolution: Revisions in Need of Revising," *William and Mary Quarterly*, Third Series, XIV (1957), 3–15.

Morgan, Edmund S., and Helen M., *The Stamp Act Crisis: Prologue to Revolution* (Chapel Hill, 1953).

Namier, L. B., *The Structure of Politics at the Accession of George III* (London, 1929).

———, *England in the Age of the American Revolution* (London, 1930).

Nickerson, H., *The Turning Point of the Revolution* (New York, 1928).

Noailles, Vicomte de, *Marins et soldats français en Amérique 1778–1783* (Paris, 1903).

Pares, Richard, *George III and the Politicians* (Oxford, 1953).

Price, Jacob, "Party, Purpose, and Pattern: Sir Lewis Namier and His Critics," *Journal of British Studies*, I (November, 1961), 71–93.

Renaut, F. P., "Le Secret service de l'amirauté britannique 1776–1783," in *L'Espionnage naval au XVIII siècle* (Paris, 1936).

Ritcheson, Charles R., *British Politics and the American Revolution* (Norman, Okla., 1954).

Spector, M. M., *The American Department of the British Government* (New York, 1940).

Taylor, Robert J., "Israel Mauduit," *New England Quarterly*, XXIV (June, 1951), 208–30.

Thomson, Mark, *Secretaries of State 1681–1782* (Oxford, 1932).

Trevelyan, G. M., *Lord Grey of the Reform Bill* (London, 1920).

Trevelyan, G. O., *The American Revolution* (New York, 1917–20, in 4 vols.).

Valentine, Alan, *Lord George Germain* (New York and Oxford, 1962).

Van Doren, Carl, *Secret History of the Revolution* (New York, 1941).

Van Tyne, Claude, *The War of Independence: American Phase* (Boston and New York, 1929).

Von Ruville, Albert, *William Pitt, Earl of Chatham* (London, 1907, in 3 vols.).

West, V. Sackville, *Knole and the Sackvilles* (London, 1931).

Whitton, Lt. Col. F. E., *The American War of Independence* (London, 1931).

Willcox, William B., "The British Road to Yorktown: A Study in Divided Command," *American Historical Review*, LII (October, 1946), 1–35.

———, "Rhode Island in British Strategy," *Journal of Modern History*, XVII (December, 1945), 304–31.

———, *The American Rebellion* (New Haven, 1954).

———, "Why Did the British Lose the American Revolution," *Michigan Alumnus Quarterly Review*, LXII (August, 1956), 317–24.

———, "Too Many Cooks: British Planning Before Saratoga," *Journal of British Studies*, II (November, 1962), 56–90.

Willcox, William B., and Frederick Wyatt, "Sir Henry Clinton: A Psychological Exploration in History," *William and Mary Quarterly*, Third Series, XVI (January, 1959), 3–26.

INDEX